The Electronics Workbench

Tools, Testers, and Tips
for the Hobbyist

The Electronics Workbench
Tools, Testers, and Tips for the Hobbyist

Delton T. Horn

TAB Books
Division of McGraw-Hill, Inc.
Blue Ridge Summit, PA 17294-0850

FIRST EDITION
THIRD PRINTING

© 1991 by **TAB Books**.
TAB Books is a division of McGraw-Hill, Inc.

Library of Congress Cataloging-in-Publication Data

Horn, Delton T.
    The electronics workbench : tools, testers, and tips for the
hobbyist / by Delton T. Horn
        p.   cm.
    Includes index.
    ISBN 0-8306-2526-7   ISBN 0-8306-2525-9 (pbk.)
    1. Electronics—Amateurs' manuals.   I. Title.
TK9965.H67   1991
621.381—dc20   91-12588
                                                        CIP

Acquisitions Editor: Roland S. Phelps
Book Editor: Laura Bader
Director of Production: Katherine G. Brown
Book Design: Jaclyn J. Boone   EL2

Contents

Introduction

EXCEPT FOR THE MOST CASUAL OF HOBBYISTS, ANYONE INVOLVED in any aspect of electronics will need to work with test equipment. There are a bewildering variety of test equipment devices available. What do they do? What equipment do you need? Which items would be nice to have, but are not a necessity? What can you do without? What equipment would be a waste of your money?

Whether you are an electronics hobbyist or a professional technician setting up your own shop, you've surely asked yourself such questions. This book's goal is to help you find the answers.

The first chapter discusses setting up a functional electronics workbench, or work area. Small items such as hand tools are also covered.

Chapter 2 will be of interest mostly to hobbyists. Its focus is on soldering and construction techniques that can be used for various electronics projects.

Chapters 3 through 11 discuss various types of test equipment, including their functions and specifications.

Chapters 3 and 4 are the longest chapters because they focus on the multimeter (chapter 3) and the oscilloscope (chapter 4), which account for about 80% of most practical electronics work. These devices are the real workhorses of the electronics workbench, and every electronics technician and serious hobbyist should have both a multimeter and an oscilloscope. These chapters will help you determine what to look for when shopping for these versatile test instruments.

Chapters 5 through 10 explore useful but less essential types of test equipment, including capacitance meters, frequency counters, signal generators, transistor testers, logic probes, and more.

Chapter 11 explores the recently implemented concept of ATE (automated test equipment), utilizing computer control and data storage and manipulation.

Finally, chapter 12 discusses some important concepts of electronics safety. It is very strongly recommended that all readers read this chapter carefully. Some of it may seem like obvious, old-hat material, but every year, countless electronics hobbyists and technicians who should know better manage to injure or kill themselves. Safety is not something that can be overdone.

This book is unlike most other electronics books. Sure, there are many books on troubleshooting and servicing techniques that mention test equipment. But those books rarely go into depth on the capabilities of such test equipment.

There have also been a number of books on specific types of test equipment, especially VOMs (volt-ohm-milliammeters) and oscilloscopes, but I don't know of any other books that provide an overview of general electronics test equipment. That is the goal of this volume.

After reading this book, you'll have a much clearer idea of what you really need to set up an electronics workbench to best suit your specific needs.

❖ 1
Arranging
the workbench

ELECTRONICS IS A VERY COMPLEX AND SOPHISTICATED FIELD, whether you pursue it as a profession or as a hobby. In the early days of electronics, the hobbyist usually didn't need very much—just a little space to work, a handful of simple components and hand tools, and maybe a soldering iron. The full-fledged technician didn't need much more, just some simple test equipment—a voltmeter, an ohmmeter, and perhaps, if he really wanted to get sophisticated, an oscilloscope or an inductance bridge.

Early electronics circuits were fairly simple. There was usually just one main signal to worry about. If that signal was OK, then the circuit was working fine.

Today's electronics circuits are generally far more complex, often with dozens or even hundreds of critical signals of various types. Countless new components perform previously unimagined functions. Some circuits are analog and others are digital, and the signals and requirements for each type are quite different.

It is clear that anyone interested in working with modern electronics needs some fairly sophisticated test equipment. Hundreds of different devices are available today, and most hobbyists (especially relative newcomers to the field) and many professional technicians are bewildered by the wide variety of choices facing them when they shop for electronics test equipment.

It's often hard to determine just what a given piece of test equipment will do, and whether it will meet your individual needs. What test equipment is essential? What test equipment is a luxury—nice to have, but not really necessary? And what test equipment is just an impressive doodad with little practical value, at least for your particular needs and interests?

This book is intended to help you answer such questions. We will look closely at many common types of test equipment and what they are used for. Standard and special functions will be discussed so you can determine which features you need, and which just increase the price without giving you anything you're ever likely to use.

We will also discuss the uses of various types of modern electronics test equipment. How are standard tests performed? What special "tricks" are possible? What precautions are necessary? With this book, you will be able to select the exact test equipment required to meet your own individual needs, regardless of what area of electronics you are interested in.

Before getting into specific types of test equipment, however, this chapter will look at the basics of laying out the most efficient electronics work area possible. The process of laying out a well-planned and convenient electronics workbench is something that is all too often overlooked by hobbyists and technicians alike. Whether you are working in electronics for fun or profit (or both), you'll get a lot more accomplished with a well-planned workbench.

The worksurface

Make sure you have plenty of workspace. Even a casual dabbler in electronics will frequently need to have two or three PC boards hooked up at once. Leave yourself adequate elbow room. If your workspace is too cramped, accidents and mistakes are much more likely to occur. You are liable to bump into something critical at just the wrong moment.

The worksurface should be smooth, so circuit boards, test equipment, and other things will sit flat. A carved design may look pretty, but it's easy to lose a small screw or tiny component in the carvings. Even if you can see it, you may not be able to retrieve it easily.

The electronics technician's worksurface should be relatively scuffproof and immune to scratches. Moving test equipment and exposed circuit boards back and forth could damage some fancy surfaces. Hand tools can also do some damage. Solder can easily splatter onto the worksurface. A durable, fireproof worksurface is essential. To keep peace in the family, it's a good idea not to work on the dining room table or other good furniture unless a protective mat of some sort is used. For some time I used a large mat designed for cooks. It was flame and heatproof and was covered with a smooth metallic foil. Moreover, it was lightweight and easily stashed behind the sofa whenever company came over.

A permanent workbench dedicated to your electronics work is the best, of course; but for many hobbyists, that is an unaffordable luxury. Many apartment dwellers, for example, just don't have the space for a permanent electronics workbench. Some ambitious hobbyists may be able to design a suitable foldaway or collapsible workbench. Otherwise, you can use a movable sheet of smooth, heatproof material as a portable worksurface.

Whether your workbench is a permanent unit in a fixed location, or a portable, temporary worksurface, it is a good idea to have a lip or raised edge around the outside rim, as illustrated in Fig. 1-1. This will prevent small screws and tiny components from rolling off the workbench onto the floor, where they can easily get lost or stepped on. At the very least, it is an inconvenience to repeatedly bend over and pick up small dropped items. A simple raised rim is very cheap and easy insurance against such nuisance problems.

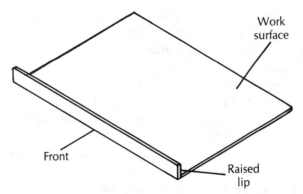

Fig. 1-1 *It is a good idea to have a raised lip around the edges of your work area to stop small parts from falling off.*

Many hardware and hobby stores sell inexpensive, lightweight strips of wood molding which are ideal for this purpose. Unless your workbench is likely to be subjected to a lot of rough treatment, the edging material doesn't have to be particularly sturdy.

Don't make the lip too high, however, or it will be awkward to work on the workbench. A 1/4- to 1/2-inch lip is probably sufficient. Assuming the worksurface is kept level, components that are likely to roll over a 1/4- or 1/2-inch rim probably won't be prone to much rolling in the first place.

These days, most (though not all) electronics projects include one or more digital ICs (integrated circuits). Many of these devices are prone to damage from static electricity. It is handy to have a pad of conductive foam mounted on one corner of your worksurface. Insert IC leads into the foam until you are ready to mount them on the circuit board. The conductive foam will electrically short the IC's leads together, preventing potentially harmful static discharges.

Use of such conductive foam is particularly important if your worksurface is at all conductive, or if your workbench is located in an area with low humidity. Static electricity is much stronger when the humidity is low.

Of course, the foam pad can be used to hold the leads of other components as well, even if they are not static sensitive. With the leads inserted into the foam pad, the parts will stay exactly where you want them, without any rolling around.

For passive components, such as resistors and capacitors, a piece of ordinary styrofoam is fine, but ordinary styrofoam should not be used to hold ICs, especially high-density devices. This is because inserting or removing the leads from the styrofoam could cause a spark of static electricity to jump to the lead, possibly damaging the delicate semiconductor crystal within the IC.

Conductive foam is definitely your best bet for holding all component leads. It may be a bit of ''overkill'' for some noncritical components, but it will never do any harm. Conductive foam pads suitable for holding IC leads are widely available from many electronics parts suppliers.

A permanently mounted soldering iron holder and a cleaning sponge are also helpful on most electronics workbenches These items will be discussed in chapter 2.

Hand tools

Whether you are constructing hobby projects from kits or from scratch, or repairing electronic equipment on either a professional or amateur basis, you'll find certain hand tools absolutely essential in your electronics work.

You won't need all of the tools described in the following few pages for every construction project or repair job; but if you do much electronics work, you will almost certainly need each of these hand tools sooner or later.

None of these tools should cost you too much. It is a good idea to use high-quality tools that will hold up reasonably well to repeated use. But there's no need to go overboard on tool quality. Often, with hand tools, you can pay 50% to 200% more just for a brand name. When doing practical electronics work, who really cares what manufacturer's name is imprinted on the handle? Is the tool well made? Is it reasonably sturdy? Is it the right tool (and size) for your specific job? These are the only questions of importance. Don't waste your money on useless cosmetics.

Pliers

Pliers are used for grasping and holding things. In electronics work, you will be using pliers for relatively small components and wires. Obviously, a heavy-duty plumber's wrench or an automotive monkey wrench will be completely useless on the electronics workbench.

The electronics hobbyist or technician will most frequently use long-nose pliers. This tool, illustrated in Fig. 1-2, is sometimes called needle-nose pliers.

Fig. 1-2 *Long-nose pliers are one of the most useful tools on an electronics workbench.*

Long-nose pliers are a very useful tool in electronics work. They are used for reaching into tight spaces, fastening wires to solder lugs, and retrieving dropped parts from the crowded corners of a chassis.

The distinctive feature of long-nose pliers is the extended grasping area. The jaws of the pliers are long and narrow. Long-nose pliers are available in a number of sizes. Some are longer and some are shorter. Some have moderately wide jaws and others are extremely narrow. If you do a lot of work in electronics, you'll probably find it handy to have two or three different sizes of long-nose pliers. But if you can only afford one, your best bet is one with longer jaws.

Before you buy any long-nose pliers, hold them up to the light and look through the closed jaws. The less light you see between the jaws of the pliers the better. If you can see quite a bit of light between the jaws, then they do not fit together properly.

However, don't make the mistake of rejecting long-nose pliers that has a ridged gripping surface at the tip and light showing through the rest of the way to the hinge. This doesn't necessarily indicate a defect or poor construction in the tool. If the jaws meet evenly over the entire ridged area, you've found good long-nose pliers.

Almost every long-nose pliers features a cutting area near the hinged base of the jaws. This cutting area is handy for cutting lightweight wires or snipping off excess lengths of component leads. Don't try to cut heavy wires with long-nose pliers. The cutting area on this type of tool is designed for light-duty use only. Trying to cut a heavy wire could dull the cutting area, and could also force the jaws of the pliers to open further than they are designed to. This can throw the jaws out of alignment or totally destroy the tool by breaking the hinge.

For occasional, light-duty electronics work, a good long-nose pliers may be all you'll ever need in the way of pliers. However, if you are serious about electronics work, you will soon find that for some jobs long-nose pliers are very awkward, and sometimes won't even do the job at all. The serious electronics hobbyist or technician usually needs a few other types of pliers, in addition to long-nose pliers. Long-nose pliers will probably be fine for about 80% of the pliers-type tasks encountered in electronics work, but that other 20% could present some problems if you don't have a few additional tools handy.

The cutting edge on long-nose pliers is often very handy, but just as often it is totally inadequate. Sooner or later in your electronics work, you will need to cut a wire or component lead in a cramped space. It may be awkward or even impossible to get the cutting area of long-nose pliers into the necessary position.

Anyone who has to cut a lot of wires or component leads will find that using the cutting area of long-nose pliers can very rapidly become awkward and uncomfortable. Obviously, a more specialized tool is needed here. For such wire-cutting tasks, you can use diagonal side-cutting pliers. The name refers to the fact that the cutting edge is along the side of a pair of diagonal (angled) jaws.

In practical, day-to-day use, the name of this gadget is often shortened to cutting pliers, or simply wire cutters. This tool is also widely known as dikes (or dykes). A typical example of this tool is shown in Fig. 1-3.

Fig. 1-3   *Cutting pliers are used to cut wires and component leads.*

Unlike most types of pliers, diagonal side-cutting pliers are not intended for grasping or holding. The sole purpose of this tool is to cut wires. The cutting edges of good diagonal side-cutting pliers are usually sharper and stronger than the cutting edges of typical long-nose pliers. Usually, dikes can cut a heavier gauge wire than long-nose pliers, but there are still practical limitations. Don't ever try to cut oversize wire with undersized diagonal side-cutting pliers. For most practical purposes, oversize wire can be considered as anything over No. 12 (AWG).

If, for some reason, you do need to cut such heavy, oversize wire, first nick it with a knife where you want to cut it, then bend the wire sharply back and forth a few times at the nicked point. The wire will break cleanly right where you want it to, and you'll avoid dulling your wire cutters or damaging the hinge and jaws.

Remember that diagonal side-cutting pliers are intended only for cutting wire. Do not use this tool to cut anything but suitably sized wire and component leads. I've seen a few technicians try to use their cutting pliers as scissors. This ridiculous practice will quickly dull the cutting edges of the pliers. Never try to use dikes as a tin snip. Dikes are not designed to cut even thin sheet metal. They will not do a good job, and the pliers are very likely to be seriously damaged by the attempt.

After you've cut a length of wire, you will often need to strip

some of the insulation off of it. Some hobbyists and a few technicians strip wires with diagonal side-cutting pliers, and X-acto
knife, or even a razor blade. In addition to being awkward and (if
a knife or razor blade is used) potentially dangerous, such makeshift approaches to wire stripping generally don't do a very good
job. It is almost impossible not to nick the wire using such methods. Such a nick could weaken the wire and possibly cause it to
break. Once again, it is best to use a tool specifically designed for
the job; in this case, wire strippers. (Technically speaking, wire
strippers aren't really part of the pliers family, although they are
quite similar.)

One of the most popular and inexpensive types of wire stripper is a very simple type with notched shear-type blades, as
shown in Fig. 1-4. This device is easy to use and rarely costs
more than a couple of dollars. It can easily be adjusted for a variety of different wire sizes. With most wire strippers of this type,
you may need to use long-nose pliers to hold the wire securely
with one hand, while using the wire stripper with the other
hand.

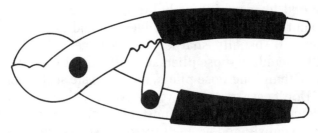

Fig. 1-4 *An inexpensive wire stripper will remove insulation neatly and efficiently, without nicking the wire.*

A common variation of this device is a combination tool
designed for both wire stripping and crimping of solderless terminals. This type of tool tends to be somewhat more expensive
than a plain wire stripper, but there are a number of household
uses for solderless connectors, so it may not be a bad investment,
especially for the general hobbyist.

The best tool for wire stripping is a rather nightmarish-look-
ing type of pliers with a viselike arrangement in one jaw to hold
the body of the wire and a set of tiny knife edges in the other jaw,
with notches in them to fit different standard sizes of wire. When
the handles are squeezed together, the two jaws are moved in

such a way that the insulation is quickly and neatly stripped from the wire.

Naturally, this type of semiautomated tool is more expensive than a simple manual wire stripper, but it is faster, more convenient to use and generally does a better job of wire stripping. This type of wire stripper never nicks wires. As a sort of fringe benefit, it is also fascinating to watch. Semiautomatic wire strippers of this type are usually priced in the $7 to $25 range, depending on the sophistication of the particular design used.

In most electronics work, you will be dealing with fairly small parts, often in small places, so long-nose pliers, as discussed earlier in this section, will be your most useful tool in this class. Sometimes, however, you may find standard snub-nosed pliers, like those shown in Fig. 1-5, a handy supplemental tool. This type of pliers can be used to hold larger components and grommets, as well as to tighten and loosen bolts.

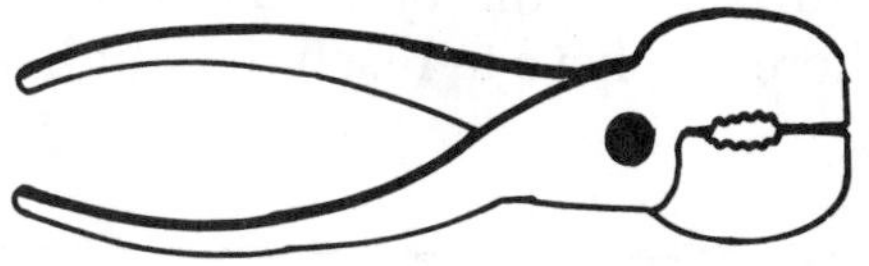

Fig. 1-5 *Standard snub-nosed pliers are sometimes useful on the electronics workbench.*

All too often an electronics hobbyist or technician finds he needs a third hand to hold something in place while he manipulates other components, test leads, or whatever. A locking plier is handy for this purpose. Ordinarily, to hold the jaws of pliers firmly against the object being held, you need to keep a tight grip on the plier's handles. With locking pliers, when you have the object and the jaws in the desired position, you flip a switch or tab on the side of the tool and the pliers stay closed when you let go of the handles.

I've found a set of hemostats to be very useful for holding small components in place. Hemostats have scissorlike handles, with small plierslike grips at the ends of the jaws. It can be easily and quickly locked in place. The strength of the grip can be adjusted so that delicate components will not be crushed.

This is not a common electronics tool, although it should be. Some electronics suppliers do carry hemostats, but if you can't find such a dealer, try a medical supplies store. I first learned about hemostats because my mother was a nurse. Hemostats are available in a wide variety of sizes useful for electronics work.

Wrenches and nutdrivers

Generally speaking, it is not a good idea to tighten or loosen nuts with pliers. It is easy to apply too much pressure with pliers. This could physically mangle and misshape a nut, especially if it is made of soft metal. Also, unless the nut is fairly small, the jaws of the pliers could be forced to open too wide, possibly damaging or even ruining the tool. In particular, never use long-nose pliers to loosen or tighten nuts, although they may be used to hold very small nuts in place while a screw is being tightened.

Pliers are also prone to slipping off a nut while you are trying to tighten or loosen it. This can scratch a painted chassis or mar the finish on a piece of equipment. It can also hurt your hand, perhaps not seriously, but painfully. Who needs it?

A better tool for this type of job is a wrench or a nutdriver. An open-end wrench, like the one shown in Fig. 1-6, is generally the most useful nut loosening and tightening tool when you can approach the nut from the side with adequate swivel room. A nutdriver, on the other hand, comes in handy in tight spaces where you have to reach the nut head on.

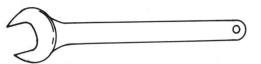

Fig. 1-6 *An open-end wrench is used to tighten and loosen nuts.*

As shown in Fig. 1-7, a nutdriver is similar to a screwdriver, except that instead of a blade, there is a socket on the end for gripping a nut. A plastic handle offers you a convenient grip on the tool. Although a few rather ingenious all-purpose nutdrivers have been marketed, most electronics hobbyists and technicians will usually buy a full set, with each individual nutdriver designed to fit a single standard nut size.

Fig. 1-7 *A nutdriver is a variation on the screwdriver.*

Both fixed open-end wrenches and nutdrivers are available in inch and metric sizes. The two most common sizes of hex-head nuts you are likely to encounter in general electronics work are the 1/4-inch and 1/2-inch sizes. The 1/4-inch nut is used most frequently with 4-40, 6-32, and 8-32 screws. This size nut is also found on a variety of sheet metal screws. The 1/2-inch nut is used in electronics work mostly for the bushings of standard potentiometers and toggle switches.

Because of the differences in how these two nut sizes are commonly used, if you really have to economize a great deal, buy a nutdriver for 1/4-inch hex nuts and an open-end wrench for 1/2-inch hex nuts. Of course, if possible, it is desirable to have both types of tools for both sizes, and possibly a few less commonly used sizes too. A small, adjustable open-end wrench may be a worthwhile investment for the serious electronics hobbyist or technician. An adjustable wrench can be set to accommodate any odd-sized nut you may run up against. Odd-sized nuts (and other parts) are frequently encountered in commercial electronic equipment from foreign manufacturers.

Some electronics hobbyists and technicians may also invest in a socket wrench set. This type of tool is sort of a cross between an open-end wrench and a nutdriver, with a semiautomated ratchet to increase the turning torque. While a good socket wrench set can be nice to have on the electronics workbench, it is scarcely essential. Nuts in electronic equipment do not have to be tightened to their maximum limit. In fact, the small, relatively soft nuts and screws used in such equipment can often be stripped and damaged by overtightening. Besides, few things are as frustrating as trying to open a piece of equipment for essential repairs after some yo-yo has tried to prove how macho he is by making the nut so tight it is virtually impossible to remove.

Socket wrench sets are typically fairly expensive and usually something not needed for electronics applications. As often as not, you won't have enough space in electronics work to provide the full swing required for the ratchet action. Sure, if you have a set of socket wrenches for other purposes, you can use them with your electronics work too, but there is generally very little point in buying this type of tool specifically for use on an electronics workbench.

Screwdrivers

The simple screwdriver is one of the most common and familiar tools used in electronics work. It is also one of the most misused tools of any type. A screwdriver is intended for one purpose, and one purpose only—to tighten and loosen screws of an appropriate size. Never use a screwdriver as a prying tool. You'll almost certainly damage the blade, especially with the smaller screw-drivers most frequently used in electronics work.

A typical screwdriver is illustrated in Fig. 1-8. This is a very simple tool. A plastic handle, usually with ridges of some sort, provides the user with a firm grip. Connected to the end of the handle is a metal shaft. (Stubby screwdrivers with very short shafts, like the one shown in Fig. 1-9, are often useful in tight spots.) The metal shaft is tapered into a blade which fits into a mirror-image slot embedded in the head of the screw.

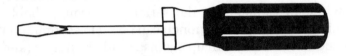

Fig. 1-8   *The screwdriver is one of the most familiar of all hand tools used in electronics work.*

Fig. 1-9   *A stubby screwdriver can come in handy in tight spaces.*

For best results, the blade should fit the screw's slot exactly. Too small or too large a blade could mar and perhaps even destroy the head of the screw, especially if it is made of relatively soft metal.

Some nonmetallic (plastic) screwdrivers are available. These are used to make adjustments in areas where a magnetized shaft could create problems. A screwdriver with a plastic shaft and blade should never be used to tighten or loosen an ordinary screw. The blade will be quickly mangled out of recognition, probably without even tightening or loosening the screw appre-ciably.

In much modern electronics work, some very tiny screws may be encountered. Special tiny screwdrivers are available for such purposes. These tools are often called jeweler's screw-drivers.

For most general electronics work, you will probably need at least two flat-bladed screwdrivers; one with a 1/4-inch blade for most ordinary screws, and one with a 1/8-inch blade for smaller screws and the setscrews found in most knobs. But screws come in a wide variety of sizes, so a full set of screwdrivers is a good investment for the serious electronics hobbyist or technician.

Like nuts, screws are available in both inch and metric sizes. Fortunately, an exactly perfect match is usually not needed, so inch-sized screwdrivers may be used on metric-sized screws, and vice versa.

You will also almost certainly need at least one (and preferably a full set of) Phillips head screwdrivers. Instead of the normal flat slot, a Phillips head screw features a star-shaped (cross) indentation for the blade of the screwdriver. A flat-blade screwdriver cannot be used with a Phillips head screw, and vice versa. These two types of screw heads are compared in Fig. 1-10.

Flat-blade   Phillips head

Fig. 1-10 *Most screwdrivers are designed for either flat-blade or Phillips head screws.*

Some knobs do not have standard slotted head setscrews, but have Allen head setscrews instead. The indentation in an Allen head screw is hexagonal in shape. The tool used for Allen head screws is the Allen wrench, or as it is sometimes called, a hex key wrench. Allen wrenches are very simple and quite inexpensive. Allen head screws come in a wide variety of sizes, so you will need a full set of Allen wrenches. Fortunately, a complete set can usually be purchased for just a few dollars.

You probably won't need to use your Allen wrenches very often, but there are times when nothing else will do the job. But a set of these tools is so inexpensive, most electronics hobbyists and technicians should be able to justify the purchase without suffering too many sleepless nights.

Electric drill and bits

A typical electronics hobbyist will sooner or later need a drill of some sort. A drill is used to prepare holes in a chassis or control panel for potentiometers, switches, screws, and other parts. This tool is less likely to be needed by a service technician repairing existing equipment.

It makes sense to buy an electric drill. A manual drill is just an invitation to frustration and fatigue. An electric drill with a variable-speed motor is preferable, if you can afford it. There are some important advantages to the lower speeds available with many modern electric drills. With slow-speed capability, you can start a hole exactly where you want it, without center-punching it first. At higher drill speeds, the bit will tend to wander from the desired spot. Also, relatively brittle materials, such as plastic and Bakelite, are often used for project cases and printed circuit boards. Such brittle materials should be drilled at low speeds to prevent chipping and cracking.

When you buy drill bits, you'll probably find it doesn't cost much more to buy a complete set than it does to buy one bit of each size you need. However, it is worth knowing that the average electronics hobbyist can usually get by with six basic drill bit sizes, and a few tiny bits for drilling component lead holes in printed circuit boards. The six standard sizes of drill bits you should keep handy are $1/8$ inch, $9/64$ inch, $3/16$ inch, $1/4$ inch, $3/8$ inch, and $1/2$ inch. This small assortment should adequately cover most of the electronics hobbyist's common needs.

Drill bits are commonly sized in $1/64$-inch graduations. The $1/8$-inch bit is useful for making holes for standard 4-40 screws. Similarly, for clearing 6-32 screws, you will need the $9/64$-inch bit, and a 8-32 screw calls for a $3/16$-inch bit. The $1/4$-inch bit is used to make holes to mount the shafts of the most common sizes of variable capacitors (less commonly used in modern electronics projects). The $3/8$-inch bit is needed to make the holes for the bushings of standard potentiometers and toggle switches. A $3/8$-inch bit is also required to make the minimum size starting hole for the jaws of a nibbling tool, which will be discussed shortly. Finally, the $1/2$-inch bit is used to make holes for pilot light assemblies and some kinds of binding posts.

Most electronics stores and supply houses carry special tiny bits for printed circuit work. These bits are exactly the right size to pass the different gauges of wire you will be using. These small printed circuit board drill bits are designed with a somewhat different cutting angle than metal-working drill bits. This allows them to drill brittle printed circuit boards more easily, and reduces the chance of these delicate bits snapping off during drilling. For some printed circuit work, a small manual drill may be preferable to an electric drill, especially if a suitable low speed is not available.

When drilling anything, but especially printed circuit boards, some sort of vise is almost essential. Vises will be discussed later in this chapter.

Nibbling tool

If there was ever a tool to gladden the heart of an electronics hobbyist, the nibbler (or nibbling tool) is it. Once again, this tool is more useful for constructing projects from scratch, rather than repairing existing equipment. Few electronics service technicians bother with a nibbling tool.

The nibbler, shown in Fig. 1-11, works like a small, tool-steel (very hard) shears, with a handle of tremendous mechanical leverage. In operation, the head of the nibbling tool is passed through a 3/8-inch (or larger) hole, and the jaws are carefully positioned for the first cut. From there the nibbler literally cuts out, or nibbles, any desired shape in metal up to 18-gauge mild steel or 16-gauge aluminum. A nibbler is obviously a very useful tool when it comes to creating a customized chassis or control panel.

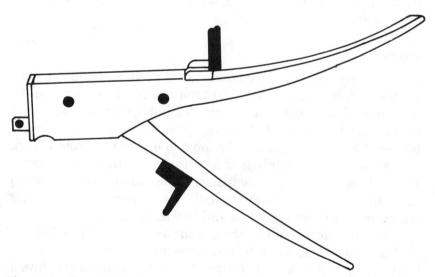

Fig. 1-11 *The nibbling tool is useful for making large or unusually shaped openings in a chassis or control panel.*

Saws

Not every piece of metal or plastic can be successfully or reliably nibbled with a nibbling tool. Often plastic boxes used to house

electronics projects are simply too thick to fit in the jaws of a nibbler. This is where a keyhole saw comes in handy. A keyhole saw
is one designed to fit into a small starting hole. This type of tool
is illustrated in Fig. 1-12.

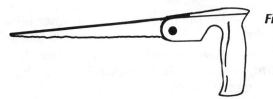

Fig. 1-12 *A keyhole saw
can be used to
enlarge or change
the shape of a
small drilled hole.*

One of the best and least expensive types of keyhole saws for
electronics work consists of an X-acto knife handle with a specially designed keyhole saw blade. It takes some effort to find
these keyhole saw blades in some areas. The surest place to find
them is in a store that caters to model airplane hobbyists.

The electronics hobbyist will also find a small hacksaw very
useful for trimming the shafts on variable capacitors and potentiometers. A vise is virtually essential for holding the component
while its shaft is being sawed. Vises will be discussed later in
this chapter.

Knives

It is certainly nice to have a good pocket knife that you can carry
around and have handy for odd repairs here and there, but for
regular workshop use, the electronics hobbyist will want an X-
acto knife with a full set of blades. The X-acto No. 11 blade will
probably be the one you use the most in electronics hobby work.

An X-acto knife consists of a standard handle (usually metal)
and various interchangeable blades. These blades are very sharp
and can easily cut through insulation with very slight pressure,
which results in fewer nicked and broken wires.

Both the electronics hobbyist and the service technician will
find a good X-acto knife useful occasionally. This tool is relatively inexpensive, and it is almost always a worthwhile investment.

You should be aware that the blades for an X-acto knife tend
to wear out and grow dull fairly quickly. As soon as you notice
that the blade isn't cutting as well as it used to, you should throw
it out (be careful how you discard it—it's still sharp and dangerous) and replace it with a new blade. This will save you consider-

able frustration, particularly if you are using your X-acto knife for delicate work, such as trimming patterns for etched circuits.

Files

Whenever you cut metal or plastic, whether by drilling, sawing, or nibbling, you are bound to leave burrs and rough edges. It is absolutely necessary to file away burrs and smooth down edges before painting. Besides, rough edges around holes look unattractive and can cut fingers.

To remove burrs and smooth cut edges, you will need large and small sizes of round, half-round, and flat files. A very narrow round file is sometimes called a rattail file. Files do not work very well when they are clogged with metal flakes, so you will also need a wire-bristled brush to clean your files periodically.

A 1/2-inch hand reamer may be a handy tool for some electronics hobbyists. It is used to enlarge holes to odd sizes. It will do the job faster and leave a more rounded hole than a file.

Other hand tools

Some electronics hobbyists and technicians may find a need for a few other tools for certain specialized work, but the tools mentioned here will cover most electronics needs. Of course, we have not yet considered any soldering tools. These will be discussed in chapter 2.

Mounting and storing hand tools

Some electronics hobbyists and technicians just leave their hand tools loose in a drawer. This is OK, but it can be a nuisance, especially if you have a number of tools and need to find a specific one in a hurry.

If you have the space for a permanent workbench, I'd recommend mounting a sheet of large perforated (perf) board. Hardware stores sell hooks that can be fitted into the holes, enabling you to hang your tools in plain sight on the board. To keep things as neat as possible, you may want to paint an outline of each tool at its spot on the board.

Certain types of tools, such as screwdrivers, nutdrivers, and certain small files may not hang very well on the perf board hooks. They will tend to fall off with the least vibration. The solution is to place a small length of wood across two or more hooks. Drill small holes in the board for each tool. The blade of a screwdriver, for example, fits through the hole, while the wider handle prevents it from falling all the way through. With tools in graduated sizes (such as screwdrivers), it is very advisable to mount them in order from largest to smallest. That way you can easily and quickly find the one you want.

If you cannot leave a permanent work area set up, the next best approach to hand tool storage is a well-organized tool box. Don't just throw your tools into the toolbox in a careless jumble. A good tool box has sections that allow you to organize your tools for convenient access.

Vises and circuit board holders

Very often while working at your workbench, you'll find you need an extra hand. A circuit board or piece of equipment will need to be held firmly in place while both of your hands are occupied manipulating tools or test leads.

Every electronics workbench, whether for a hobbyist or a professional service technician, should be equipped with one or two small vises. Do not use the heavy-duty vises intended for use in woodworking applications. The jaws of the vise on an electronics workbench should be soft, pliant rubber (or a similar material) to avoid scratching or otherwise marring the cabinet of a piece of equipment being held.

Be careful never to overtighten the vise. The item being held could bend, crack, or even snap in two. Some objects, such as circuit boards, can easily be crushed.

It is usually pretty risky to put an ordinary printed circuit board in a standard vise. A few manufacturers offer special small vises intended for just this purpose. There is also a related device called a third hand, or a circuit board holder. This gadget consists of a sturdy base with two (or sometimes more) movable arms that can be easily positioned in any convenient way. At the end of each arm is a large alligator clip (or similar clamp) that is used to hold a circuit board. The mobility of the arms permits you to hold the board at almost any angle, so this type of holding device is even more versatile than a standard vise.

Vises can be mounted on the edge of a workbench with a secondary viselike holder, or they can be permanently bolted in place. Some small vises have a vacuum base of some sort. They can be firmly mounted on any smooth, dry surface. Later, the vacuum can be broken and the vise can easily be moved. Most third-hand circuit board holders have vacuum bases, although a few are designed to be screwed down to a permanent surface.

Component cabinets

Whether you are building projects from scratch or repairing existing equipment, you will need to keep an assortment of electronic components on hand. If you are a hobbyist who only builds projects from complete kits, this section will not apply to you.

Electronic components are small and come in a wide variety of values. If you are not organized, you'll cause yourself a lot of unnecessary frustration and wasted time searching for the specific component you need.

Obviously, throwing all of your components into a shoe box would not be very efficient. But if you try to use separate boxes for each type of component, the system will quickly become terribly unwieldy. Fortunately, almost any hardware store sells multi-drawer cabinets for storing small parts. This type of cabinet is also sold in sewing and fishing stores.

The cabinet consists of (usually) 10 to 40 pull-out plastic drawers. Resistors, capacitors, transistors, ICs, and so forth easily fit into the drawers. The entire cabinet is fairly compact, and several cabinets can often be stacked. My workbench has three cabinets—one for resistors, one for capacitors, and one for semiconductors (transistors, diodes, and ICs).

You can label each drawer to identify the values or type numbers contained in each compartment. Most of these cabinets come with suitable adhesive labels for exactly this purpose. Component values can be grouped in whatever way you find convenient. My resistor cabinet consists of 40 drawers, arranged in eight rows of five drawers each. The resistor values are divided into five groups from 1 to 10. This grouping is repeated for each row, with each row increasing in value by a factor of 10. This system is laid out in detail in Table 1-1. You can copy this system exactly, modify it to suit your own individual needs, or devise your own storage system. The important thing is to have a system that allows you to locate the desired component quickly and efficiently, with a minimum of fuss and bother.

There is one important restriction to the use of these parts cabinets. Be very, very careful how you store CMOS (complementary metal-oxide semiconductor) IC chips. These devices are very sensitive to damage from static electricity discharges. Unless you

Table 1-1   Typical arrangement of resistor values in a 40-drawer cabinet.

<0.3	0.31–0.45	0.46–0.6	0.61–0.75	0.76–1.0
1.1–3	3.1–4.5	4.6–6.0	6.1–7.5	7.6–10.0
10.1–30	31–45	46–60	61–75	76–100
101–300	310–450	460–600	610–750	760–1000
1.1K–3K	3.1K–4.5K	4.6K–6K	6.1K–7.5K	7.6K–10K
11K–30K	31K–45K	46K–60K	61K–75K	76K–100K
110K–300K	310K–450K	460K–600K	610K–750K	760K–1M
1.1M–3M	3.1M–4.5M	4.6M–6M	6.1M–7.5M	>7.6M

All values are in ohms: K = kilohms (× 1,000); M = megohms (× 1,000,000).

are completely sure your cabinet's drawers are made from non-conductive plastic (and this is not normally the case), do not store unprotected CMOS ICs in them. When in doubt, wrap the chip in aluminum foil or insert its leads into a small piece of conductive foam. It's better to be safe than sorry. A storage system that damages or destroys the items it is supposed to store is obviously not a good idea.

Test equipment and test leads

With a permanent electronics workbench, you should spend some time determining the best arrangement for your test equipment. This is not normally much of an issue with a temporary or portable arrangement, since the test equipment can be set up differently each time, depending on the specific tests you need to make during that particular work session.

Obviously, on a fixed workbench, the most frequently used test equipment (usually the VOM (volt ohm milliammeter) or DMM (digital multimeter) and the oscilloscope) should be the most accessible, while the more exotic, less commonly used equipment should be in the harder to reach corners.

A power supply should be placed in a central position, so it is convenient to access from any point on the workbench. Your workbench power supply should have full current limiting and overpower protection. Whether you are building projects from scratch or repairing existing electronic equipment, momentary short circuits are almost inevitable from time to time. If the power supply willingly pumps out high amounts of current, considerable damage can be done, leading to time-consuming and often expensive repairs. In some cases, certain devices can be damaged beyond repair.

Test equipment that is often used together should be placed near each other. For example, a signal generator will often be used in the same test procedures as an oscilloscope, so it makes sense to keep these two pieces of test equipment side by side.

When arranging the test equipment on your workbench, make sure that all controls are accessible. Some equipment have controls on the back or the bottom of the case. (This represents poor design, in my opinion.)

Make sure all of your test equipment gets adequate air circulation. If several devices are packed closely together and used simultaneously, the heat will tend to accumulate to high levels. A small fan to keep your test equipment cool may be a good idea on a large, heavily equipped workbench.

Be careful never to mount any piece of equipment so that air vents are blocked. Those air vents are there for a reason—they permit air to circulate through the case. If the air vents are blocked, a considerable amount of heat may build up in the equipment. This is likely to lead to premature failure.

A power strip is a good idea for powering the test equipment on your workbench. Flicking one switch ensures that everything is off when you're through working for the day. If possible, get a power strip with automatic overvoltage protection and a built-in circuit breaker. This will help to protect your valuable and possibly expensive equipment.

Store your various test leads so that they do not get tangled. Such tangling of test leads is not only a time-consuming nuisance, but untangling them can put unnecessary strain on the test leads, shortening their useful life span. A good idea is to drape them loosely over individual pegs or hangers. If you have a piece of perf board to store your tools (as discussed earlier in this chapter), you can easily add a few more hooks to keep your test leads handy and accessible.

Of course, it makes sense to store specialized test leads near the equipment they are intended to be used with. For example, high-capacitance probe leads should be kept near the oscilloscope, not near the transistor tester.

Questions of safety

By all means, don't scrimp on safety with your electronics workbench. It's never worth the risk. Make sure all equipment is securely in place. You don't want anything to fall. Heavy equipment could injure someone who happens to be nearby when it falls. Of course, the falling equipment itself is likely to be damaged or even destroyed when it hits the floor.

If children might be in your work area at any time, make absolutely sure that inquisitive little hands can't reach anything dangerous. This includes delicate equipment that they could damage without being hurt themselves. If that does happen, you'll have no one to blame but yourself.

If appropriate, consider buying a humidifier or dehumidifier to suit the environment of your particular workbench. As a rule of thumb, humidity should be in the 40% to 60% range, if possible. (Admittedly, this is not always possible.) If the humidity is much lower than this, static electricity is likely to build up, leading to stray discharges which could easily damage or destroy CMOS ICs or other delicate electronic components. If you have this type of problem, get a humidifier. Unless you are in a very extreme desert environment, you probably should leave the humidifier running on its "low" setting.

On the other hand, too much humidity can be just as bad (albeit in different ways) as too little humidity. Humidity, as you should know, is a measure of the amount of moisture (or water vapor) in the air. Too much moisture can speed up rusting and corrosion of certain electronic components and metal or plastic parts. Condensation of the water vapor from a high-humidity environment can cause sticking or slippage of moving parts, or even dangerous short circuits between closely spaced wires or printed circuit traces.

Excess humidity is most likely with a workbench in a basement. A dehumidifier to remove excess moisture from the air is often a very good investment, and in certain areas it may be absolutely essential.

Of course, actual water (whether spilled or as the result of flooding) should be absolutely guarded against, especially when electrical power is applied to anything on the workbench. The shock hazard from even just a little bit of water in the wrong place can be enormous, and sometimes deadly.

Make sure that all electrical equipment on your workbench (both test equipment and especially any circuits you might be working on) has adequate short-circuit protection. Everything should be protected by a fuse or a circuit breaker. For expensive equipment, multiple fusing isn't always overkill. For example, an oscilloscope will usually have a built-in fuse. Plug it into a power strip with a circuit breaker anyway. This protection is added to the main circuit breakers or fuses of your house's electrical wiring system.

Short circuits are particularly likely when you are working on an open circuit board, so you really can't have too much protection here. Whenever possible, use a power supply with current limiting and a built-in fuse plugged into a power strip with a circuit breaker; and always keep a careful eye on what you are doing.

Never, ever defeat the purpose of any fuse or circuit breaker. Do not bypass it, even temporarily. Never substitute a fuse of a higher value. If you do, some expensive component is likely to blow out to protect the fuse, and you certainly don't want that. You also run a far greater risk of receiving a dangerous electrical shock if you bypass a fuse or circuit breaker or use a fuse with too high a rating. It is never worthwhile to take such foolish chances.

With a little forethought and common sense, you can set up your electronics workbench for maximum efficiency and safety. Take your time setting up your work area. I guarantee that you'll end up paying for any carelessness or sloppiness sooner or later. In some cases you could pay with your life or serious (or at least painful) bodily injuries. In other cases, you will pay with unnecessarily damaged equipment or components. You will almost certainly pay with increased frustration and needlessly wasted time. Take the time now to set up your electronics workbench so that it works for you. In the long run, you'll be glad you did.

❖ 2
Soldering aids and construction helps

ONE THING IS CERTAIN. IF YOU WORK WITH ELECTRONICS IN any capacity whatsoever, you're probably going to have to do some soldering. This chapter discusses equipment and methods for good soldering, which is useful for both electronics hobbyists and electronics service technicians. Both hobbyists and technicians will want to pay close attention to the section on soldering-related problems.

We will also look at a few construction aids; this will be primarily of interest to hobbyists. Professional service technicians may want to skim through that section, or perhaps skip it altogether.

Solder

There are many different types of solder, intended for various purposes, many of which are outside the realm of electronics. For example, acid-core solder is often used for soldering pipes. This type of solder must never be used in any electronics work. The acid contained in the core of this solder is highly corrosive. It will quickly and thoroughly destroy most electronics components and eat holes through circuit boards. Acid-core solder is not intended for electronics work and should never be used for this purpose.

For electronics work, rosin-core solder should be used. As the solder is heated to its melting point, the rosin vaporizes and cleans the joint as it is made. This ensures a good, reliable electrical connection between the wires being soldered together.

Most electronics hobbyists and technicians use solder that comes in a wirelike form containing a core of rosin in the center. This type of solder is very easy and convenient to use. Some technicians and hobbyists, however, prefer to use solid, coreless solder, with separately applied rosin flux. I think most of us would find this approach unnecessarily messy and awkward for general electronics, but if you prefer it, there is nothing wrong with it. The separate rosin flux is usually in the form of a semiliquid paste.

There is one special case in which the use of solid solder and a separate rosin flux is called for. This is when you need to solder something directly to an aluminum chassis. For most low-frequency circuits, chassis grounds are normally achieved with solder lugs and screws. The metal screw and solder lug make electrical contact with the metal (usually aluminum) chassis, and the necessary wires are soldered to the solder lug. This works fine when we're dealing with low-frequency, low-power signals.

For some high-power or high-frequency circuits, however, this method does not make adequate electrical contact with the chassis. Stray capacitances (which become important at higher frequencies) may be created, causing the circuit to perform improperly. In such circuits, it is sometimes necessary to solder the circuit wires directly to the chassis (which is typically made of aluminum). Unfortunately, you cannot use ordinary rosin-core solder for this purpose. The joint will not hold because the oxide coating the aluminum chassis resists the cleaning effects of the rosin flux.

There is a special aluminum-soldering flux available which cleans away aluminum oxide and permits the solder to flow properly when heated. This flux is in the form of a separately applied paste. Solid (coreless) solder should be used with any separate flux paste.

Basically, solder is an alloy of tin and lead. The relative amounts of these two metals in the solder determine its characteristics, especially its melting point. For electronics work you need a solder that melts at relatively low temperatures. This is because many electronics components (especially semiconductors) are very sensitive to heat and can be damaged or destroyed if soldering is done at too high a temperature. Another important reason to keep the soldering temperature as low as possible is the close spacing of the solder joints in most electronic circuits. There is not room for large amounts of heat to dissipate safely.

If too low a temperature is used, the solder will not melt completely, and it won't flow properly over the joint. The rosin flux may not vaporize enough to perform its necessary cleaning action. The result is a cold solder joint, and a poor electrical connection.

The ideal alloy for electronics work is a 63-37 solder. This means the solder is composed of 63% tin and 37% lead. This type of solder is known as eutectic solder, and has the lowest possible melting point of any tin-lead solder. Because of it's low melting point, cold solder joints are rare if eutectic solder is used. Unfortunately, true eutectic solder is generally quite hard to find and usually rather expensive. Apparently, it is difficult to manufacture this particular alloy.

Most practical electronics soldering is done with a 60-40 alloy. This type of solder is made of 60% tin and 40% lead. It has no special name, but is often called "electronics solder," or something similar. The melting point of this type of solder is not as low as that of eutectic solder, but it is still reasonably low. With proper soldering technique, cold solder joints shouldn't be too much of a problem. We will discuss cold solder joints in more detail later in this chapter. Rosin-core 60-40 solder is widely available from almost any store that caters to electronics hobbyists and technicians. Radio Shack, for example, carries a wide variety of sizes.

In a pinch, you can probably get away with a 50-50 alloy solder, but never use any solder with a higher proportion of lead then this. The required temperature to fully melt the solder is too high to be safe for electronic circuits.

Electronics solder is usually sold in a wirelike form on a roll. A wide variety of sizes (diameters) are available. Use common sense when selecting a solder size. If you are making small solder joints, such as for the pads of an IC on a printed circuit board, you'll want the finest, thinnest solder available to avoid solder bridges and shorting of the joint to an adjacent joint. On the other hand, if you are soldering wires to large solder lugs, it will take you forever with a very thin solder. In this case, you will want to use a thicker solder wire.

If you do more than occasional electronics work, it is probably a very good idea to keep several different sizes of solder on hand. Many hobbyists and technicians mount holders for their rolls of solder (like miniature paper towel holders) on their workbench. This keeps the solder handy, but out of the way at all times.

When buying a roll of solder, it usually makes sense to buy the largest roll available, unless your electronics work is very infrequent. The per foot cost of solder goes down considerably as the size of the roll increases. It is not very economical to buy solder in small quantities. For one thing, you end up paying a lot extra for all the packaging. In very small quantities (less than about 25 feet), this can account for more than half the price of the solder.

You may occasionally run across tape solder. This type of solder is in the form of little strips of tape that are wrapped around the joint to be soldered. Tape solder has an extremely low melting point and can be melted with a match. This can be handy for a quick and dirty repair in an emergency situation, but it doesn't do a very good job for most general electronics work.

Soldering irons and guns

There are two broad categories of tools used for soldering. The differences between the two are slight, and different sources may define them somewhat differently. The two basic types of soldering tools are known as soldering irons and soldering guns.

A soldering iron has a heated tip at the end of a shaft. On the opposite end of the shaft is an insulated handle, as illustrated in Fig. 2-1. Very small soldering irons are sometimes called soldering pencils or pencil irons. The only difference here is the overall physical size of the tool.

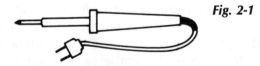

Fig. 2-1 *Most electronics hobbyists use a pencillike soldering iron.*

Typically, current flows through a soldering iron, heating the tip as long as power is applied to the tool. In most cases, power is applied through a cord plugged into an ac outlet.

A soldering gun is functionally similar to a soldering iron, but the handle is in the shape of a gunlike grip, as shown in Fig.

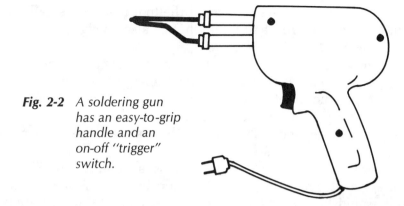

Fig. 2-2 *A soldering gun has an easy-to-grip handle and an on-off "trigger" switch.*

2-2. Usually, though not always, a soldering gun will have a trigger that serves as an on-off switch.

On some models, current is fed to the tip (heating the tip) only when the trigger switch is held in. Releasing the trigger on this type of soldering gun stops further current from flowing through the device. The tip will then cool down.

More commonly, the trigger serves as a push-type on-off switch. Pushing the trigger switch once allows current to flow through the soldering gun, heating the tip. The current will continue to flow through the tool until the switch is pressed again (or the power source is removed, of course). Pushing the trigger switch a second time turns off the soldering gun. Current no longer flows through the tool, and the tip cools down. On some units, a small indicator light mounted somewhere on the tool (usually on the handle or on a separate base) glows to let you know that the soldering gun is on and power is being applied to the tip. This is a handy feature and can help prevent accidents. With a standard soldering iron, the only way to turn the tool off is to unplug it from the power source (ac outlet).

With any soldering iron (or gun), always remember that the well-established laws of physics dictate that it takes a finite amount of time for the tip to heat up when power is applied or to cool down when power is removed. Do not expect instant on-off operation with this type of tool. It just isn't possible.

Considerable care is required when using any soldering iron or gun. Bear in mind that the tip gets extremely hot when power is applied to the tool. Carelessness could be extremely dangerous.

Both soldering irons and soldering guns are available in a wide variety of sizes. Some have interchangeable tips. There are two sizes of importance to consider when choosing a soldering iron (or gun)—the physical size of the tool itself (especially the tip, but the shaft width and length may also be significant) and the "electrical size," or wattage.

Any soldering iron (or gun) is designed to convert electrical energy into heat. The more electrical energy the tool uses, the greater the amount of heat produced. The wattage of a soldering iron (or gun) is an indirect measurement of the amount of heat the tool can generate. The higher the wattage, the greater the heat.

For large, heavy-duty soldering jobs, a large, relatively high-wattage soldering iron (or gun) should be used. A low-wattage unit would be inefficient for soldering wires to an aluminum chassis, for example. Cold solder joints would be almost inevitable under such circumstances.

On the other hand, for soldering components onto delicate circuit boards, a small, low-wattage soldering iron (or gun) must be used. In tight areas, too large a tip may prevent you from directly applying the heat to the joint being made. Too high a wattage will produce too much heat, possibly damaging certain electronic components, especially semiconductors. Excessive heat can also cause printed circuit traces to peel off the surface of the board. In short, this is another case of using the right tool for the job.

For most modern electronics work, you can probably get by with just a single, relatively small, low-wattage (25- to 30-watt) soldering iron. The pistol handle of a soldering gun may be awkward and inconvenient when servicing certain types of equipment. If possible, choose a soldering iron with interchangeable tips. Use a fine-point tip for delicate circuit board work and a broader, flat-edged tip for soldering wires to solder lugs, large transformers, and the like.

Some modern soldering irons and soldering guns feature a rheostat that allows you to manually adjust the wattage (and therefore the heat at the tip) for various applications. Another nice feature is a small indicator light that glows whenever power is applied to the tool. This is especially handy for units with a trigger on-off switch, as previously discussed.

Recently, small battery operated and rechargeable soldering irons have been made available. These units are, of physical necessity, always on the low-wattage type. They would be a time-consuming nuisance on a regular workbench. Batteries would be consumed very rapidly, or frequent recharging would be required. These tools are not intended for regular day-to-day use. But, for occasional field work (away from your bench), battery operated and rechargeable soldering irons can be extremely handy, especially if you ever need to make an emergency soldering repair without convenient access to an ac outlet.

Proper soldering technique

Soldering is not a particularly difficult skill to learn. If you have no experience with soldering, it is probably a good idea to practice with some scrap pieces of wire and junk components before you begin an actual project or kit or attempt to make a repair in an existing electronic circuit.

While soldering is fairly simple to do, poor soldering technique is one of the leading causes of problems with kits and projects that do not work. Bad solder joints show up as problems in commercially available electronic equipment too; a lot more often than you may think.

Most of the soldering done in factories today is done by machine or by people on an assembly line. Soldering machines occasionally apply too much or too little solder, and they don't notice if the circuit board to be soldered is in the wrong position or oriented at the wrong angle. Small flaws in the soldering machinery, or in the solder itself, can also cause a bad solder joint.

A factory assembly line is usually manned by unskilled or semiskilled workers, especially in some (certainly not all) overseas factories. The work is monotonous and the workers are encouraged to keep the line moving as fast as possible to produce the maximum number of completed units in the shortest possible time. Any human being is fallible. A few bad solder joints in any large run are probably inevitable, and the worker generally has no chance (and no encouragement) to check his work.

Better factories do use some form of quality control on the finished product. Sometimes, this is done by pulling a random unit from the line and checking it thoroughly. Deluxe models are usually individually checked to make sure that basic functions work.

Some problems will inevitably slip by the best quality control program. It's not unheard of to buy a brand new piece of electronic equipment in its original factory packaging, and discover it doesn't work from the word go. This is usually due to some sort of soldering problem somewhere within its circuitry.

More commonly, a cold solder joint may let the unit work fine for awhile, then, because of the poor, unstable electrical connection within the cold solder joint, the unit suddenly stops working. The problem may then be continuous or intermittent (the symptoms come and go). A technician must repair the equipment, even though it came from the factory with the flaw. This type of problem is one reason why all reputable manufacturers offer at least some minimal form of warranty on electronic equipment.

Cold solder joints and other soldering problems will be discussed in more detail later in this chapter. First, let's take some time to consider how proper soldering should be done.

To get good solder joints, you first need to prepare and clean your soldering iron (or gun). Flakes of old solder and miscellaneous crud can rapidly build up on the tip of a soldering iron (or gun). Heating this garbage wastes energy and insulates the tip from the joint to be soldered. Sometimes this accumulated gunk can slowly corrode the metal of the tip, resulting in a pitted, unevenly heated surface.

Before plugging in your soldering iron (or gun), make it a practice to briefly examine the tip. If it looks bad, it is bad. When in doubt, assume the worst. If the tip is crusty and corroded, use a fine-toothed file to clean away the accumulated crud. File down to the bare copper of the tip. If you don't want to bother with filing, or if the tip has already been filed several times and doesn't have much metal left, discard the tip and replace it. This is another good reason to buy a soldering iron (or gun) with interchangeable tips. If the tip is permanently mounted, the entire tool must be discarded when the tip goes bad. Usually, the heating unit is still perfectly good, so this is unquestionably a wasteful approach.

Once you've got a nice, bright tip, heat up your soldering iron (or gun). Wait until it is fully heated before you attempt to use it.

Once the full operating temperature is reached, you must tin the tip. Tinning is nothing more than coating the tip with an even coat of fresh solder. If the tip is not tinned, the solder will not flow over the joint properly. It will be sucked up to the tip.

As you are soldering, periodically pause between joints and wipe the tip with a rag or moist sponge to keep the solder on the tip bright and shiny. This should be done quickly because the tip is very hot and you want to avoid burning yourself or setting the cleaning rag or sponge on fire. The rag or sponge should be moist, but not dripping wet.

Special chemically treated cleaning sponges are available from many electronics dealers, including Radio Shack. Usually the sponge is sold in a nonskid holder. Many soldering iron holders have a built-in cleaning sponge. This permits convenient one-handed operation.

Periodically check the tip of the soldering iron (or gun) as you work. Occasionally, during a moderate to long soldering session, you may have to retin the tip. When you are through working and have unplugged your soldering iron (or gun), wipe the tip as it is cooling to keep the tinning layer of solder clean and shiny.

This may seem like a lot of fuss and bother, but these simple steps will greatly extend the life of your soldering iron (or gun) and the tip. Soldering iron (gun) tips may not be terribly expensive, but such costs can add up quickly if you are careless. More importantly, these procedures will ensure faster heating and good solder joints, which should be vitally important to any electronics hobbyist or technician.

Now we're ready to consider the actual process of soldering. Any good solder joint requires a firmly fixed base of some sort. This might be a pad on a printed circuit board, a solder lug, a tie point on a terminal strip, a push-in terminal on a piece of perf board, or a pin on the base of a transistor or tube socket. With very few exceptions, it is not a good idea to connect two (or more) electronic components except by soldering them to a good, fixed support.

If a piece of insulated wire is to be soldered, you need to strip away some of the insulation from the end of the wire. Some wire has special insulation that vaporizes when it is heated during soldering. If you are unsure of the type of insulation used, always assume that the insulation must be removed before soldering. Attempting to solder ordinary insulation will result in a bad solder joint and melted bits of insulation dripping all over the circuit board. It will also gunk up the tip of your soldering iron (or gun). Some of the ordinary insulation will be vaporized during soldering; the fumes will, at best, smell bad and in some cases may be somewhat poisonous. They certainly aren't going to do any good. Don't attempt to heat vaporize any insulation that was not specifically designed for that. Strip the insulation from the wire before soldering. Wire-stripping tools were discussed in chapter 1.

It is usually a good idea to tin the ends of the wire or the component leads before making the actual solder joint. This is especially important when stranded wire is used, but it is a good idea for solid wire too. It may not always be necessary, but it never hurts, and it's better to be safe than sorry. It just takes a couple of seconds.

Tinning a wire or component lead is just like tinning the tip of a soldering iron (or gun). Melt a little solder and allow it to flow evenly over the wire or component lead to be soldered.

Once you have the ends of your wire or component lead prepared, the next step is to fasten it firmly to the support point, as shown in Fig. 2-3. It is important to make a good mechanical connection if you want to guarantee a good, reliable electrical connection. Soldering the joint shown in Fig. 2-4 will almost certainly lead to problems when operating the finished circuit.

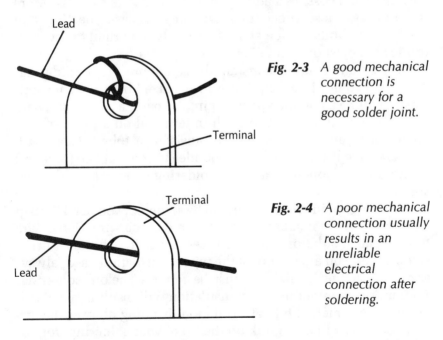

Fig. 2-3 *A good mechanical connection is necessary for a good solder joint.*

Fig. 2-4 *A poor mechanical connection usually results in an unreliable electrical connection after soldering.*

Bend the wires and leads and crimp them slightly. The mechanical strength of the joint should come from the physical connection. Don't rely on the solder to physically hold the joint together. On printed circuit boards, all you have to do is push the wire or component lead through the hole drilled in the board, and bend the end against the copper to secure it.

Before applying any heat to the joint, take a moment to ask yourself, What will the heat of soldering do to the components attached to this joint? Many electronic components can be damaged or destroyed by excessive heat, and sometimes even by the normal heat of soldering. This is especially true of semiconductor components, such as transistors, diodes, and ICs. If there is any possibility of heat damage to any components near a joint to be soldered, be sure to use a heat sink of some sort. Soldering heat sinks will be discussed later in this chapter.

Specially designed heat sinks for soldering purposes are widely available from electronics dealers. In some cases, you can use a makeshift heat sink fashioned from a paper clip, or you can use an alligator clip or hemostat (see chapter 1). In a real pinch, you can lean a screwdriver blade or the jaws of your pliers against the component to be protected from the heat of soldering. Obviously a heat sink that can be clipped on will make the job much easier.

Once you have a good physical joint, and delicate components are suitably protected, you are ready to apply heat to the joint. The object is to heat the joint so that when the solder is touched to it, the solder will melt and flow over the joint. This is illustrated in Fig. 2-5. Notice that you should not apply the solder to the tip of the iron (or gun) and let it flow down onto the joint. Doing this will not give you a good, clean solder joint. On occasion it may be convenient to apply a surplus drop of solder to the tip of the soldering tool to aid in the heat flow, but the bulk of the solder must be applied directly to the joint.

After you've gained a little experience, you will be able to tell whether the solder is flowing properly by observing the way it covers the joint. The melted solder should wet all the surfaces it comes in contact with, just like a drop of water would. If the solder stands up and beads on the surface, then the joint isn't hot enough and the solder connection is incomplete.

This is the most common cause of a type of soldering failure known as a rosin joint. At first glance, the joint looks solid, yet all that is holding the parts together is a thin film of rosin flux. The joint certainly won't hold for long.

One quick and dirty test is to jiggle the joint after it has cooled. If the soldering was done properly, the joint should be quite solid. Do not jiggle the joint before it has fully cooled, how-

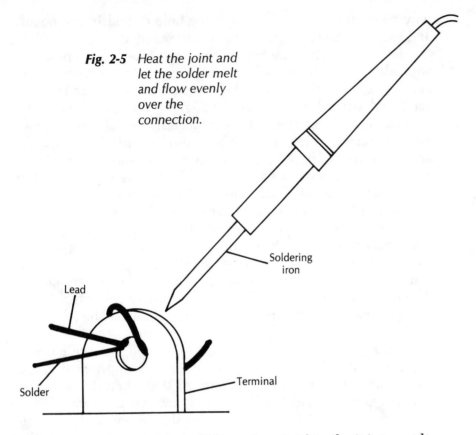

Fig. 2-5 *Heat the joint and let the solder melt and flow evenly over the connection.*

Soldering iron

Lead

Solder

Terminal

ever. This could cause air bubbles to form within the joint, resulting in a cold solder joint.

It is not possible to illustrate a cold solder joint, but the experienced electronics hobbyist or technician soon gets pretty good at recognizing them. A good solder joint looks clean, smooth, and shiny. A bad (cold) solder joint looks rough, dull, and pitted. Unfortunately, in some cases a solder joint may look good, but may still be a cold solder joint.

Cold solder joints usually result in unreliable electrical connections at the joint, which can often cause intermittent problems. They can create a very high resistance in the connection which can easily throw off the operation of the circuit. In some cases, a cold solder joint can act like a diode, introducing unwanted audio from nearby radio stations into audio amplifier circuits. Enormous problems can be created by such unwanted signals in digital circuits.

Do not use too much solder when making the joint. Use just enough solder to fully wet the whole joint. Large globs of solder can interfere with pins in sockets and can easily cause shorts with adjacent solder joints. Such solder bridges can be a particular problem on printed circuit boards with tiny, closely spaced traces. Solder bridges can show up in commercially manufactured electronic equipment too.

Often a stray globule of solder will adhere someplace harmless. Later, after the equipment has been fully assembled, the globule of solder can break free and land almost anywhere. This can cause an intermittent (and occasionally a permanent) short circuit. Make sure your soldering work is neat. Don't let any stray globules of solder get away from you.

Soldering problems

As stated earlier in this chapter, bad soldering is one of the major causes of problems in electronic equipment. This is especially true of hobbyist projects and kits, but such problems also occur in commercially manufactured equipment. Occasionally a joint will not have sufficient solder, or in some cases, may not have been soldered at all. The latter problem is most likely to come from a factory with an automated soldering machine. The electrical connection of such an unsoldered joint will be weak and unreliable. Intermittent operation problems are the likely result.

The problem can usually be located with a simple visual check of the circuitry exhibiting the intermittent operation. In a large system there may be hundreds or even thousands of joints, but a good electronics technician can usually narrow the problem down to a specific area or subcircuit based on the specific symptoms. The solution to such problems is to apply more solder to the connection.

On most printed circuit boards, the traces are very closely spaced. It is very easy for solder to overlap two or more traces, producing a short circuit. This is called a solder bridge. Solder bridges are most likely to show up in hobbyist projects and kits. In a commercial factory, the quality control program should catch such problems. If a piece of equipment with a solder bridge should happen to reach a dealer's shelves, it will exhibit problems right out of the box. Once again, a visual inspection is the best way to find solder bridges. A magnifying glass and a good, strong light can help considerably.

It really is not too difficult to avoid forming solder bridges when constructing a circuit. Just work slowly and carefully.

Don't use too much solder. Use just enough to adequately cover the joint. Any excess beyond this is wasteful and just asking for solder bridge problems. As you make each joint, take a moment to examine it carefully before moving on to the next joint. A little extra time taken here could save you hours of frustrating trouble-shooting and repair time later.

A related problem is the temporary or intermittent solder bridge. This is caused by a loose globule of solder rolling around the circuitry. If a stray drop of solder lands in the wrong place when soldering, it can adhere to the surface, then later break off, leaving it free to land anywhere within the circuitry. The loose bead of solder can easily get caught so that it touches two or more traces on a printed circuit board or other conductors. The metal-lic solder will conduct electricity between the traces creating a short circuit.

A visual inspection can usually solve this problem. Just remove the loose bit of solder and the problem should clear up. You should be aware, however, that certain short circuits can cause permanent damage to some components in the circuit, so more extensive repairs may be needed. Suspect a loose globule of solder when you have an intermittent problem and the symptoms change or you hear a small rattling sound when you sharply rap or gently shake the equipment.

The real bane of every electronics hobbyist's and techni-cian's existence is the cold solder joint. A cold solder joint is formed when the solder is not sufficiently heated to flow prop-erly around the joint. Essentially, instead of a solid joint, there is a bubble inside, as illustrated in Fig. 2-6. The electrical connec-tion is unreliable. In some cases there may be no electrical con-nection at all. More commonly, the connection will periodically make and break, causing intermittent symptoms. Sometimes the circuit works just fine and other times it acts up. Occasionally, a cold solder joint will let the circuit work properly for awhile,

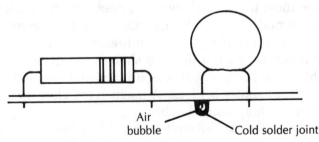

Air bubble   Cold solder joint

Fig. 2-6 *A cold solder joint does not make a good electrical connection.*

then it will suddenly go bad and the circuit won't work properly until the joint is repaired.

In some cases, a cold solder joint can be spotted visually. A good solder joint will look clean, smooth, and shiny. If a joint looks dull and pitted, it's usually safe to assume that it is a cold solder joint. Unfortunately, some cold solder joints look perfectly fine, but inside they're defective.

The normal cure for a cold solder joint is to simply reheat the solder and allow it to flow around the joint properly. In some cases you may need to add a little more solder. With a very bad joint, it's often advisable to remove the old solder (desoldering tools are discussed later in this chapter) and redo the joint.

I've found that in repairing electronic equipment with possible cold solder joints, it's worthwhile to reheat any suspect joints. In several "tough dog" repairs, I finally just reheated all the solder joints in the troublesome portion of the circuit, and as often as not, this has cleared up the problem. Obviously the problem was one (or more than one) cold solder joint. Who knows which of the joints I reheated was the troublemaker? And who cares? Often it takes less time and trouble to reheat all the solder joints than to try to pinpoint the specific problematic cold solder joint. As long as no semiconductor components are overheated (use heat sinks), no harm is likely to be done by reheating a good solder joint.

Heat sinks

Many electronic components are heat sensitive. Too much heat can cause some resistors or capacitors to change their value. More importantly, some components (especially semiconductors) can be permanently damaged or destroyed by too much heat.

During soldering, a great deal of heat is concentrated into a small area. The metallic lead of the component being soldered conducts the heat into the body of the component. To avoid problems from overheating delicate electronic components, it is important to direct the heat someplace else, where it can dissipate into the surrounding air safely. This is done with a device called a heat sink.

A heat sink is a metallic object that can be physically connected to the lead between the joint being soldered and the body of the component. Because the metallic conducting surface of the heat sink is larger than the surface area of the component lead, the heat sink absorbs most of the excess heat energy from the joint being soldered. The heat is then dissipated into the surrounding air.

You can create a temporary heat sink with almost any metallic tool. For example, you can hold a screwdriver blade or pliers against the component lead being soldered. Unfortunately, this requires an extra hand during the soldering process and is often awkward, and in some cases this trick may be impossible to pull off.

It's better to have a heat sink that clamps onto the component lead, leaving your hands free for other purposes. A hemostat (as described in chapter 1) will often do the job quite well. You can use a simple alligator clip as a heat sink, or you can fashion a makeshift heat sink from a paper clip. A paper clip heat sink is particularly handy for solder DIP-type (dual in-line pin) ICs. The paper clip can be fitted around all of the pins on one side of the chip so you don't have to move it after soldering each individual pin.

Whenever possible, it is best to use a tool designed specifically for the job at hand, especially if you do a lot of soldering. Specially designed heat sinks for soldering purposes are widely available from most electronics dealers. These are special spring-loaded clips designed for a large surface-to-air contact area for maximum heat dissipation. A typical heat sink of this type is illustrated in Fig. 2-7. These commercially marketed heat sinks are available in a wide variety of useful sizes.

Fig. 2-7 Spring-loaded heat sinks are useful when soldering heat-sensitive components, such as semiconductors.

Another way to avoid destroying delicate (and expensive) semiconductor components is to use sockets. This isn't very practical for simple semiconductor devices, such as diodes and inexpensive transistors, but sockets are extremely helpful for ICs.

Some electronics hobbyists and technicians don't believe in the use of IC sockets except in special cases where the chip must be changed frequently (like a PROM (programmable read-only memory) IC). They argue that often the socket will cost as much as or more than the IC being protected. But it isn't so much a matter of protecting the IC, as protecting your time and sanity. If there is a problem and an IC has to be replaced, desoldering and resoldering each of the pins can be a real time-consuming nuisance. Why bother with it?

You don't even have to do the damage while soldering. Every once in awhile, you'll run into a dud chip. Even if it works at first, if you need to replace it later, you'll be thankful for an IC socket.

There are some cases when IC sockets are definitely not advisable. In certain high-frequency circuits, a socket can introduce some problematic stray capacitances into the circuit. Also, in some portable equipment, there may be a problem with the chips bouncing out of the socket.

In most electronic circuits, however, the regular use of IC sockets sounds like a worthwhile idea to me. In fact, when repairing commercial equipment without sockets, I'll often add a socket when I have to remove and replace an IC. I consider it a very worthwhile investment. You might call it a form of insurance against future trouble. Of course, in some very tightly spaced circuits, there simply isn't room for a socket.

When an IC socket is used, there is no need for a heat sink. The socket itself isn't sensitive to the heat of normal soldering, and the semiconductor chip is not inserted until after all the soldering has been done, so the risk of heat damage to the component is neatly avoided.

I've occasionally heard one rather curious objection to the use of IC sockets. Supposedly they make it easy to insert the IC backwards. Well, yes; but it's just as easy to solder it into the circuit backwards. Carelessness is carelessness, and sockets have nothing to do with it. Always check the orientation of any polarized component before applying power to the circuit.

There is, however, one risk that is more or less unique to IC sockets. Sometimes one or more pins can get bent up under the body of the IC, instead of fitting into the hole in the socket. Insert and remove all ICs into and out of sockets very carefully to avoid such problems.

Soldering aids

Besides heat sinks, and the soldering iron and soldering gun themselves, there are a number of tools available to aid in the soldering process. Some of these soldering aids are extremely simple, but quite useful. For examples, Radio Shack sells an inexpensive set of several soldering aid tools. This set includes an awl to help poke through circuit board holes that have gotten filled with solder, picks to chip away unwanted solder, and a small wire-bristle brush for cleaning away small loose globules of molten solder. Such tools are far from essential. Most electronics hobbyists and technicians get by without them, but they can make certain soldering jobs a lot easier. Because these soldering aids carry such low price tags, they are not really a luxury. There's really no good reason not to include a set of such tools on your workbench.

If you use your soldering iron more than two or three times a year, you definitely should get a soldering iron holder. This is simply a metal stand to safely hold the hot soldering iron while you are inserting new components onto a circuit board or preparing the next joint to be soldered. A holder prevents the soldering iron from rolling around or coming in contact with anything it shouldn't—like delicate, heat-sensitive electronic components or anything flammable. A loose soldering iron can even melt away the insulation on or burn through its own power cord. This is an incredibly dangerous fire and shock hazard. A soldering iron holder is also convenient. The handle of the soldering iron is always in a fixed place, ready to be grabbed, without risking a burn from the hot shaft and tip. Here again, a perfectly adequate soldering iron holder won't cost you more than a few dollars, so it can hardly be considered a frivolous luxury.

Some electronics hobbyists and technicians solidly mount their soldering iron holder to a fixed position on their workbench. Others prefer the option of moving the soldering iron around on the workbench, within handy reach while they're soldering and out of the way when they're doing other work, such as using test equipment. Your choice will ultimately depend on your personal preferences, the size of your work area, and the type of electronics work you usually do.

Special chemically treated sponges for cleaning the tips of hot soldering irons (or soldering guns) are available. Usually, the sponge is contained in a nonskid holder of some sort. Some deluxe soldering iron holders feature built-in cleaning sponges.

Probably the most important types of soldering aid tools are desoldering tools. These devices are also sometimes known as solder suckers. Suppose you've used a little too much solder on a joint, or maybe you have to clean up a solder bridge between traces on a printed circuit board. In making electronic repairs, you will often need to remove the solder from a joint so you can replace a defective component. The question is, How do you get rid of all the old solder? The solution is to heat the joint so that the solder to be removed is melted. Then, the unwanted solder is sucked away by a desoldering tool.

There are three basic types of desoldering tools in widespread use in modern electronics work. Listing them from the least to most expensive, they are the desoldering braid, vacuum bulb, and spring-loaded desolderer. Even a spring-loaded desolderer (the most expensive type) will only cost about $4 to $15, depending on its design and sophistication.

Desoldering braid is a lot like a broad, flat stranded wire. A number of tiny wire strands are wound together into a fairly wide braid. By placing the end of a clean braid against a hot joint covered with molten solder, capillary action draws the liquid solder up into the braided wires, removing it from the joint. After you have desoldered the joint, the used portion of the braid is cut off and discarded. Desoldering braid is usually sold on spools, like ordinary wire.

Some electronics hobbyist and technicians find desoldering braid very easy to use. Some can even use a moderately heavy piece of stranded wire in a pinch. Others just can't get desoldering braid to work properly. If not held properly, it just smears the molten solder around without removing it from the joint. Many electronics hobbyists and technicians find that desoldering braid does not clean the desoldered joint adequately. Some people find this method convenient and handy, while others find it awkward and totally inadequate. I suggest you try it. If it feels comfortable for you and does a good job of desoldering, great. If not, you'll probably want to use a different approach to desoldering.

A vacuum bulb desoldering tool is simply a plastic or rubber bulb with a hollow teflon tip. The bulb is squeezed to force the air out of it through the tip. The tip is placed against the molten solder to be removed. Releasing the bulb creates a small vacuum. Air and molten solder are sucked up through the teflon tip into the bulb. The tip is then removed to empty the accumulated bits of solidified solder from inside the bulb.

It takes a little practice to hold the vacuum bulb properly, but most electronics hobbyists and technicians can quickly learn the trick and find this desoldering tool usually does a good job. A word of caution—the teflon tip can often get clogged with solder that can quickly solidify in the tip, rather than in the body of the bulb. A clogged tip can usually be cleared out by forcing a heated wire or needle through the opening, pushing the solder into the bulb.

A few soldering irons feature a special attachment for a built-in vacuum bulb desolderer. This permits more convenient, one-handed operation.

A spring-loaded desolderer is even easier and more convenient to use. This gadget is shaped something like a very fat pencil. Usually the body is made of clear plastic so you can see when the tool needs cleaning. As a fringe benefit, this also allows you to watch the mechanics involved in this type of desoldering tool.

Before using this tool, you must first move a small lever so that a large spring is locked in place. The spring is physically connected to a plastic plug that forces air out of the body of the tool and blocks the tip. Like the vacuum bulb, the spring-loaded desolderer has a hollow teflon tip.

The joint to be desoldered is heated until the old solder melts and starts to flow. The tip of the desolderer is placed against the molten solder and a trigger button is pressed, releasing the compressed spring. Typically, only a very light force (perhaps a single finger) is required to release the trigger. When the spring inside the tool is released, it very rapidly pulls the plastic plug out of the way. This happens so fast that a small, momentary vacuum is created in the tip of the tool, causing the liquified solder to be sucked into the body of the tool.

There is some variety between desoldering tools of this type, but they all use the same basic principles. The spring-loaded desolderer is very easy to use, and almost always does an excellent job of cleaning up unwanted solder.

As with the vacuum bulb desoldering tool discussed earlier, the teflon tip of a spring-loaded desolderer can become clogged with bits of solder. The obstruction can be cleaned out with a piece of heated wire or a needle. The tip is usually removable, permitting you to clean the inner parts of the desolderer and remove accumulated bits of rehardened solder.

Construction techniques

There are several methods of construction used in building electronic circuits. We will briefly discuss a few of the more popular of these construction techniques in this section.

Breadboarding

In the very early days of radio and electronics, hobbyist circuits were assembled on wooden bases. Since so many hobbyists used a kitchen breadboard as the base, this construction technique came to be known as breadboarding.

On these early, primitive breadboards, brackets were used to hold controls and tube sockets above the surface of the wooden base. Wires and small components (such as resistors, coils, and capacitors) were simply run from terminal to terminal.

The term breadboard is still used to indicate a hobbyist construction technique in which a prototype or temporary circuit can be quickly assembled and easily modified. Breadboarding is a very useful construction method when you want to experiment with alternate component values in a circuit.

Modern breadboarding is usually done with a special solderless socket. This type of socket features many holes that can hold component leads or wires snugly and firmly. The holes are internally connected in a specific pattern. For example, all of the holes in a single row on one side of the socket may be shorted together.

Any breadboarded circuit is temporary. The connections are not stable enough physically for long-term use. This is not a permanent construction technique.

Perforated boards with push-in terminals

In many ways, the modern perforated circuit board (perf board) is a direct descendent from the wooden breadboards used by the early radio experimenters. In some cases, component leads are pushed through the holes in the board and soldered directly to one another using point-to-point wiring. Usually, it is more advisable to use push-in terminals, or flea clips. These are just two different names for basically the same thing. Some people make a minor distinction in which flea clips are smaller than push-in terminals.

Perforated circuit boards are widely available with two basic hole sizes and several different patterns of hole spacing. For most electronics work, perf boards with 0.062-inch or 0.093-inch holes are used. There are also various different kinds of push-in terminals that are made to be inserted into these holes. Most electronics hobbyists will probably use the kind that are designed to grip a wire or component lead while it is soldered in place. You may also find considerable use for the quick-disconnect type of push-in terminals. This type of push-in terminal is handy for patching together prototype circuits before you decide on a final design. This is similar to breadboarding (discussed earlier).

The advantages of perf board construction are the relatively short time it takes to go from the original idea or schematic to the finished circuit and the fact that perforated circuit boards can be stripped of all components and connections and reused almost indefinitely. It is also fairly easy to make modifications or corrections to a circuit using this type of construction technique.

But nothing is perfect, of course. Perf board construction has some disadvantages too, especially the lack of heat dissipation (compared to metal chassis construction) and the relative bulk of the finished circuit (compared to printed circuit construction). Both of these alternate construction techniques will be covered later in this section.

The basic technique for building circuits with perforated circuit boards and push-in terminals is simple and straightforward. The first step is to get a rough idea of how much space the circuit will take up by physically laying out your components on the board in approximately the same pattern as in the finished circuit.

The next step is to sketch the circuit layout to scale. An easy way to do this is to place a piece of paper on a plain piece of perforated board (of the same type you will be using for the circuit, of course) and rub a soft pencil lightly over the surface. This will leave you with a pattern matching the holes in the board. You can then draw your circuit layout with the holes showing up in the right positions.

Determine where you will need to drill larger holes in the perf board for control shafts, standoffs, and other large components and hardware items. It is a very good idea to use lockwashers under all nuts and on all control shaft bushings, especially if the finished project is likely to be moved around a lot.

At this point, you are ready to install the electronic components for your circuit and solder their terminals together via the push-in terminals. Solder each new joint as you install the components. As soon as you have all of the wires for a particular terminal in place, solder the joint. Don't wait until all of the components are installed to start soldering. This way you will avoid the frustration of wires springing loose as you work.

It is usually a good idea to install the least heat sensitive components onto the circuit board first, if possible. Install the resistors and capacitors first, and save the semiconductors for later. Install inexpensive diodes and transistors before any expensive ICs. Of course, sockets may be soldered into the circuit along with the resistors and capacitors.

Perforated boards with adhesive-backed circuit traces

A compromise between straight perforated board construction (discussed above) and printed circuit board construction (discussed later in this chapter) is a construction technique using ordinary perf board with conductive tape and pads with pressure-sensitive adhesive backing. There are several variations on this basic idea. A wide variety of pressure-sensitive adhesive-backed conductors are marketed under the trade name Circuit Stik, among others. There are a variety of precut pads with the proper spacing to allow the immediate insertion of transistors in standard cases, DIP ICs, round can ICs, and various common discrete components (resistors, capacitors, and so forth). There are also several widths of copper tape with adhesive backing that can be used to interconnect the various component pads in the finished circuit. The final product is a circuit board that looks very much like a printed circuit board, but it is easier and less messy to make in single quantities than true printed circuit boards.

The primary advantages of this construction method are neatness, the speed of recreating the layout on the actual perforated board, and the relatively low inductance in the circuit's interconnecting leads. Because the adhesive-backed pads and tape can be easily peeled off of the board, it is fairly easy to make corrections and modifications to a circuit constructed using this system.

This construction method is a particularly good one for the beginning electronics hobbyist. Experience can be gained in laying out pseudo printed circuit boards without all the fuss, bother, and messy chemicals associated with etching true printed circuit boards. If you later decide to reproduce the circuit, it is fairly easy to transfer a successful layout using this construction method to a printed circuit master. Multiple duplicate circuit boards can then be reproduced for copies of the project.

But this construction method, like any other, is far from perfect. There are some significant disadvantages. The biggest disadvantage is that the stick-on pads and conductive tape are relatively expensive. In addition, sometimes the adhesive backing on the pads and connecting tape does not stick as well as it should. Pads and connecting strips can come loose from the board during soldering, or even during later use of the circuit. Fortunately, most peeling problems can be successfully forestalled by carefully burnishing all of the stick-on elements in place. Also, it is important not to let the natural oils from your fingertips get onto the surface of the board before applying the adhesive-backed pad or tape.

Component leads can be soldered directly to the stick-on pads. There is no need to use push-in terminals on circuit boards using this construction method.

Point-to-point wiring

For some fairly simple circuits using just a handful of components, you can use point-to-point wiring. No real base for the circuit is used in this construction technique. The leads of the components are simply soldered together.

To give the circuit some degree of mechanical stability, solder terminals or solder lugs are usually employed. A solder terminal is a strip of bakelite (or occasionally some other type of plastic) with a metallic screw-down foot for mounting onto the case or chassis of the project. One or more metal loops, or terminals, are provided as connection points for the leads to be soldered.

There is no particular difference between solder terminals and solder lugs. They are basically the same thing. In some sources, however, a minor distinction is made. A solder terminal, according to these sources, has two or more connection loops, while a solder lug has only one. Some typical solder terminals and solder lugs are illustrated in Fig. 2-8.

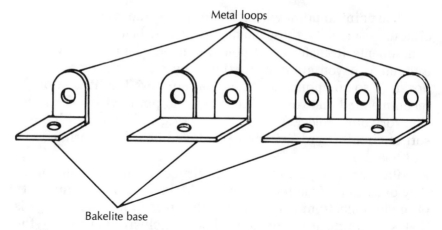

Metal loops

Bakelite base

Fig. 2-8 *A variety of solder terminals and solder lugs are available.*

In constructing the circuit, the leads to be soldered are mechanically connected to the metal loop, or terminal, as shown in Fig. 2-9. Once all of the wires for that joint are attached to the terminal, the connection is soldered.

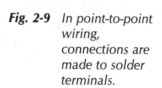

Fig. 2-9 *In point-to-point wiring, connections are made to solder terminals.*

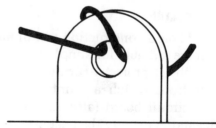

The point-to-point wiring construction method is really only suitable for very simple circuits. For a circuit of any complexity, you can very easily run into problems with "rat's nest" wiring. Rat's nest is a fairly self-explanatory name for jumbled wiring that goes every which way, full of tangles. Such jumbled wiring is next to impossible to trace if any error in wiring is made or if the circuit needs to be serviced or modified at a later date. The tangles of rat's nest wiring can also put undue strain on wires and solder joints, possibly resulting in breakage and premature circuit failure.

Loose, hanging wires can create their own problems in many circuits, such as stray capacitances and inductances. Such stray capacitances and inductances between adjacent wires can allow signals to get into the wrong portions of the circuit, resulting in erratic or incorrect operation of the circuit.

The point-to-point wiring technique is fine for small, simple circuits, especially those made up primarily of large, passive components (transformers, potentiometers, large-value capacitors, etc.). If you are constructing a circuit using more than a dozen or so components or one that employs ICs, it is strongly recommended that you don't use point-to-point wiring construction for your project. Use a construction technique with some sort of circuit board—either a perforated board or a printed circuit board.

Projects using point-to-point wiring are not as common as they once were. One reason for this is the increased complexity of modern electronic circuits. Another reason for this change is that semiconductors are now almost exclusively used as the active components in most modern electronic circuitry. Point-to-point wiring is a much more suitable construction technique for circuits built around vacuum tubes. The tubes themselves are large, making them awkward to mount on circuit boards, and the large base of the average tube socket can support a number of standard passive components, such as resistors and capacitors.

Printed circuits

The perf board construction techniques discussed earlier in this section are suitable for simple to moderately complex, one-of-a-kind hobbyist projects. For moderate to complex circuits, or for circuits from which a number of duplicates will be built, a printed circuit board (also called a PC board) gives very good results and is usually the best overall construction technique.

In modern electronics, there is little question that the printed circuit is the most widely used construction method. Virtually all of today's commercially manufactured electronic equipment use printed circuit boards. Strictly speaking, the term printed circuit is something of a misnomer. So-called printed circuit boards are not made by any process resembling the one used to print this book. Instead, the circuit traces on the board are etched in an acid bath.

A nonconductive board (usually made from some form of plastic or glass) is used as a base for the circuit. Copper traces on one side (or, in very complex circuits, on both sides) of the board act as connecting wires between pads surrounding drilled holes for the component leads. Very steady, stable, and sturdy connections can be made, since the component leads are soldered directly to the supporting board itself.

All printed circuit boards start out covered on one or both sides with a solid layer of copper. The unwanted portions of the copper are etched away in an acid bath, leaving the desired circuit traces.

There are several methods for making printed circuit boards. The simplest is to draw the desired circuit traces onto the copper with a special resist pen. The special ink in this pen protects the copper it covers from being eaten away in the acid bath. It is very important to cover the desired circuit traces thoroughly with the resist ink to prevent undesired holes in the finished traces.

A similar method uses press-on resist decals, which are rather like the adhesive-backed conductive pads and tape used to create pseudo printed circuit boards using perf boards, as discussed earlier in this chapter.

Both of these methods of direct application of resist are practical only for one of a kind projects. When duplication of a circuit is the goal, the printed circuit boards are prepared via photographic techniques. This covers the desired places of the board with a chemical resist that prevents etching.

In all cases, once the resist has been applied, whether directly or photographically, the board is then soaked in an acid bath that eats or etches away the unprotected (and undesired) copper from the face of the board. The etched board is then removed from the acid bath and the resist is washed off, leaving the desired circuit traces on the finished printed circuit board.

Great care must be taken when laying out a printed circuit board to eliminate wire crossings as much as possible. The copper traces are not insulated. Obviously, two traces cannot cross over each other without shorting to each other. (Unless, of course, the traces are on opposite sides of the board. Two-sided printed circuit boards are used for very complex circuits.) If a crossing of conductors is absolutely essential, and that does happen with some frequency, an external wire jumper must be used. This wire jumper is usually mounted on the component side of the board, just as if it was an actual electronic component.

Normally, most of the electronic components in the circuit are mounted on the opposite side of the board from the copper traces. The component leads are fitted through holes drilled in the board. The leads are then soldered directly to the copper pad on the opposite side of the board. The excess lead is snipped off with wire cutters to reduce the chances of a short circuit and to create a neater, more professional appearance. Printed circuit board construction results in strong mechanical connections and very short leads. Short leads can significantly minimize interference and stray capacitance problems.

Whenever you solder to a printed circuit board, whether during the original construction of the circuit or as part of a later repair, be very careful not to use too much heat or to apply heat from the soldering iron for too long a time. Excessive heat can cause the copper foil trace to lift off the board. Such an unsupported trace is very fragile and is almost certain to break.

Solder bridges between adjacent traces can be a problem on printed circuit boards with closely placed traces. Be careful not to use too much solder. Always make sure the solder flows where it belongs.

Tiny, near-invisible hairline cracks in the copper traces can also be quite problematic if you're not careful. Generally, fairly wide traces that are widely spaced are the easiest to work with and the most reliable. However, this isn't always practical with all circuits—especially where ICs, with their closely spaced lead pins, are used. If insufficient resist was used in preparing the printed circuit board, hairline cracks are likely to be formed during the acid bath or etching process. Cracks can form at a later time on any printed circuit board, especially if it is subjected to mechanical stress, such as being dropped.

Universal printed circuit boards

There is a fairly recent variation of printed circuit construction. Designing and etching a customized printed circuit board can be a time-consuming and somewhat tricky job. Now you can buy various universal PC boards. These boards are pre-etched with a generalized pattern of copper traces, and can be used for many different circuits.

Wire wrapping

There is one type of permanent circuit construction that does not require soldering. This is the recently developed wire-wrapping method. It is used primarily in circuits using large numbers of ICs and relatively few discrete components (resistors, capacitors, transistors, diodes, etc.).

In a wire-wrapped circuit, a thin wire (typically 30 gauge) is wrapped tightly around a square post. The edges of the post bite into the wire itself, making a good mechanical and electrical connection without soldering. The components in the circuit are fitted into special sockets that connect their leads to the square wrapping posts. While some wire-wrap sockets for small discrete components are available, for the most part, wire-wrap sockets are used with DIP-type IC chips. If there are one or two discrete components in the circuit and you can't locate a suitable socket, you can use a hybrid construction by soldering the socketless components directly, using point-to-point wiring, while the ICs are placed in wire-wrap sockets. In circuits involving many discrete components, the wire-wrapping method of construction generally tends to be rather impractical.

Wire-wrap sockets for ICs can be used in regular soldered circuits. There is nothing that says you can't solder ordinary wire to the square posts of a wire-wrap socket. This can be handy in some cases, because the leads on a wire-wrap IC socket are considerably longer than those on an ordinary IC socket, or on the IC itself. The disadvantage of using wire-wrap IC sockets in this way is that they are considerably more expensive than regular soldered sockets. Typically, a wire-wrap socket costs one and one-half to two times as much as a comparable socket intended for a soldered circuit.

There are several advantages to the wire-wrapping method of circuit construction. Obviously, since there is no soldering, the possibility of excess heat from the soldering iron damaging or destroying the delicate semiconductor crystals in expensive ICs is eliminated. For the most part, wire-wrapped connections can be made (or unmade) quickly and easily. Moreover, it usually is not difficult to make changes or modifications in the circuit.

Special wire-wrap tools are required to make the wrapped connections properly. They cannot be made by hand. If you are very agile, you can make wire-wrap connections with needle-nose pliers, but this will almost certainly be time-consuming and generally more trouble than it's worth. Mechanical wire-wrap tools are available for just a few dollars. Automated wire-wrap tools are also available.

As always, there are some important disadvantages to the wire-wrapping method of circuit construction. The use of discrete components in the circuit is problematic and awkward at best. The thin wire-wrapping wire is very fragile and quite easily broken. It is also very easy to get such thin gauge wire hopelessly tangled if you don't work very carefully and methodically. In complex circuits, the wiring can be rather difficult or even impossible to trace. Using different colored wires can help when it comes to tracing wires for later modifications or repairs. Finally, since the wire-wrap wire is so very thin, it can only carry very low-power signals. Signal radiation and interference problems may also show up when high-frequency signals are used within the wire-wrapped circuit.

Bricklaying

Recently, a new method of circuit construction has been developed for complex systems using dozens or hundreds of ICs. This construction method is called bricklaying.

Essentially, multiple ICs are stacked up like bricks, as shown in Fig. 2-10. The leads of the chips are bent outward, instead of angled down as they are for most construction methods. The bodies of the ICs are epoxied together, and connections are soldered directly to the bent out leads.

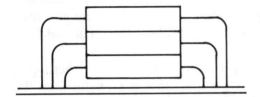

Fig. 2-10 *A fairly new, but not recommended, type of circuit construction is called bricklaying.*

Obviously, an individual chip can never be removed or replaced in a circuit using bricklaying. Repairs of such circuits are limited to substituting entire modules or circuit boards. Of course, this involves replacing several components that are perfectly good. This means such repairs are inherently more expensive in terms of parts, but servicing time is cut down considerably.

Bricklaying is a suitable construction method only for large-scale industrial equipment where downtime for repairs cannot be tolerated. The primary advantage of bricklaying is that a large circuit can be crammed into a smaller physical space.

This construction method is mentioned here solely in the interest of completeness. You may, from time to time, come across electronic equipment that uses bricklaying. Despite the fact that a few ''how to'' articles on bricklaying have been published in some of the electronics hobbyist magazines, I do not think this is a practical or reasonable construction technique for any hobbyist project. Actually, I'm not entirely convinced it is such a hot idea for industrial use either. Packing the ICs so close together severely limits their heat dissipation characteristics and may well subject them to premature failure. I'd say that the brick-laying method of construction should be used only in those rare cases when nothing else will do the job; otherwise, forget it. I will acknowledge, however, that many people in the electronics field disagree with me on this.

Construction helps

Finally, we will look at a few specialized tools and aids that will be of interest to electronics hobbyists because they are helpful in the construction of projects. For the most part, these tools and construction helps will not be of much interest to the electronics technician, who basically just repairs existing equipment. Most of these construction helps have already been mentioned in passing in our discussion of the various construction techniques in the last few pages.

Push-in terminals and flea clips help keep any circuit constructed on a piece of perforated board neat. They can often ensure a stronger mechanical connection than soldering directly to the component leads. Some push-in terminals have spring-loaded clips to permit easy solderless connections and disconnections. Naturally, such spring-loaded terminals are considerably more expensive than ordinary push-in terminals designed for soldering. Flea clips are just very small push-in terminals. There is little other significant difference between flea clips and push-in terminals.

Press-on adhesive-backed conductive strips and pads were discussed in the section on perf board construction. These items are great for creating prototype circuit boards that can later be transferred to a true printed circuit board for reproduction of the circuit. They can also be useful in some cases for quick and dirty repairs and modifications of existing printed circuit boards. The most obvious application here is the use of a strip of conductive tape to replace a damaged or peeling copper trace on a board.

Conductive paint is also available. You could paint all the traces to create a pseudo printed circuit board, but this would be incredibly expensive, and therefore impractical. This, like conductive tape, is really only good for occasional touch-ups. If you make a printed circuit board and discover that the resist didn't adequately cover the area to be protected, or if the board was left in the acid bath too long, conductive paint can be used to fill in the holes in the traces.

Conductive paint can also be of interest to service technicians, because it can be used to repair peeling or cracked traces on a printed circuit board. It can also be used to make small modifications in a printed circuit board. You can use conductive paint in place of jumpers on the component side of a single-sided printed circuit board. If you do this, make sure none of the component leads short to the painted jumper trace.

Copper and silver conductive paint are available. The silver paint is considerably more expensive, but it conducts better. Remember that the painted trace will not conduct as well as a true copper trace or a wire.

In the section on wire wrapping, we mentioned that special wire-wrapping tools are available for use with this construction method. The same tool is generally used to both wrap and unwrap connections.

A wire-wrapping tool is needed to tightly wrap the wire around the square posts. If the wire is not wrapped tightly enough, the edges of the square post will not bite into the wire, and both the electrical and mechanical connection will be weak. If you are very agile, you can make wire-wrap connections with needle-nose pliers, but this will almost certainly be time-consuming and generally more trouble than it's worth.

Mechanical wire-wrapping tools usually cost about $5. Automated wire-wrapping tools do a better, more reliable job, and can really be a relief when you have to wrap a few hundred connections in a large circuit. These wire-wrapping tools usually operate on batteries, but some plug-in devices are available.

Wire-wrapping tools can also be used with a special wire that is intended to be soldered. This type of wire does not need to have its insulation stripped off for soldering. The heat from the soldering iron vaporizes the specially designed insulation.

So far, in the first two chapters of this book, we have looked at the electronics workbench itself and a number of small items that are used on the workbench. Now we are ready to move on to the major pieces of electronic test equipment. What will you need, and for what purpose? What test equipment is essential, what is a luxury, and what is a waste of money for your purposes? In the following chapters we will explore these questions for the many common types of electronic test equipment available to the modern electronics hobbyist and technician.

❖ 3
Multimeters

THERE ARE MANY DIFFERENT TYPES OF TEST EQUIPMENT USED IN electronics work, but by far the most widely used and versatile electronic testing instrument is the multimeter. In fact, for many casual electronics hobbyists, a multimeter is the only piece of test equipment they own. A multimeter can be used for at least 75% of the average service technician's or electronics hobbyist's testing needs.

The name multimeter suggests that this type of test equipment is a multiple-function device. A multimeter can measure each of the three basic parameters of electrical circuits—voltage, current, and resistance. In fact, a simple passive multimeter is generally known as a VOM (volt-ohm-milliammeter). Various multimeters using active circuitry are also widely available.

Before discussing actual multimeters, we will first examine the three basic functions of the multimeter—the voltmeter, the milliammeter, and the ohmmeter.

The milliammeter

The heart of most analog multimeters is the d'Arsonval meter. This type of meter, which measures current, got its name from its inventor—Jacques A. d'Arsonval. The internal construction of this type of meter is illustrated in Fig. 3-1. A permanent magnet in the shape of a horseshoe is positioned around a tiny coil of wire wound on a small piece of soft iron. This coil is known variously as the armature or the movement of the meter. These terms

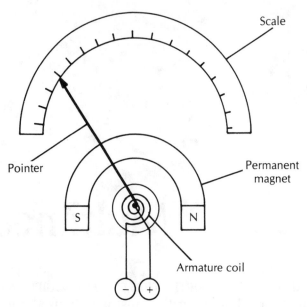

Fig. 3-1 *The basic analog multimeter is designed around a d'Arsonval current meter movement.*

are fully interchangeable in this context. The movement coil is mounted on a pivot that allows it to move freely.

When an electrical current flows through the armature coil, the movement develops a magnetic field by the principle of induction. The north pole of this induced magnetic field faces the north pole of the permanent magnet, and the coil's south pole faces the south pole of the permanent magnet. Because like magnetic poles repel each other, the movement is forced to turn on its pivot so that its magnetic poles no longer face the like poles of the permanent (and fixed position) magnet. Just how far the movement turns on its pivot depends on the relative strength of the magnetic fields involved. Naturally, the magnetic field of the permanent magnet will have a constant level. The strength of the magnetic field induced in the armature coil is directly proportional to the strength of the electrical current being fed through the coil. Therefore, the physical motion of the armature is directly proportional to the amplitude of the applied electrical current.

A pointer can be mechanically attached to the center of the armature so that the amount of applied current is indicated on a calibrated scale. The stronger the applied current, the further the pointer will move across the face of the scale. This scale is marked in equal units spaced and numbered so that the current value can be read directly from the meter's face.

A small spring mechanically opposes the rotation of the armature. This small amount of physical opposition is easily overcome by the applied current and its resulting magnetic field. However, when current stops flowing through the coil, the spring forces the movement (and thus, the pointer) to return to the zero (no input signal) position.

The current applied to a d'Arsonval meter must have the correct polarity. If the polarity of the current is reversed, the south pole of the electromagnet (armature) will be facing the north pole of the permanent magnet, and vice versa. Since unlike magnetic poles attract each other, the armature and its attached pointer will not move.

Some specially designed meters can be adjusted so that the zero position is in the center of the scale. This allows the pointer to move in either direction, thus indicating current of either polarity—positive or negative. Most standard meters, however, do not have this dual-polarity capability.

A d'Arsonval meter's movement is mechanically quite delicate and fragile. Meters are usually enclosed in protective cases (generally made of transparent plastic), but they can still be permanently damaged if dropped or otherwise mishandled. Also, the coil in the armature is made of very fine wire so that it will be light and move easily. This means that the armature wire cannot carry very much current. If too much current is applied to a d'Arsonval meter's movement, the armature can very quickly be ruined. Fortunately, there are several practical methods of decreasing the current actually applied to the meter by a known amount, still allowing the meter to give an accurate reading.

With a reasonable amount of care, a d'Arsonval meter movement is sturdy enough for practical use, and can usually last and give reliable readings for a number of years. d'Arsonval meters are sometimes called moving-coil movement meters for reasons which should be quite obvious from the above discussion.

When a meter is used to measure electric current, it is usually referred to as an ammeter, from ampere meter. Since the ampere is a rather large unit for most practical electronic circuitry, milliammeters or microammeters are frequently used instead. The only real difference is the scale used. A milliampere (mA) is one-thousandth of an ampere, and a microampere (μA) is one-millionth of an ampere.

To measure current flow the ammeter must be inserted into the circuit itself. In other words, the meter is placed in series with the circuit component whose current flow is being measured. This is shown in Fig. 3-2. Remember that in any series circuit, the current flow is equal at all points. If an ammeter is placed in series with the rest of the circuit, the same current that flows through the circuit will flow through the meter and be indicated by the movement's pointer.

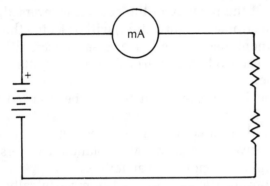

Fig. 3-2 *A current meter must be in series with the circuit being tested.*

Because the ammeter is placed in series with the circuit, its internal resistance must be as low as possible to avoid upsetting the normal current flow. The meter movement inevitably acts as an additional resistance element in the circuit.

For example, let's suppose we have a circuit with a total resistance of 10,000 ohms powered by a 10-V source. The nominal current through the circuit can be found using Ohm's law:

$$I = E/R$$
$$= 10/10,000$$
$$= 0.001 \text{ A}$$
$$= 1 \text{ mA}$$

When the ammeter is inserted into the circuit, its internal resistance adds to the resistance of the circuit. Electrically, the ammeter "looks" like an extra series resistor. For instance, if the meter's resistance is 5000 ohms, the total resistance in the circuit becomes 15,000 ohms (10,000 + 5,000) when the ammeter is placed in series with the regular circuit. This changes the current flowing through the circuit to

$$I = E/R$$
$$= 10/15,000$$
$$= 0.00067 \text{ A}$$
$$= 0.67 \text{ mA}$$

The current value has dropped 33%. Obviously, this is a significant difference.

On the other hand, let's assume the ammeter's internal resistance is only 50 ohms. In this case, the addition of the meter in
series with the circuit increases the total circuit resistance to only
10,050 ohms (10,000 + 50). Under these circumstances, the current flow will be

$$I = E/R$$
$$= 10/10,050$$
$$= 0.000995 \text{ A}$$
$$= 0.995 \text{ mA}$$

This is within 0.5% of the correct nominal current value (1 mA).
Clearly, for an accurate current reading, the ammeter's internal
resistance must be as low as possible.

Because an ammeter must be used in series with the circuit
it is testing, one of the connections in the circuit has to be physically disconnected so the meter can be inserted into the circuit.
Often this requires desoldering. For this reason, among others,
current measurements generally aren't made nearly as frequently
as voltage or resistance measurements.

Quite often it is necessary to measure a current that is larger
than the available ammeter will handle. Remember, the armature
coil can be burned out if the applied current is too high. This
problem can be taken care of with a shunt resistance. A shunt
resistance is nothing more than a resistor in parallel with the
meter movement, as illustrated in Fig. 3-3.

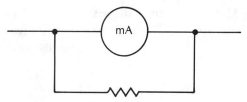

Fig. 3-3 *A shunt resistor can be used to increase the range of a current
meter.*

By carefully selecting the proper ratio between the shunt resistance and the internal resistance of the meter itself, we can safely measure virtually any amount of current flow. Most practical ammeters are actually milliammeters or microammeters with an appropriate shunt resistance. The tiny coil in a standard meter movement usually can't carry a full ampere (or more) without suffering damage.

The shunt resistance is generally quite small. As an example, let's suppose we have a milliammeter with an internal resistance of 50 ohms and a full-scale reading of a 1 mA (0.001 A). This means that an applied current of 1 mA will cause the maximum possible deflection of the armature and pointer. A greater current than this could damage the delicate meter movement.

Now, suppose we need to use this meter to read currents up to 100 mA (0.1 A). The meter itself can handle only 1% of the desired full-scale reading, so obviously, the shunt resistance will have to carry the other 99%. Using Ohm's law, we can calculate the full-scale voltage that must be dropped across the 1-mA meter:

$$E = IR$$
$$= 0.001 \text{ A} \times 50 \text{ ohm}$$
$$= 0.05 \text{ V}$$

For a full-scale reading of 0.1 A, the shunt resistor will have to carry a current of 0.099 A. Since the shunt resistance is in parallel with the meter, the voltage drop will be the same across both items. We already know the voltage drop across the meter movement's internal resistance (0.05 V), so we can rearrange Ohm's law to solve for the necessary shunt resistance:

$$R = E/I$$
$$= 0.05/0.099$$
$$= 0.5 \text{ ohm (approximate)}$$

Adding a shunt resistor with a value of 0.5 ohm in parallel with the 50-ohm 1-mA milliammeter raises its full-scale reading to 100 mA. It also lowers the total effective resistance of the meter to

$$1/R_t = 1/R1 + 1/R2$$
$$= 1/50 + 1/0.5$$
$$= 0.02 + 2$$

$$= 2.02$$
$$R_t = 1/2.02$$
$$= 0.495 \text{ ohm}$$

Of course this lowered meter resistance will be an advantage when the modified meter is placed in series with a working circuit.

It should be obvious from the preceding example that the full-scale reading of an ammeter cannot be increased by too large a factor, or the required shunt resistance value will become impractically small. In fact, even the example we presented here would not be too practical, since resistance values below about 10 ohms are fairly rare, and they are rather expensive when they can be found.

When a shunt resistance is used to change the full-scale reading of an ammeter, the calibration markings on the meter's scale will no longer be accurate. However, when the increase factor is an exact multiple of ten, as in our example, this is not much of a problem. The same calibration markings can be used and the appropriate number of zeros can be added mentally. For instance, if the meter in our example gave a reading of 0.5 mA (0.0005 A), it means the actual measured current was equal to

$$I = 0.5 \times 100$$
$$= 0.05 \text{ A}$$
$$= 50 \text{ mA}$$

Of course, all shunt resistors should have the tightest tolerance possible. For serious testing, 1% tolerance resistors are generally essential, and 0.1% tolerance resistors are highly desirable. However, 5% tolerance resistors may be adequate in some noncritical applications. The tolerance of a shunt resistor should never be greater than 5%.

In most multimeters, the milliammeter section is given several ranges by switching various shunt resistors in and out of the meter circuitry. A front-panel switch is used to select the appropriate shunt resistor for the desired meter range.

The voltmeter

A voltmeter is a measurement device for determining the electrical voltage at a specific point in a circuit. To measure the voltage in an electronic circuit, the voltmeter is placed in parallel across a resistance element within the circuit, as shown in Fig. 3-4. The resistance element does not have to be an actual resistor. Remember that anything less than a theoretically perfect conductor will exhibit some resistance, so the voltmeter can be placed in parallel across almost any electronic component. The deflection of the meter's pointer will be proportional to the voltage drop across the resistance element.

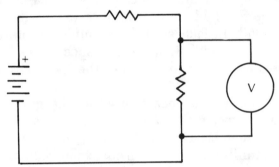

Fig. 3-4 *A voltmeter must be in parallel with the circuit being tested.*

Actually, the meter movement itself is measuring the amount of current flowing through its built-in coil, but Ohm's law permits us to directly convert this current into a proportionate voltage reading. Electrical current is defined by the ratio of the voltage to the resistance: $I = E/R$. Because the resistance element in parallel with the meter presumably has a constant resistance value, the current flowing through the meter will be directly proportional to the voltage drop across the resistance element.

In an ammeter, the meter's internal resistance should always be kept as low as possible, because the meter is used in series with the circuit being tested. A large meter resistance produces a relatively large voltage drop that would not be present if the meter was not in the circuit.

In a voltmeter, on the other, the internal resistance should be as large as possible. This is because this type of meter is used in parallel with the circuit being measured. In most practical voltmeters (including those on virtually all multimeters), a rather large-value fixed resistor is internally connected in series with the meter movement, as shown in Fig. 3-5. This large resistor is called a multiplier and it serves two important functions: it protects the meter movement from excessive current and it helps prevent problems from circuit loading.

Fig. 3-5   *Most practical voltmeters include a multiplier resistor.*

We can best understand the problem of circuit loading by examining a specific example. Suppose we want to take voltage measurements in the simple resistor/source voltage circuit shown in Fig. 3-6A. Let's assume that each of the two resistors in this simple circuit has a value of 1,000 ohms and the voltage source is 10 V. The total resistance in this circuit is

$$R_t = R1 + R2$$
$$= 1,000 + 1,000$$
$$= 2,000 \text{ ohms}$$

The current flowing through the circuit can be found with Ohm's law:

$$I = E/R$$
$$= 10/2,000$$
$$= 0.005 \text{ A}$$
$$= 5 \text{ mA}$$

Rearranging the Ohm's law equation, we can find the voltage drop across one of the resistors:

$$E = IR$$
$$= 0.005 \times 1,000$$
$$= 5 \text{ V}$$

Because the two resistors have exactly the same value, the voltage drop across each individual resistor is the same.

Now, when we use the voltmeter to measure the actual voltage drop across R2, we place the meter in parallel across the resistor, as shown in Fig. 3-6B. Electrically, the meter "looks" like another resistance element in parallel with R2, as illustrated in Fig. 3-6C.

Let's say the voltmeter has an internal resistance of 50 ohms. The parallel combination of the meter resistance and R2 works out to

$$1/R_t = 1/R2 + 1/R_m$$
$$= 1/1,000 + 1/50$$

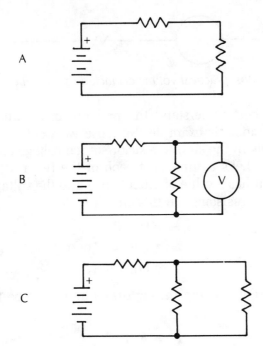

Fig. 3-6 *This simple circuit illustrates the problem of voltmeter loading: A)*
The circuit; B) Adding the voltmeter; and C) The equivalent circuit.

$$= 0.001 + 0.02$$
$$= 0.021$$
$$R_t = 1/0.021$$
$$= 47.6 \text{ ohms}$$

Notice that the effective resistance of R2 in the circuit has been
decreased considerably. We can round this resistance off to 48
ohms.

Now the total effective resistance in the circuit is

$$R_t = 1,000 + 48$$
$$= 1,048 \text{ ohms}$$

The reduced circuit resistance changes the current flow to

$$I = E/R$$
$$= 10/1,048$$
$$= 0.0095 \text{ A}$$
$$= 9.5 \text{ mA}$$

The actual measured voltage drop across the R2-R*m* combination is

$$E = IR$$
$$= 0.0095 \times 48$$
$$= 0.46 \text{ V}$$

The voltage reading shown on the meter will obviously be extremely inaccurate when compared to the normal (no meter) voltage drop across R2. This voltage reading is so far off, it is utterly useless.

Now suppose an extra multiplier resistor is placed in series with the voltmeter's movement, so that the total resistance of the meter is 20,000 ohms. In this case, the effective parallel combination of R2 and the meter resistance works out to

$$1/R_t = 1/R2 + 1/R_m$$
$$= 1/1,000 + 1/20,000$$
$$= 0.001 + 0.00005$$
$$= 0.00105$$
$$R_t = 1/0.00105$$
$$= 952 \text{ ohms}$$

This is clearly much closer to the original nominal value of 1,000 ohms for R2. Now the total circuit resistance equals 1,952 ohms and the current flowing through the circuit equals

$$I = E/R$$
$$= 10/1,952$$
$$= 0.0051 \text{ A}$$
$$= 5.1 \text{ mA}$$

So the measured voltage drop across R2 now gives a meter reading of

$$E = IR$$
$$= 0.0051 \times 952$$
$$= 4.88 \text{ V}$$

This is much closer to the nominal voltage drop value of 5 V.

If we increase the meter's resistance even further, to 1,000,000 ohms (1 megohm), the parallel combination comes even closer to the value of R2 alone—just slightly over 999 ohms. This gives us a much more accurate voltage reading on the meter.

For the most accurate readings, the meter should be essentially nonexistent (electrically invisible) as far as the circuit's operation is concerned. This is impossible to achieve in practice, so we try to come as close to the ideal as we can. For a voltmeter, increasing the meter's resistance (using a multiplier resistor) increases the accuracy of the measurement.

If you are comparing voltages between similar circuits (as in servicing, when you compare a defective unit to a working standard), the meters used in each circuit should have the same readings. If the difference between the meter resistances is large, you may not be able to compare the readings in any meaningful way.

Passive multimeters usually have voltmeter resistances of 20,000 to 50,000 ohms/V. Active multimeters, such as VTVMs (vacuum tube voltmeters) or DMMs (digital multimeters) (discussed later in this chapter), provide much higher voltmeter resistances and, therefore, greater measurement accuracy.

The ohmmeter

The third section of a multimeter is the ohmmeter. An ohmmeter measures dc resistance. Of course, since a standard d'Arsonval meter movement is used in most analog ohmmeters, what is actually being measured by the meter is still current. The design of the ohmmeter takes advantage of Ohm's law to convert the current measurement into a resistance readout on the meter's face. The user does not have to do any Ohm's law calculations when using an ohmmeter. The scale is calibrated to read the resistance directly in ohms.

In one respect, ohmmeters work backwards when compared to ammeters or voltmeters. With ammeters and voltmeters, the pointer normally rests at the far left (facing the meter) of the scale, representing the minimum possible value (zero). This makes sense. When no signal is applied to the meter, we should expect a reading of zero. As larger signals are applied to the meter's test leads, the pointer moves up the scale (to the right), indicating a higher current or voltage reading.

The normal rest position for an ohmmeter is still at the far left of the scale, but this position now indicates the maximum possible resistance reading (infinity). As the pointer moves up the scale, lower resistance values are indicated. At the far right of the scale is the 0-ohms position. This may seem quite odd at first glance, but it actually makes perfect sense. The minimum resistance (0 ohms) is obtained with a dead short. If there is no circuit path between the test leads (an open circuit), the resistance between the leads is theoretically infinite. Normally, when the ohmmeter is not being used, the leads are not touching, so the circuit between them is open. The rest (no input signal) position of the meter should indicate an infinite resistance reading.

A very simple ohmmeter circuit is shown in Fig. 3-7. The variable resistor labeled R_m is included to calibrate the meter. Notice that unlike basic ammeters and voltmeters, the basic ohmmeter has its own built-in voltage source, usually a small battery.

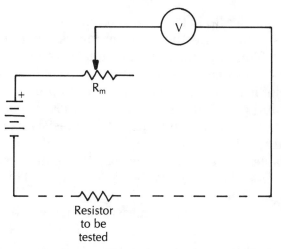

Fig. 3-7 *An ohmmeter includes a built-in voltage source.*

To understand how an ohmmeter works, we'll look at a specific example. We will assume that the meter movement used in the ohmmeter circuit has a full-scale reading of 1 mA (0.001 A). We will also assume that the battery has a voltage of 3 V, and the total internal resistance of the ohmmeter circuit is 3,000 ohms.

During a test reading, Ohm's law tells us that the current applied to the meter movement will be equal to the battery voltage divided by the sum of the meter circuit's internal resistance and the external resistance being measured. That is

$$I = E/(R_m + R_x)$$

Where

R_m = the internal resistance of the ohmmeter circuit, and

R_x = the unknown external resistance to be measured.

When we short the two test leads together, we are effectively measuring an external resistance of 0 ohms. The current flowing through the meter in this case equals

$$
\begin{aligned}
I &= 3/(3{,}000 + 0) \\
&= 3/3{,}000 \\
&= 0.001 \text{ A} \\
&= 1 \text{ mA}
\end{aligned}
$$

So in our example, the meter's pointer will move all the way to the far right end of the scale, giving a resistance reading of 0 ohms.

Potentiometer R_m in the ohmmeter circuit is used to position the meter's pointer directly at the zero mark when the test leads are shorted. This adjustment will calibrate the ohmmeter. As the battery ages, its voltage drops and the setting of R_m has to be read-justed periodically to keep the ohmmeter in proper calibration.

Continuing with our example, if the test leads are disconnected from one another (infinite external resistance), no current will flow through the meter because there isn't a complete circuit path available. Of course, in this case the pointer remains at its rest position at the far left of the meter's scale. This position is labeled *infinity* or ∞.

Most practical resistance measurements will be somewhere between the extremes of a dead short and a completely open circuit (no circuit path). Let's say we connect a 3,000-ohm resistor between the test leads of our sample ohmmeter. The current now flowing through the meter will be equal to

$$
\begin{aligned}
I &= 1/(3{,}000 + 3{,}000) \\
&= 3/6{,}000 \\
&= 0.0005 \text{ A} \\
&= 0.5 \text{ mA}
\end{aligned}
$$

When measuring an external resistance equal to the meter's internal resistance (3,000 ohms in our example), the pointer will move to the center of the scale. The lower the external resistance between the ohmmeter's test leads, the further up the scale the pointer will move.

There is another important difference between an ohmmeter and an ammeter or voltmeter. Current and voltage readings can be read off the meter in a direct, linear fashion. Doubling the signal will cause the meter's pointer to move twice as far. An ohmmeter, however, requires an exponentially calibrated scale. A simple linear scale just won't work. This is illustrated in Table 3-1, which compares the current flowing through the meter for various test resistances. This nonlinear response occurs because the ohmmeter's internal resistances is, of necessity, a constant value. It is actually the ratio of the internal resistance and the external resistance that is being indicated by the position of the meter's pointer.

Table 3-1   Comparison of current for various test resistances.

E	R_m	Test resistance	R_t	I (mA)
3	3,000	0	3,000	1.00
3	3,000	500	3,500	0.86
3	3,000	1,000	4,000	0.75
3	3,000	1,500	4,500	0.67
3	3,000	2,000	5,000	0.60
3	3,000	2,500	5,500	0.55
3	3,000	3,000	6,000	0.50
3	3,000	3,500	6,500	0.46
3	3,000	4,000	7,000	0.43
3	3,000	4,500	7,500	0.40
3	3,000	5,000	8,000	0.38
3	3,000	5,500	8,500	0.35
3	3,000	6,000	9,000	0.33
3	3,000	6,500	9,500	0.32
3	3,000	7,000	10,000	0.30
3	3,000	7,500	10,500	0.29
3	3,000	8,000	11,000	0.27
3	3,000	8,500	11,500	0.26
3	3,000	9,000	12,000	0.25
3	3,000	9,500	12,500	0.24
3	3,000	10,000	13,000	0.23
3	3,000	10,500	13,500	0.22
3	3,000	11,000	14,000	0.21
3	3,000	∞	∞	0.00

The internal resistance can be altered to change the overall range of the ohmmeter. For example, if the meter circuit's internal resistance is 10,000 ohms, a midscale reading would indicate an external resistance of 10,000 ohms, instead of the 3,000 ohms of our previous example. But within any given range, the internal resistance is fixed as far as the actual testing is concerned.

Because of the built-in battery in the ohmmeter circuit, resistance readings should normally be taken with no power applied to the circuit or component under test. The ohmmeter can be damaged by an external voltage or current signal. In some cases, the ohmmeter voltage could also do some harm to the circuit being tested if it is "fighting" the circuit's normal signal voltages.

When measuring the resistance of a component wired into a circuit, you may find you get a too-low reading. This is because some other circuitry is in parallel with the resistance element being measured. Remember the parallel combination of two or more resistances is always less than any of the original component resistances. To prevent such misreadings, one end of the component to be tested should be lifted up from the circuit, if possible. This will ensure an accurate resistance reading, without errors from any parallel resistances in the circuit. Such parallel resistances are not always obvious at first glance.

The problem of ac signals

It is important to remember that a standard ohmmeter is designed to read dc resistances only. It cannot accurately measure ac impedances or inductances, which change with the signal frequency. Special ac impedance meters are available, but they are expensive and require fairly complex circuitry.

There is also a problem in measuring an ac current or voltage with a simple dc meter like those described so far in this section. This is because any ac signal, by definition, is continuously changing its value. Many multimeters have settings for measuring ac voltages and (sometimes) ac currents. Because of the way the scales on these ac meters are calibrated, the reading will be accurate only if the input signal is a sine wave. The indicated value will be the RMS (root mean square) value of the sine wave. For other waveshapes, this RMS value will not be accurate. This type of ac meter may give a too-high or a too-low reading.

For serious and precise measurement of ac signals, your best bet is to use an oscilloscope. That piece of equipment will be discussed in detail in chapter 4.

VOMs

Rather than use separate ammeters, voltmeters, and ohmmeters, most electronics technicians and hobbyist use all-in-one multimeters. The most common and least expensive type of multimeter is the VOM (volt-ohm-milliammeter). This type of multimeter is strictly passive in its circuitry. It has no active components.

Basically, a VOM consists of a physically large current meter, with several different calibrations marked on its scale face, and a multiposition range/function switch. The scale markings are often in contrasting colors to make it easier to read the appropriate values. For example, my VOM uses green for the ohm values, red for ac voltages, and black for dc voltages and currents.

The range/function switch determines the meter's mode. Usually the following functions are offered:

- dc milliammeter,
- dc voltmeter,
- dc ohmmeter,
- ac milliammeter, and
- ac voltmeter.

On some less expensive models, one or both of the ac modes may be omitted. The range/function switch selects the appropriate shunt or multiplier resistors and other relevant components, such as a battery for ohmmeter measurements and rectifying diodes for ac current and voltage measurements. Usually, any of several different shunt or multiplier resistors may be selected to give multiple overlapping ranges to each function.

An illustration of a fairly typical VOM is showing in Fig. 3-8. The VOM on my workbench has a 19-position range/function switch, with four metering functions—dc resistance, ac voltage, dc current, and dc voltage. The specific ranges offered on this particular instrument are summarized in Table 3-2. This VOM also has a switch that cuts the displayed voltage and current readings in half. For example, when this switch is on, a full-scale reading on the 2.5-Vdc scale will indicate a measured voltage of 1.25 V.

The VOM is used with a pair of test leads. Usually, long probes are on the end of these test leads, but other tips are available for special purposes. Normally, one of the test leads has red insulation and the other has black insulation. The test leads plug into two sockets on the front panel of the VOM. The black lead should also be connected to the "common" jack. This jack may be marked "COM," "Ground," or " – " on some VOMs. All measurements are made referenced to the common point. Since most

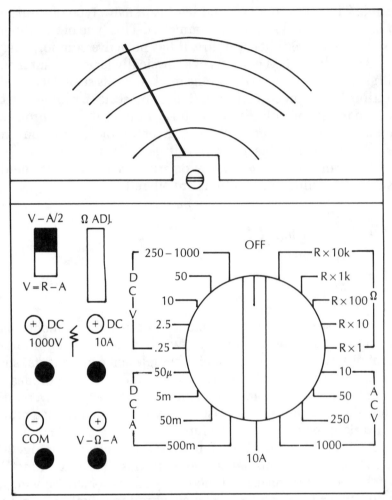

Fig. 3-8 *A typical analog VOM.*

VOMs can only measure positive voltages and currents, the black test lead should be connected to the most negative end of the portion of the circuit to be monitored on the meter.

The red test lead is usually plugged into a jack marked " + ," "TEST," or "V-Ω-A." This is the positive end of the test connection. The meter can be severely damaged if too large a current or voltage is applied to this jack. Many VOMs, including the one shown in Fig. 3-8, have additional large-signal jacks. For example, on my VOM there is a warning that the normal positive jack has absolute maximum ratings of 1,000 Vac, 250Vdc, and 500 mA dc. A special, secondary test jack is used to measure dc voltages between 250 and 1,000 V. Yet another auxiliary jack is used

Table 3-2   Ranges for a typical VOM.

Switch position	Function	Range
1	Off	—
2	Ohms	R × 10K
3	Ohms	R × 1K
4	Ohms	R × 100
5	Ohms	R × 10
6	Ohms	R × 1
7	ac V	10
8	ac V	50
9	ac V	250
10	ac V	1000
11	dc A	500 mA
12	dc A	50 mA
13	dc A	5 mA
14	dc A	50 μA
15	dc V	0.25
16	dc V	2.5
17	dc V	10
18	dc V	50
19	dc V	250 and 1,000

to measure large currents, up to 10 A. You could safely make low-value voltage and current measurements using these special large signal jacks, but you would not get meaningful readings because the meter's pointer won't move very far across the scale.

The same common jack is used for all resistance, voltage, and current measurements, regardless of the range. The only other control on the front panel of most VOMs is the calibration control for the ohmmeter section. Usually, this is a small thumb wheel connected internally to a trimming potentiometer.

When using a VOM it is vitally important to be careful that the range/function switch is set correctly before attempting any test measurement. If it is set for too high a range, no harm will be done, but the meter's pointer won't move very far and may be difficult to read the value from the scale. For current and voltage measurements, it is usually best to start out at the highest available range, then carefully adjust the range downwards until you get a clear, unambiguous reading on the meter's face. If the meter is set on too low a range, the applied voltage or current could slam the pointer over to the far end of the scale, possibly bending the pointer or damaging the armature coil.

When you are measuring dc voltage, make sure the range/function switch is set for a dc voltage range. Do not attempt to make a dc voltage reading on an ac scale, or vice versa. Also, do not apply a voltage to the meter's test leads, when the switch is set to a current or resistance range. Similarly, if you are trying to measure current, make sure the switch is selecting an appropriate current range. Serious damage can be done if you attempt to make a voltage or current measurement when the multimeter is set up to read resistance. With very few exceptions, all resistance tests should be made with no power applied to the circuit under test.

When using the ohmmeter section of your multimeter, you will notice that the scale is very nonlinear. Higher values are crammed into a small space at the far left (facing the meter) of the scale, while lower values are increasingly spread out as you move up the scale (to the right). It is usually best to start measuring an unknown resistance on the lowest range ($R \times 1$) and work your way up to higher ranges ($R \times 10$, $R \times 100$, $R \times 1K$, $R \times 10K$) until you get a clear, readable indication on the meter's scale.

Remember, the ohmmeter section works from an internal battery. If this battery starts to go bad, measurement accuracy will be lost. You may not be able to calibrate the ohmmeter when the battery gets weak. The battery in a VOM is for the ohmmeter only. It has no effect at all on the voltmeter or ammeter sections of the VOM. In fact, you could remove the battery altogether and still make voltage and current readings.

The impedance rating for any multimeter is a very, very important specification. It is usually given in ohms per volt. The higher this rating, the more accurate the meter readings will be. Some real cheap VOMs with ratings of 1,000 ohms/V are available, but they are virtually useless for practical electronics work. Such a VOM isn't good for much beyond testing battery voltages.

Most inexpensive VOMs are rated for 20,000 ohms/V. For a long time, this was considered the standard rating for this type of test equipment. More and more newer models, however, are rated at up to 50,000 ohms/V.

There are several significant advantages to the VOM as a piece of test equipment. Of course, it is very versatile, as are all multimeters. The VOM is generally quite inexpensive, especially when compared to most other types of multimeters. You can purchase a good-quality VOM for about $20 to $60. The chief differences between various models are the physical size of the meter's scale (larger scales are easier to read), the number of ranges, and the overall quality of the meter movement itself.

VOMs are rugged. The meter's armature is fairly delicate. As long as the instrument is not dropped from a significant height or onto a hard surface, or subjected to serious abuse, it should last a long time, even in field use where it gets banged around.

Portability is another one of the VOM's assets. Because it includes no active circuitry it tends to be very lightweight and compact. It does not require any external power source or heavy batteries. The ohmmeter section is usually powered by an AA cell or a 9-V transistor battery. Since the VOM's circuitry is passive, there is never any warm-up time required for the instrument to stabilize itself. Accurate readings can be taken right away.

The chief downfall of the VOM is in its accuracy. With a typical accuracy or sensitivity rating of 20,000 to 50,000 ohms/V, the VOM offers only fair accuracy when compared to other types of multimeters.

VTVMs

Until recently, the second most popular type of multimeter was the VTVM (vacuum tube voltmeter). In fact, for a long time, this was the only available alternative to the VOM.

Unlike the simple VOM, the VTVM includes active circuitry to measure voltage and resistance. While there are a few occasional exceptions, most VTVMs do not include a milliammeter section to measure current.

As the name suggests, this instrument's active circuitry is built around vacuum tubes. As vacuum tubes have declined in popularity, the VTVM has become something of a rarity in modern electronics. Solid-state equivalents of the VTVM, using FETs (field effect transistors) in place of vacuum tubes, will be discussed in the next section of this chapter.

The biggest advantage of the VTVM is that the input signal to be measured is amplified, increasing the sensitivity and, therefore, the accuracy of the instrument considerably. A typical accuracy/sensitivity rating for a VTVM is 11 megohms (11,000,000 ohms). This is obviously a very significant improvement over the VOM's 20,000 to 50,000 ohms/V. VTVMs can often safely measure larger voltages than VOMs can.

A VTVM can measure ac voltages at higher frequencies than most VOMs can. The accuracy of ac voltage measurements tends to decline sharply on most VOMs when the signal frequency exceeds a few hundred hertz.

The VTVM's advantages are also the direct cause of its disadvantages. Because active circuitry is involved, a power supply is required for the VTVM. This will usually be an ac power supply requiring access to a line current socket. This limits the portability of the instrument, as does its relatively large size and weight. Vacuum tubes are rather bulky. They are also easily broken because they are made of glass. The vacuum tubes emit quite a bit of heat, and this heat must be properly dissipated to avoid serious problems. Vacuum tubes also require at least some warm-up time before they stabilize. The technician must turn on the VTVM 10 to 15 minutes before he can take any accurate readings.

It used to be that most electronics hobbyists used VOMs, while the majority of electronics technicians kept a VTVM on their workbench because of its greater accuracy. Service technicians usually also kept a VOM in their toolbox for field work, but the VTVM was the multimeter of choice for serious electronics work. With the development of solid-state multimeters, such as the FET voltmeter and the digital multimeter (both of these instruments will be discussed shortly), the disadvantages of the VTVM began to outweigh its advantages. VTVMs are rapidly becoming obsolete, although a handful of them are still being manufactured.

FET voltmeters

As vacuum tubes began to vanish from the general electronics market, a solid-state version of the VTVM was increasingly desirable. The result of this need was the FET voltmeter. This device looks very much like an ordinary VOM, but it includes active amplification circuitry to improve the sensitivity. The active circuitry in this type of test equipment is designed around a semiconductor component known as the FET (field effect transistor). Unlike ordinary (bipolar) transistors, the FET has electrical characteristics that are quite similar to those of vacuum tubes.

The FET voltmeter offers a higher accuracy/sensitivity rating than ordinary VOMs. A few FET voltmeters have a sensitivity rating as low as 100,000 ohms/V, but 1 megohm /V (1,000,000 ohms/V) is a much more common rating for this type of instrument. Some deluxe FET voltmeters have sensitivity ratings as high as 10 megohms /V (10,000,000 ohms/V).

Because of the active circuitry in an FET voltmeter, power must be applied to the instrument during all tests. Since the solid-state components in the FET voltmeter consume far less current than vacuum tubes, a small lightweight battery is usually adequate. In most FET voltmeters, a simple 9-V transistor battery is used as the power source.

The biggest disadvantage of the FET voltmeter compared to the VOM is that the cost of this instrument is somewhat higher. Typically, an FET voltmeter will cost about $20 more than a VOM with similar features and ranges. Of course, this higher price buys you greater measurement accuracy.

Digital multimeters

Anyone who is even slightly familiar with the modern world of electronics knows that the buzz word today is "digital." It seems like everything is going digital, whether there is a good reason for it or not. So no one should be even mildly surprised by the existence and growing popularity of DMMs (digital multimeters). A DMM performs essentially the same functions as a VOM or VTVM, except the measured values are indicated directly on a digital readout rather than read from the position of a pointer on an analog scale.

Digital multimeters feature high input impedances. The input impedance is essentially the same as the accuracy/sensitivity ratings we have mentioned throughout this chapter. Even an inexpensive DMM will have an input impedance of at least 1 megohm (1,000,000 ohms).

The earliest DMMs were quite expensive and fairly limited in their capabilities. Today, some DMMs are available in the $50 to $100 price range, although many deluxe models cost far more. Even an inexpensive DMM will tend to outperform a standard VOM or FET voltmeter on most basic tests. (There are some tests were an analog multimeter is definitely preferable to a DMM. Such cases will be discussed in the next section of this chapter.)

Some deluxe DMMs have additional test features. For example, many currently available models measure conductivity as well as resistance. Conductivity is the reciprocal or resistance:

$$\text{Conductivity} = 1/\text{Resistance}$$

A conductivity measurement makes it possible to measure very, very small resistances, such as that of a length of simple copper wire. No practical conductor ever has a resistance of zero.

(We're ignoring superconductors here, of course, since they are not yet practical for use in most electronic circuitry.)

A few DMMs have built-in capacitance testers (see chapter 5) or frequency meters (see chapter 6). Others have capabilities for testing even more exotic functions. Most DMMs, however, are designed to measure the "big three" of electronics—voltage, current, and resistance.

Early DMMs usually employed seven-segment LEDs (light emitting diodes) for the digital readouts. This worked fine, but LED displays require fairly large amounts of current, especially if large numerals are to be displayed for easy readability. Naturally, this increased the overall power consumption of the instrument. Also, LED readouts can be rather difficult to read in some bright lighting conditions because of reflections.

Most modern DMMs use LCDs (liquid crystal displays) in place of the LED readouts formerly used. LCDs consume considerably less power than LEDs, allowing larger numerals to be displayed.

It can be difficult to read LCDs in dim lighting, but since few electronics technicians do much of their work in the dark, this isn't likely to be much of a problem. However, many DMMs feature backlighting for their displays to improve the readability.

Digital multimeters are now available in a wide variety of sizes and formats to suit all sorts of electronics needs. The hobbyist or technician should select the instrument that suits his particular purposes.

Most inexpensive DMMs are handheld battery operated units designed for maximum portability. This type of DMM is perfect for field work. Many handheld DMMs are small enough to fit easily into a toolbox, or even a pocket. A typical handheld DMM is shown in Fig. 3-9.

Larger DMMs for use on a permanent workbench are also available, ranging from the relatively simple (as in Fig. 3-10) to the very sophisticated (as in Fig. 3-11). Most benchtop DMMs can be operated by either battery or ac power.

Analog vs. digital

These days there seems to be an urge to convert all electronics circuitry into digital form. Many functions that were once served by analog circuitry now use digital circuitry. In some cases, this is a real and valuable improvement. In some cases, digital circuitry

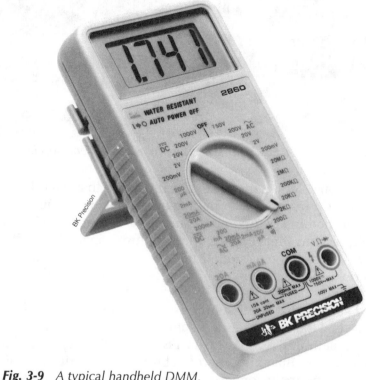

Fig. 3-9   *A typical handheld DMM.*

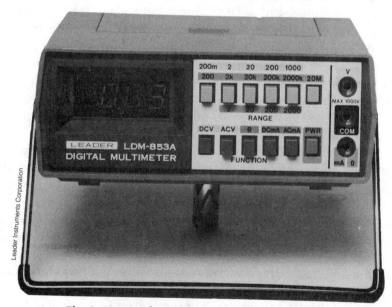

Fig. 3-10   *A relatively simple benchtop DMM.*

Fig. 3-11   *This is a sophisticated benchtop DMM.*

can be used to implement certain functions that would be difficult or even impossible to implement by analog means.

But nothing is a perfect panacea, and that includes digital
electronics. In some cases, converting from analog to digital circuitry results in no particular improvement. There are even some
functions where a digital circuit doesn't work as well as an analog circuit.

I suspect that the first impulse among many electronics hobbyists, and even a few service technicians, is to go for a shiny new
DMM, shunning a VOM or an FET voltmeter as old-fashioned
and obsolete. But this is a very short-sighted attitude that may
well hurt you in the long run. There are some serious trade-offs to
be considered between analog and digital multimeters.

The advantages of a DMM are pretty clear. The measured
value is indicated directly and precisely in numerical form, usually to several decimal places. With an analog meter, you have to
estimate where on the scale the pointer is aimed; fine decimal
precision isn't possible. Moreover, you have to be sure you are
looking at the meter face head-on to prevent parallax errors. If
you look at the meter from an angle, the pointer's position will
appear to move a little.

On the other hand, in most practical electronics work, approximate measurements are perfectly adequate. In most circuits,
it doesn't really make any practical differences if the voltage is
11.93, 12.0, or 12.15 V, as long as it is reasonably close to a nominal value of 12 V. Component tolerances will cause some fluctua-
tion in values from circuit to circuit, so reference values are only
approximate.

In many cases, the exact measured value isn't as significant
as the amount of change in value. A good example is using an
ohmmeter to test a capacitor. This procedure is discussed in the

next section of this chapter. Essentially, when the ohmmeter's test voltage is applied across the capacitor's leads, the pointer will jump to a very low resistance value, then slowly move back to a higher resistance value. This process is very clearly visible on an analog meter; but on a DMM, the result is just a blur of numbers changing too rapidly to be read.

Ideally, if you do more than casual work in electronics, you should own both a digital and an analog multimeter. While there is considerable overlap in their functions, they are each good for different purposes. If you can't afford both, I'd recommend that you go with an analog VOM or FET voltmeter. It will be cheaper than a DMM and generally more versatile. If you are working seriously enough in electronics to require the precision of a digital readout, you definitely should invest in a simple analog VOM as a back-up.

That's not to say any electronics hobbyist or technician wouldn't find advantages in having a DMM handy. But its advantages tend to be in the area of luxuries rather than absolute necessities. The special tests made possible on an analog meter will probably be more important for most people working with electronics than the advantages of the DMM.

Digital circuitry is great, but it is important to keep things in perspective. There is no reason to throw out all analog circuitry and devices. In fact, there are good reasons not to. Analog is better for some things than digital, just as digital is better for other purposes. It makes sense to use both technologies, choosing the one most appropriate for the specific task at hand.

Multimeter applications

The potential applications for a multimeter are virtually endless. Of course, the most common and obvious uses are to make direct voltage, current, and resistance measurements, as described earlier in this chapter. But there are many more ways for a resourceful electronics hobbyist or technician to use a multimeter.

Voltage measurements

Voltage measurements are made with the multimeter placed in parallel across the resistance element(s) whose voltage drop is being measured. The higher the input impedance (sensitivity rating) of the multimeter, the more accurate the voltage reading will be, because the parallel resistance of the meter affects the total effective resistance seen by the circuit's voltage source. Obviously, the component being measured for voltage drop should not be disconnected from the circuit because it is necessary to apply power to the circuit under test.

In most cases, all voltage measurements should be referenced to the circuit's ground (0-V point). This will usually be the most negative potential in the circuit. The black lead is connected to a good ground point (sometimes the chassis), while the red lead is moved about as a probe to measure the voltage at various points in the circuit. When measuring negative voltages, the multimeter's test leads should be reversed. That is, the red lead should be connected to the circuit's ground, while the black lead is used as the probe to test the negative voltages at specific places in the circuit.

Be careful to set the polarity of your multimeter correctly. A strong voltage of the wrong polarity could damage the armature coil by forcing it to try to turn the wrong way.

When using a VOM, DMM, VTVM, or FET voltmeter to make a voltage measurement, it is vitally important to be careful that the range/function switch is set correctly before applying the external voltage to be tested. If the meter is set for too high a range, no harm will be done, but the meter's pointer won't move very far and it may be difficult to read the value from the scale. For most practical voltage measurements, it is advisable to start out at the multimeter's highest available range, then carefully adjust the range downwards until you get a clear, unambiguous reading on the meter's face. If the meter is set on too low a range, the excessive applied voltage could slam the pointer over to the far end of the scale, possibly bending the pointer or damaging the armature coil.

When you are measuring dc voltage, make sure the range/function switch is set for a dc voltage range. Do not attempt to make a dc voltage reading on an ac scale, or vice versa.

Current measurements

For analog multimeters, at least, current measurements represent the instrument's most basic and direct operating mode. In actual practice, however, they tend to be used more commonly for voltage or resistance readings.

One reason for this is the built-in inconvenience of current measurements. The meter must be placed in series with the circuit being tested with power applied to the circuit. This means a circuit connection must be physically broken to insert the meter, as illustrated in Fig. 3-12.

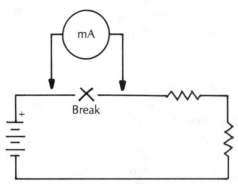

Fig. 3-12 *To make a current measurement, a break must be made in the circuit to insert the meter in series.*

The signal applied to the multimeter's test leads must be of the correct polarity to prevent potential damage. The red test lead must be positive with respect to the black test lead. A strong applied signal of the wrong polarity can damage the armature coil of your multimeter by forcing it to try to turn the wrong way.

Whenever you make a current measurement with a multimeter, you must be very careful to set the range/function switch correctly before applying power to the circuit being tested. If the meter is set for too high a range, no harm will be done, but the meter's pointer won't move very far and it may be difficult to read the value from the scale. Generally speaking, when making current measurements, it is a good idea to begin with the multimeter set for its highest available range. If necessary, you can then adjust the range downwards until you get a clear, unambiguous reading on the meter's face. If the meter is set on too low a range, the strong applied signal could cause the meter's pointer to slam violently over to the far end of the scale. This could bend the pointer or damage the multimeter's armature coil.

When you are measuring dc current, make sure the range/function switch is set for a dc current range. Do not attempt to make a dc current reading on an ac scale, or vice versa. Most simple VOMs are not designed to measure ac current, although a few models do have this capability.

Resistance measurements

Resistance measurements, like voltage measurements, are made in parallel with the resistance element (electronic component) being measured. Of course, power should not be applied to the circuit under test during resistance measurements. Resistance readings are normally taken with no power applied to the circuit or component under test. When used as an ohmmeter, your multimeter can be damaged by an external voltage or current signal. In some cases, the ohmmeter voltage could also do some harm to the circuit being tested if it is "fighting" the circuit's normal signal voltages.

Resistance measurements can be taken across almost any electronic component, either in or out of circuit. When you make a resistance measurement of a component wired into a circuit, you may find that you get a too-low reading. This occurs because some other circuitry is in parallel with the resistance element being measured. Remember the parallel combination of two or more resistances is always less than any of the original component resistances.

To prevent such problematic misreadings, one end of the component to be tested can be lifted up from the circuit, if possible. This will ensure an accurate resistance reading, without errors from any parallel resistances in the circuit. Such parallel resistances are not always obvious at first glance. Semiconductors can be particularly troublesome in this way.

Whenever you use the ohmmeter section of an analog multimeter, you must remember that the resistance scale runs backwards compared to the voltage and current scales. This is not a problem for DMMs, which simply display the current value presently being measured in direct numerical form.

On an analog multimeter's resistance scale, the pointer normally rests at the far left (facing the meter) of the scale, representing the maximum possible value (infinite resistance). As the resistance being measured decreases, the meter's pointer moves up the scale (to the right). At the far right of the scale is the 0- ohms position. This position is reached by the pointer when there is a dead short between the multimeter's test leads.

Testing capacitors

A moderate- to large-value capacitor can be tested with the ohmmeter section of an analog multimeter. This test will not reveal the actual capacitance of the component being tested, but it will indicate if the capacitor has excessive leakage or is open, the two most common capacitor faults. In a pinch, this ohmmeter capacitor test can be used to get a rough idea of the component's time constant, which is related to the capacitance value.

This test can be done on capacitors wired into a circuit, but the results will be far more reliable if the capacitor is taken out of circuit. If the capacitor is wired into a circuit, parallel resistances might obliterate the desired characteristics of the reading.

Before testing the capacitor, you must make sure that it is fully discharged. This can be easily accomplished by shorting the capacitor's leads together. With a loose component with full-length leads, you can just touch them together. If this is not possible, you can use a screwdriver, pliers, or even a length of spare wire to short the capacitor's leads together to discharge it. A dead short like this will discharge the capacitor very quickly.

Once the capacitor has been discharged, connect the ohmmeter's leads to either end of the capacitor. If you are testing a polarized capacitor (such as an electrolytic capacitor or a tantalum capacitor), make sure the red test lead is connected to the capacitor's positive lead and the black test lead is connected to the capacitor's negative lead.

While connecting the multimeter's test leads to the capacitor, carefully watch the meter's pointer. As soon as the connection is made, the pointer will jump to a very low resistance reading. Almost instantly, the resistance will begin to increase, and the pointer will climb back up to a very high resistance reading. The speed of this upward resistance climb is roughly proportional to the capacitance of the device being tested.

If the meter's pointer stays at a very high resistance value without the jump to a low value, the capacitor is open. For very small-value capacitors, the pointer jump may be too fast for you to see. Compare your test results with a known good capacitor of the same type and value. If the pointer jumps to a low resistance value and stays there, the capacitor is shorted. Discard this component.

You'll find that many capacitors will exhibit the jump, but the final resistance value won't be all that high. This indicates a lot of leakage in the capacitor. Again, it is best to compare your results with a similar capacitor that you know is good. Different types of capacitors will exhibit differing amounts of leakage.

Electrolytic capacitors usually have a leakage resistance between about 75,000 and 100,000 ohms. I'd be highly suspicious of any capacitor (of any type) that showed a leakage resistance of less than about 50,000 ohms.

It usually takes a little practice to get consistent results with this test procedure. It is not difficult, but it does require a fairly sure hand to cleanly connect the test leads to the capacitor to be tested.

This test is only suitable for analog multimeters. If you try to test a capacitor with a DMM you'll get a blur of numbers that change too rapidly for you to read them.

Of course, using a multimeter to test capacitors is just a quick and dirty procedure at best. For better and more accurate results, you should use a dedicated capacitance meter. These devices will be discussed in chapter 5.

Testing coils and transformers

The separate turns of wire in a coil or transformer must be electrically insulated from each other. If two turns of wire short against each other, any wire between the shorted turns is useless.

If you know the nominal resistance for a coil or transformer winding, you can measure it with the ohmmeter section of your multimeter. (Either an analog multimeter or a digital multimeter may be used for this test.) If the measured resistance is significantly less than the nominal value, or if it is virtually equal to 0 ohms, then the coil or transformer winding is shorted. The component should be replaced.

You will probably need to perform such tests with your multimeter set to its lowest available resistance range. An analog multimeter will only give reliable results for fairly large (many turns) coils. The conductance scale available on many DMMs can be helpful in testing small coils.

With transformers, you should also test for a short between either end of each winding (and the center tap, if used) and the transformer's core. You should measure a very high resistance here. A typical minimum value for a good transformer's winding-to-core resistance is 25 megohms (25,000,000 ohms). The exact value will depend on the specific design of the individual transformer. If any part of the transformer's winding shows less than 1 megohm (1,000,000 ohms) to its core, it's a safe bet that the transformer is bad and potentially dangerous. Discard it and use a new transformer with appropriate voltage and current ratings.

It can also be useful to measure the resistance between the primary and secondary windings of a transformer. A good transformer will show a fairly high resistance in this test. Typical values run from about 20 megohms (20,000,000 ohms) to over 100 megohms (100,000,000 ohms).

Another multimeter test for a power transformer (not an impedance transformer) can be used to determine the turns ratio. The ac voltmeter section of the multimeter is used for this test. Either an analog or a digital multimeter can be used for this purpose.

Simply apply a known ac voltage to one of the transformer's windings and measure the ac voltage at the other winding. Ignore any center taps for the time being. The turns ratio of any power transformer is always equal to the ratio between the voltages in the primary and secondary windings:

Turns ratio = Primary voltage/Secondary voltage

For example, let's say you feed an ac voltage of 25 V into one winding of a transformer and then measure 5.2 V at the other winding. In this case, the turns ratio is

$$\text{Turns ratio} = 25/5.2$$
$$= 4.8$$

We can use some simple algebra to find out the secondary voltage for this transformer when ordinary line current is applied to the primary winding (as in normal operation).

Secondary voltage = Primary voltage/Turns ratio

In our example this works out to

$$\text{Secondary voltage} = 117/4.8$$
$$= 24.375 \text{ V}$$

The rated secondary voltage for this transformer is probably 24.5 V, a fairly standard value.

For safety reasons, it is a good idea to use a smaller than normal ac voltage (not house current) as the input signal for this test. The reason for this is that it is possible to get the primary and secondary windings reversed. If this happens, the result is a step-up transformer, instead of a step-down transformer. Let's say we used 117-Vac house current as the test signal and applied it to the transformer's secondary winding by mistake. At the opposite winding, there would be an ac voltage of

$$\text{Output voltage (step-up)} = \text{Input voltage} \times \text{Turns ratio}$$
$$= 117 \times 4.8$$
$$= 561.6 \text{ V}$$

This high voltage could be very dangerous to the person making the test, and could possibly overheat and damage the transformer being tested or the multimeter. Use a low input voltage to be safe. There's no sense in taking unnecessary chances.

When making this type of test out of circuit, you can expect to get a higher than normal secondary voltage from the transformer. This is because the multimeter places such a small current load on the transformer. For a more accurate test of a transformer's output voltage, be sure to use an appropriate load resistance comparable to the circuit the transformer would normally be used in.

Testing semiconductors

A multimeter can also be used to test simple semiconductor components, such as diodes and bipolar transistors. The ohmmeter section of the multimeter is again used for these tests. These semiconductor resistance tests can be made in circuit, but you will get more reliable results if you remove the component from the circuit before testing it. Any parallel resistances in the circuitry can throw off the readings considerably; possibly making your results confusing or even totally meaningless.

As with all ohmmeter tests, no power should be applied to the semiconductor component being tested. To prevent possible damage to some low-power devices, use an ohmmeter with a very low-voltage battery—preferably 1.5 V, instead of a 9-V transistor battery. As a rule of thumb, make your semiconductor resistance tests with the multimeter set on its highest resistance range. The higher internal meter resistance on this range will cause more of the test voltage to be dropped internally, limiting the current flow through the component under test. Obviously, you don't want to risk damaging or destroying the component you are trying to test.

To test a semiconductor diode, attach the multimeter's red lead to the anode and the black lead to the cathode. This will forward bias the component. The multimeter should indicate a fairly low resistance—typically under 1,000 ohms. There will be considerable variation in the forward-biased resistance with different types of diodes. With some units, the forward-biased resistance will be only 10 ohms or so, or even just a few tenths of an ohm.

Now, reverse the polarity of the diode. Connect the multimeter's red test lead to the cathode and the black test lead to the anode. Now the diode is reverse biased, and the multimeter should give a very high resistance reading. The reverse-biased resistance reading should be considerably higher than the forward-biased resistance reading. With most diodes, the difference will be at least a factor of 10, or more.

Again, the actual reverse-biased resistance depends on the specific type of diode being used. Some diodes may have reverse-biased resistances as low as 100 ohms or so, while others will exhibit reverse-biased resistances of several megohms (millions of ohms).

For the most reliable tests, you should compare the resistance readings from your tests to those for a diode of the same type that is known to be good. As a general rule, however, if the measured resistance is significantly lower when the diode is forward biased than when it is reverse biased, then the component is probably OK.

This test procedure can also be used to quickly determine the correct polarity of an unmarked diode. When you get the lower resistance reading, you know that the multimeter's red test lead is connected to the anode and the black test lead is connected to the cathode.

The same basic procedure can be used to test bipolar transistors. A bipolar transistor consists of two PN junctions, as illustrated in Fig. 3-13. The transistor looks a little like a pair of back-to-back diodes. A diagram for an NPN transistor is shown in Fig. 3-14. For a PNP transistor, the polarities are simply reversed, as illustrated in Fig. 3-15. Each of the PN junctions in a bipolar transistor can be tested as if it was a diode. You only concern yourself with two of the transistor's leads at a time.

For a NPN transistor, you should get a low resistance reading when the black test lead is connected to the base of the transistor and the red test lead is touched to the transistor's emitter. Reversing the polarity of the leads (red to base and black to emitter) should reverse bias the PN junction, resulting in a very high resistance reading.

For a PNP transistor, these readings should be reversed. You

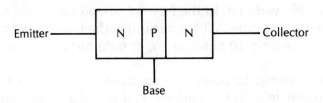

Emitter ———— | N | P | N | ———— Collector

Base

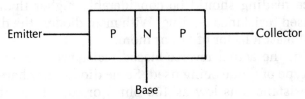

Emitter ———— | P | N | P | ———— Collector

Base

Fig. 3-13   *A bipolar transistor consists of two PN junctions.*

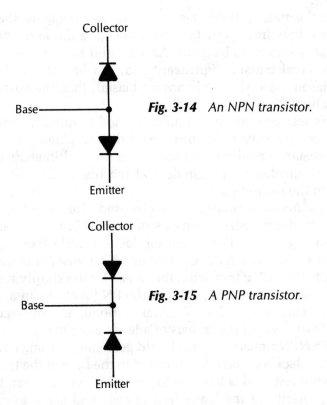

Collector

Base ————

Fig. 3-14   *An NPN transistor.*

Emitter

Collector

Base ————

Fig. 3-15   *A PNP transistor.*

Emitter

should get a high resistance reading when the base is negative
with respect to the emitter, and a low resistance reading when the
base is positive with respect to the emitter.

The other PN junction in a bipolar transistor is between the base and the collector. Test this in the same way as you tested the base/collector junction. For an NPN transistor, you should again get a low resistance reading when the black test lead is connected to the base of the transistor and the red test lead is touched to the transistor's collector. Reversing the polarity of the leads (red to base and black to collector) should reverse bias the PN junction, resulting in a very high resistance reading.

Of course, these resistance readings will be reversed for a PNP transistor. There should be a high resistance reading when the base is negative with respect to the collector, and a low resistance measured when the base is positive with respect to the emitter.

In each of these tests, the differences between the two resistance readings should be quite large. A typical PN junction in a bipolar transistor might give a resistance reading of about 20 ohms when it is forward biased, and a resistance reading of well over 100,000 ohms when the junction is reverse biased.

Testing a diode or bipolar transistor with an ohmmeter using these procedures is just a crude check. This test procedure tells you nothing about the operating parameters of the semiconductor component being tested. It is either functional or nonfunctional. It may be functional, but its characteristics may be so far off spec that it may not operate properly in certain circuits.

Identifying wires in a multiconductor cable

Sometimes the electronics technician might have to do some work on a system with long runs of multiconductor cable. If the original installer used color-coded wires, or applied labels to the individual wires, there will be no problem. All too often, however, multiconductor cable is installed without any identification of the individual wires. Occasionally, even if labels were applied during installation, they age and fall off. If the various individual wires in a multiconductor cable are not clearly identified, the service technician may have some difficulty identifying just what is connected to what.

A VOM (or any other multimeter) can be used to identify the individual wires in the cable. Connect a pair of test leads with alligator clips to a standard 9-V battery. You may want to add a pilot lamp or a milliammeter in series with the battery.

The actual test procedure requires two people, one at either end of the run of cable to be identified. Person A has the battery,

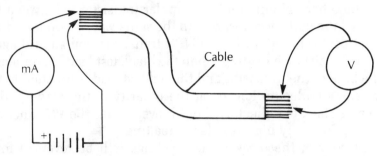

Fig. 3-16 *Two people can use a multimeter to identify unmarked wires in a run of multiconductor cable.*

and person B has a voltmeter set to a 10-V range. The basic test setup is illustrated in Fig. 3-16.

Person A connects the test leads from the battery to any two of the wires in the cable. Person B now experiments with various combinations of wires at his end of the cable. He checks each combination of wires with the voltmeter. When he finds the right two wires, the pointer will move. If the polarity is reversed, the meter's pointer will try to move backwards. This will almost always be visible. Person B should reverse the positions of his meter's test leads to confirm he has the right connection. His voltmeter should measure 9 V. If the cable is very long, there may be some voltage drop, but it probably won't be significant. If a pilot lamp is used at the battery end, it will light up, alerting person A that the correct connection has been made. A milliammeter will serve the same purpose. No current will flow from the battery until the correct connection is made at the other end of the cable.

Adhesive-backed labels should be affixed to each wire as it is identified. Then person A moves the battery leads to two of the remaining wires, and person B repeats the test procedure at his end. This process continues until all the individual wires in the cable have been identified and labeled.

Persons A and B have an agreed upon labeling code. A practical approach is to make the positive wire in each test pair an odd number (1, 3, 5, etc.) and the negative wire an even number (2, 4, 6, etc.). Of course, the label numbers should be assigned in numerical order. That is, the first identified pair is made up of wires 1 and 2, the second pair uses wires 3 and 4, the third is 5 and 6, and so forth. Once all of the identifying labels are securely in place, they will make any subsequent service calls more convenient and less time-consuming.

Power tests

Electrical power can be defined in terms of any two of the three basic electrical parameters—voltage, resistance, and current. The standard power equations are

$$P = IE$$

$$P = RI^2 = R \times I \times I$$

$$P = E^2/R = (E \times E)/R$$

Because a multimeter can test voltage, resistance, and current, power measurements can be made with this type of test instrument.

To measure the output power of an audio amplifier, you will need to use a multimeter with an ac voltmeter section and a signal generator. Signal generators will be discussed in chapter 7. A signal generator is simply a circuit that produces a steady tone at a specific, consistent frequency and amplitude. In this test, the signal generator is used as the original signal source for the audio amplifier being tested. It would be very difficult to make this test with an ordinary music source as the input signal. Music signals consist of continuously changing multiple frequencies, with the amplitude varying widely from moment to moment. We need a consistent signal here, not one that sounds good. The signal generator should be connected to the amplifier's auxiliary input jack and set for a frequency of 1,000 Hz, although this does not have to be a precision adjustment. Anywhere in the neighborhood of 1,000 Hz will do just fine. For most modern audio amplifiers, the signal generator should be set up for a 1-V signal amplitude to drive the amplifier to its full output power.

A wirewound power resistor is connected across the output terminals of the amplifier being tested. This resistor should be rated to withstand the full rated power of the amplifier, with some room to spare. The resistance of this load resistor should match that of the amplifier's output. For most modern audio amplifiers, this will be 8 ohms. The usual loudspeaker should be disconnected from the amplifier for this test. The ac impedance of a loudspeaker will prevent the simple calculations we will be using later. A dc resistance is much, much easier to work with. The test setup is illustrated in Fig. 3-17.

Once the signal generator and the load resistor have been connected, turn on the amplifier. Any tone controls on the amplifier should be set to their nominal flat settings. Initially, set the ampli-

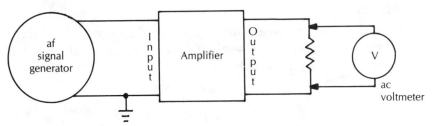

Fig. 3-17 *The basic test setup for measuring an audio amplifier's output power.*

fier's volume control to about its halfway point and measure the ac voltage across the load resistor. Since the load resistance is a known value (generally 8 ohms), the measured voltage can be used to calculate the actual output power of the amplifier using the equation

$$P = E^2/R$$

Let's say we measure 6.5 V across the load resistor. This means the output power is equal to

$$P = 6.5^2/8$$
$$= 42.25/8$$
$$= 5.28 \text{ W}$$

The first test is made at half volume to make sure everything is connected properly and the ac voltmeter won't be overloaded. Feel the load resistor with a finger tip. If it feels hot, shut down the amplifier and replace the load resistor with one that can take a much larger wattage. In the next part of the test, we'll be feeding more power into the load resistor. If the load resistor burns out, some amplifier circuits could be seriously damaged.

Once you've determined that everything is safe, repeat the test with the amplifier's volume control set just slightly below its maximum level. Virtually all audio amplifiers will distort the signal at their top volume, so that last little bit of power isn't particularly useful. It's just there for headroom for peak signals. Most audio amplifiers have volume controls calibrated from 1 to 10. Set the volume control to 9 for this test.

Measure the ac voltage across the load resistor again. It should be significantly higher than the voltage measured at half volume. It probably won't be double the previous voltage. However, with a few amplifier designs, the output voltage may be more than doubled.

Continuing with our example, let's say our test amplifier now puts out 11 V. This means the amplifier's maximum power is equal to

$$P = 11^2/8$$
$$= 121/8$$
$$= 15.125 \text{ W}$$

Make your measurements fairly quickly. For safety's sake, you shouldn't leave the amplifier running at high power into the load resistor for long. Try not to keep the power on more than a minute or so.

You should be aware that this is just a quick and dirty approach to measuring an audio amplifier's output power. Manufacturers and commercial laboratories use much more sophisticated power measurements. However, this test will often do for just a rough check of an amplifier.

One limitation of this test is that it gives no indication of how well the signal is being reproduced by the amplifier. The signal may be reproduced at a high power level, but with so much distortion that it is utterly unrecognizable. You can check for distortion in the amplified signal with an oscilloscope (see chapter 4).

❖ 4
Oscilloscopes

THE MULTIMETER (DISCUSSED IN THE PRECEDING CHAPTER) IS SO versatile and useful, it can almost be considered the electronics technician's right arm. If that is so, then his left arm is the oscilloscope.

The word oscilloscope is made up of *oscillation*, meaning a fluctuating signal, and *scope*, meaning a visual instrument. An oscilloscope, in other words, lets you view fluctuating (ac) signals in an electronics circuit.

The multimeter is best suited for dc measurements, although it can be used for some ac measurements. The oscilloscope, on the other hand, is designed primarily for ac (fluctuating or oscillating) signals, although it can be used for certain dc measurements.

Drawing waveshapes

The oscilloscope, as shown in Fig. 4-1, is designed around a cathode-ray tube (CRT), which is a simple version of the tube used in TV sets. The front end of the tube bulges out to serve as a screen. The inner surface of this screen is coated with a phosphorus substance that emits a glow when it is stimulated by electrons striking it. A steady stream of electrons is emitted from an electron gun mounted at the rear of the CRT. We will discuss the electron gun in more detail in the next section of this chapter.

A magnetic yoke is placed around the neck of the CRT to deflect the path of the electron beam, causing it to strike different

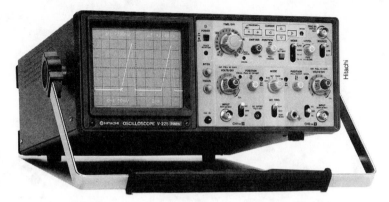

Fig. 4-1   *An oscilloscope permits the user to directly view a waveshape on a televisionlike screen.*

points on the screen. If no signal is applied to the yoke, then the oscilloscope will display a steady glowing dot at the center of the screen.

Usually, a steady sawtooth-wave signal, like the one shown in Fig. 4-2, is used to move the electron beam from side to side across the face of the screen. This is called the horizontal control signal, or the sweep frequency. To an observer facing the screen, the image starts at the far left of the screen, in response to the lowest portion of the sawtooth waveform. As the sawtooth signal increases its voltage, the electron beam is moved proportionately across the screen. The phosphors continue to glow briefly after they've been stimulated by the electron beam, so it appears that a continuous line is being drawn across the screen.

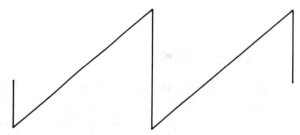

Fig. 4-2   *A sawtooth wave is usually employed as the sweep signal for an oscilloscope.*

When the sawtooth-wave signal reaches the peak voltage point of its cycle, the electron beam is deflected all the way over to the far right edge of the screen. The signal voltage then drops almost instantaneously from its maximum level to its minimum level, so the electron beam is whipped back over to the far left side of the screen. This return path is so fast, it is scarcely visible. Some oscilloscopes include special blanking circuitry to completely shut off the electron beam during this return portion of the horizontal control signal. The horizontal motion of the electron beam is often referred to as the x-axis.

The normal sawtooth-wave horizontal control signal is generated within the oscilloscope itself. Several different frequencies can be selected, determining how fast the line will be drawn from the far left to the far right of the screen. Most oscilloscopes allow the user to bypass the internally generated horizontal signal and use any external signal to control the horizontal signal and use any external signal to control the horizontal movement of the electron beam. This can be useful for certain tests.

The vertical control signal is usually the external signal that is being monitored by the oscilloscope. The voltage of this signal at any instant determines how far up or down the screen the electron beam is deflected. As the horizontal control signal moves the electron beam from left to right, the vertical control signal moves it up and down. The vertical motion of the electron beam is often referred to as the y-axis.

If the vertical control signal is an ac signal, its waveshape will be drawn across the face of the oscilloscope. For instance, if the vertical control signal is a sine wave, the screen of the oscilloscope might look something like Fig. 4-3.

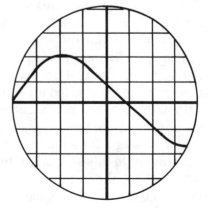

Fig. 4-3 *A typical sine wave input as displayed on an oscilloscope.*

The relative frequencies of the horizontal (x-axis) and vertical (y-axis) control signals determine how many complete cycles of the waveform will be displayed on the screen. In fact, you can

determine the frequency of an unknown vertical signal by counting the number of complete cycles displayed, and dividing that
value into the known frequency of the horizontal control signal.

The electron gun

The basic structure of an electron gun in a typical CRT is shown
in Fig. 4-4. There are five main components to the electron gun.
They are the heater (or filament), the cathode, the control grid,
the focusing anode, and the accelerating electrode.

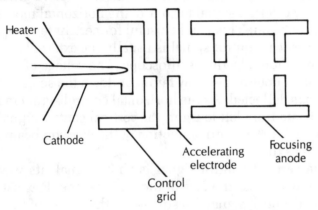

Fig. 4-4   *The five main components of an electron gun.*

The electron gun requires a very high voltage to operate. The
oscilloscope's circuitry includes a special high-voltage dc power
supply specifically for the electron gun.

The heater (filament) is fed a large, continuous voltage causing it to heat up. The heat from the filament allows the cathode to
emit electrons when it is fed an appropriate negative voltage. The
strength of the electron beam from the cathode is partially determined by the voltage fed to the control grid.

The focusing anode focuses the electron beam. That is, the
voltage applied to this section of the electron gun forces the electrons from the cathode to follow a very narrow beam path. The
emitted electrons are then speeded up by the voltage applied to
the accelerating electrode.

The electron beam then passes through the body of the CRT
and is deflected by the signals from the surrounding electromag-
netic yokes. The electrons are moving at such a high speed that

the deflection signals bend the beam but don't stop it. The electrons speed forward until they hit the phosphor-coated screen, causing the appropriate phosphors to glow.

Standard oscilloscope controls

The controls featured on an oscilloscope vary somewhat from model to model. Deluxe oscilloscopes usually offer special features, requiring extra controls. But virtually all practical oscilloscopes include some version of the following controls. You should realize that some manufacturers may use different terms for some of these basic functions. Don't be thrown by this.

The standard oscilloscope controls include:

- Vertical gain, which determines how much deflection from a baseline a given input voltage will cause.
- Vertical position, which allows the baseline (no signal position) to be moved up and down the face of the screen.
- Horizontal gain, which sets how much deflection will be caused in the right or left dimension. This control is only used when an external signal is used to control the sweep frequency, rather than the oscilloscope's built-in sawtooth-wave oscillator.
- Horizontal position, which moves the displayed waveform from right to left on the screen.
- Coarse frequency, which sets the approximate frequency range for the built-in sweep oscillator.
- Fine frequency, which fine tunes the exact frequency of the built-in sweep oscillator.
- Sync, which sychronizes the display pattern with another signal source.
- Intensity (brightness), which determines how bright the displayed line(s) will be.
- Focus, which is used to adjust the clarity of the displayed line(s).

Some oscilloscopes are designed to simultaneously display two separate signals, one in the top half of the screen and the other in the bottom half of the screen. This type of instrument is called a dual-trace oscilloscope, and it is very useful for comparing input and output signals or signals from different portions of a circuit being tested.

The circuitry of an oscilloscope

The fundamental sections of an oscilloscope's circuitry are illustrated in Fig. 4-5. As you can see, there are six main sections: the CRT, the high-voltage power supply, the low-voltage power supply, the horizontal deflection amplifier, the vertical deflection amplifier, and the time-base oscillator. We have already discussed the CRT in some detail earlier in this chapter.

The high-voltage power supply is needed to feed the high signal voltages required by the CRT's electron gun. The low-volt-

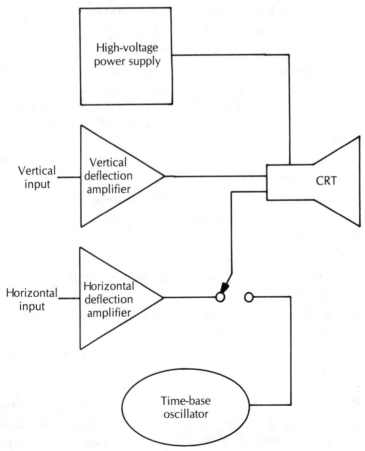

Fig. 4-5 *A block diagram for a typical oscilloscope.*

age power supply drives the remaining electronic circuitry in the oscilloscope.

The horizontal deflection amplifier preconditions the horizontal signal so it can drive the CRT's yoke and direct the electron beam in the horizontal dimension (x-axis). The horizontal signal may be an external signal or it may be the oscilloscope's internally generated sawtooth-wave oscillator, which is included in the time-base oscillator section.

The vertical deflection amplifier similarly preconditions the externally applied vertical signal so it can drive the CRT's yoke and direct the electron beam in the vertical dimension (y-axis).

The screen of an oscilloscope is usually covered with a cross-hatch of horizontal and vertical lines dividing the screen into discrete areas, which are called granules or divisions. These dividing lines make it easier to read and interpret the signals displayed on the oscilloscope's screen. If there are five vertical divisions from right to left, and one complete signal cycle is displayed in each granule, then you know that the input signal has a frequency exactly one-fifth the oscilloscope's current sweep frequency.

Oscilloscope specifications

As with any type of electronic equipment, different models of oscilloscopes vary widely in their specifications (performance capabilities). Many different specs are given by various test equipment manufacturers, but for most purposes, the electronics hobbyist or technician will need to be concerned with just five basic specifications when choosing an oscilloscope. These are bandwidth, rise time, input impedance, sweep time, and deflection factor.

The bandwidth is probably the most important single specification for oscilloscopes, and the price of the instrument tends to increase with improvements in the bandwidth. The bandwidth of an oscilloscope is a measurement of the maximum identifiable signal frequency that the scope can display. Higher frequency signals may be displayed, but it will be difficult or impossible to identify the individual cycles of the high-frequency signals. There can also be considerable attenuation of input signals beyond the oscilloscope's rated bandwidth.

For basic analog electronics work, an inexpensive 5-MHz (5,000,000 Hz) oscilloscope is fine. This is certainly sufficient for analog audio and low-frequency radio work. However, the increasing popularity of digital circuitry limits the usefulness of the 5-MHz oscilloscope. For digital circuits, an oscilloscope with a bandwidth of at least 20 MHz (20,000,000 Hz) is usually required. For serious electronics hobbyists and technicians, the standard for oscilloscopes is rapidly becoming 40 MHz (40,000,000 Hz) or 50 MHz (50,000,000 Hz). Of course, such wide bandwidth oscilloscopes cost considerably more than the electronically simpler 5-MHz models. For all oscilloscopes, the lower end of the bandwidth is 0 Hz, or dc.

With the bandwidth rating, there will usually be a decibel feature. This indicates the maximum attenuation of the signal amplitude within the specified bandwidth. The lower this figure, the better the oscilloscope.

The rise time is an important specification for any oscilloscope that will be used with high-frequency signals. It is a measurement of how rapidly the scope's traces can follow quick changes in the signal. The lower the rise time, the better the oscilloscope. For most modern oscilloscopes, the rise time is in the nanosecond (ns) range. A nanosecond is equal to one-billionth of a second.

The input impedance determines how much the oscilloscope will load the circuit under test. The oscilloscope's probes are placed in parallel with the circuitry being monitored, so the higher the instrument's input impedance, the less the circuit being measured will be affected by the presence of the scope. The impedance problem in testing is discussed in some detail in the section on voltmeters in chapter 2. A typical input impedance rating for a modern oscilloscope is 1 megohm (1,000,000 ohms) in parallel with 20 pF. The capacitance is of significance in ac circuits for similar reasons as the resistance in both dc and ac circuits.

The sweep time is the reciprocal of the sweep frequency generated by the oscilloscope's internal time-base oscillator. This specification is given in a range of seconds (or microseconds) per division. The specifications for a typical oscilloscope might list 0.1 μs/division to 0.5 s/division. Obviously, the wider the available range of sweep times, the more versatile the oscilloscope will be, but it is important to also consider how many range steps are offered. It may be very difficult to accurately calibrate and adjust an oscilloscope with a wide sweep time range, but just a few range steps.

The sweep time ratings will often be accompanied by a percentage error factor, such as ±3%. That means that the 0.5-s/division scale might be off by as much as 0.015 seconds (15 ms). Of course, for the sweep time rating, when we speak of "divisions," we are referring to the x-axis.

The deflection factor rating is similar to the sweep time rating, except it is given in volts (or millivolts) per division along the y-axis. A typical modern oscilloscope might have a deflection factor specification of 1 mV/division to 5 V/division, ±3% in 10 steps. Once again, the wider the specified range of deflection factors and the higher the number of range steps, the better and more versatile the oscilloscope will be.

Multitrace oscilloscopes

Most standard oscilloscopes are designed to display just one signal trace at a time, as shown in Fig. 4-6. Some deluxe models can simultaneously display two signal traces, one above the other, as illustrated in Fig. 4-7. This type of instrument is known as a dual-trace oscilloscope, for perfectly obvious reasons. A typical dual-trace oscilloscope is shown in Fig. 4-8.

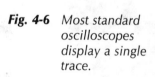 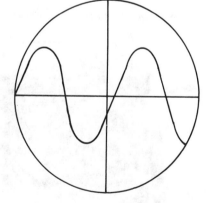

Fig. 4-6 *Most standard oscilloscopes display a single trace.*

A dual-trace oscilloscope is useful for comparing signals from two different points in a circuit. Comparing input and output signals for a specific stage is one common application. A dual-trace oscilloscope can also be very handy in matching up timing signals—making sure different electronic events are occurring in the proper sequence.

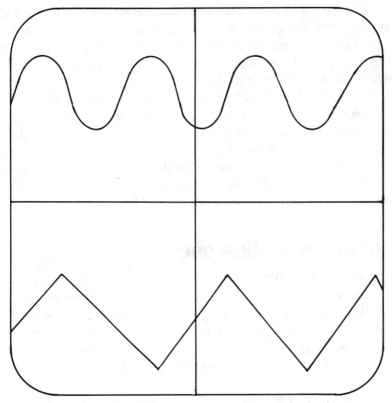

Fig. 4-7 *Many deluxe oscilloscopes can simultaneously display two traces.*

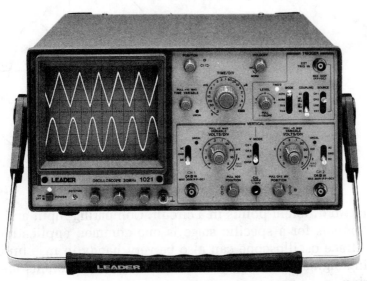

Fig. 4-8 *A typical dual-trace oscilloscope.* Leader Instruments Corporation

A true dual-trace oscilloscope has two separate and independent electron guns mounted within its CRT. This is quite expensive, however, so most so-called dual-trace oscilloscopes actually only simulate the dual-trace effect. These pseudo dual-trace oscilloscopes usually feature two modes or methods of displaying the two signals with a single electron beam. These are known as the alternate mode and the chopped mode.

In the alternate mode, one complete trace of the upper signal (one complete cycle of the sweep frequency signal) is displayed, then one complete trace of the lower signal (a second complete cycle of the sweep frequency signal) is drawn. On the next sweep frequency cycle, the upper signal is redrawn. This alternating pattern continues indefinitely.

In the chopped mode, the electron beam is rapidly jumped back and forth between the upper and lower traces. A little bit of the upper trace is drawn, then a little bit of the lower, then a little more of the upper, and so forth. The chop switching normally works so fast that the eye cannot catch the tiny breaks in the drawn traces, and each trace appears to be a solid line.

The chopped mode works best for low sweep frequencies. The chop switching frequency should be significantly higher than the sweep frequency to avoid noticeable breaks in the displayed traces.

The alternate mode, on the other hand, is usually best when high sweep frequencies are employed. If a low sweep frequency is used in the alternate mode, the upper trace will fade away before the oscilloscope has finished drawing the lower trace, and vice versa. If a high sweep frequency is used, both signal traces will appear to be simultaneously displayed.

In some applications requiring very critical timing of different signals the alternate mode can be somewhat misleading. While the two traces appear to be simultaneously displayed, they are actually separated by a time period equal to one complete sweep cycle. This could be significant in a few high-speed digital switching circuits. Usually, either the alternate mode or the chopped mode may be used without problems, depending on the appropriate sweep frequency used.

Both the alternate mode and the chopped mode use the same basic circuitry, as illustrated in Fig. 4-9. Two vertical preamplifiers are used—one for each trace. An electronic switch (sometimes called a chopper circuit) selects which of the two vertical

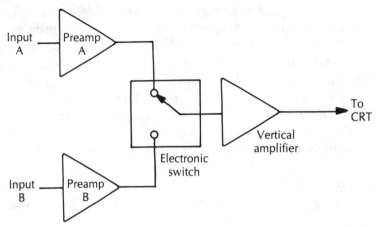

Fig. 4-9 *Both the alternate mode and the chopped mode in a dual-trace oscilloscope use the same basic circuitry.*

inputs will drive the main vertical drive amplifier (which controls the electron gun in the CRT) at any given instant.

The only operational difference between the alternate mode and the chopped mode is the speed at which the electronic switch is controlled. In the alternate mode, the electronic switch reverses its setting once per sweep cycle, while in the chopped mode, the switching takes place many times within each individual sweep cycle.

Each of the two vertical preamplifiers is fed a dc offset voltage. This is used to separate the two displayed waveforms on the screen. One vertical preamplifier is fed a positive offset voltage, so its signal is displayed above the scope's center line, while the other vertical preamplifier is fed a negative offset voltage, so its signal is displayed below the scope's center line.

Most multitrace oscilloscopes offer only two simultaneous traces; but more are possible, especially in the alternate mode. The only limits are the persistence of the phosphors (how long they glow after they are stimulated by the electron beam) and the physical size of the CRT screen. Multiple displays take up quite a bit of room, of course. Four-, eight-, and even sixteen-trace oscilloscopes are not uncommon today, although they are fairly expensive. A multitrace oscilloscope is shown in Fig. 4-10. This is an analog/digital oscilloscope. This type of instrument will be discussed toward the end of this chapter. The biggest disadvantage here is that each display is time shifted with respect to the other signals shown on the screen.

Fig. 4-10   *An analog/digital multitrace oscilloscope.*

More than four simultaneous traces are not practical for chopped mode display. Because the oscilloscope is switching back and forth between the displayed traces in the chopped mode, details of the displayed signals may be lost during the switching process if too many simultaneous displays are used.

Top-of-the-line oscilloscopes sometimes offer true dual-trace capabilities. As stated earlier, this involves having two separate electron guns in the CRT, and two complete sets of electronic circuitry. Essentially, this type of instrument is really two complete oscilloscopes in a single package sharing a single screen face.

Some recent super-deluxe oscilloscopes can display four or even more simultaneous traces. Naturally, such instruments are very expensive. Unless you frequently have a definite, inescapable need for more than two traces, such an oscilloscope should probably be classed as an unnecessary luxury. If you're rich, great. Otherwise, make do with a less expensive scope.

Digital oscilloscopes (discussed later in this chapter) often feature multiple-trace displays at somewhat lower cost than comparable analog equipment. But these instruments are still quite expensive and out of the financial reach of most electronics hobbyists and many professional electronics technicians.

Oscilloscope probes

An oscilloscope has two test leads. One is simply a ground clip, which is connected to the ground (zero-potential point) of the circuit under test. The other test lead is the probe, which is touched to the circuit point to be monitored. The signal at that point in the circuit is then displayed on the oscilloscope's screen.

The oscilloscope's leads are almost always shielded cables. This is necessary to avoid problems with noise pickup. Such shielding is particularly important when monitoring low-amplitude signals, or if the circuit being tested generates high-frequency signals of any kind.

Long cables between the probe and the oscilloscope can significantly increase noise pick-up problems. The capacitance of the cable itself also becomes a significant factor with long cable lengths, reducing the measurable signal frequency of the test setup. Short test leads are always preferred, if possible, for the specific test setup.

Because of the oscilloscope's high input impedance, a simple shielded cable can be used as a test lead for many simple tests. But for most oscilloscope work, a specially designed probe of some type is used.

The simplest and most common type of oscilloscope probe is the 1× probe. This device is sometimes called a 1:1 probe. Basically, it is a simple cable used to directly connect the circuit point being tested to the high-impedance input of the oscilloscope. The scope's high input impedance avoids loading problems, which could possibly throw off the normal operation of the circuit being tested. The test cable is designed for low capacitance and a minimum of signal loss.

The combined effect of the 1× probe and the oscilloscope's input impedance acts like a low-pass filter. Low-frequency input signals aren't particularly affected; but as the signal frequency increases, its amplitude is increasingly reduced. Some ac signals can be phase shifted by this pseudofilter. That is, the beginning and ending points of each cycle can be moved in time. This phase shift can interfere with making accurate measurements of critical timing signals. Another effect of this filtering action is that the sides of square-wave, rectangular-wave, and pulse-wave signals can become slanted. The rise and fall times of these signals are increased by the probe capacitance, as illustrated in Fig. 4-11.

The maximum bandwidth for a 1× probe is about 5 MHz (5,000,000 Hz), although the filtering effects will begin to show up at frequencies lower than this. For some tests with certain low-frequency signals, these filtering effects will not be a prob-

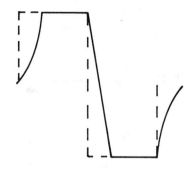

Fig. 4-11 *Probe capacitance can increase the rise and fall times of pulse signals.*

lem. In many cases, they won't even be noticeable. But just as often, these effects will become major problems. The solution is to use a more sophisticated probe.

An improved oscilloscope probe for use with high-frequency signals is the 10× probe. This device is also known as a 10:1 probe, a divider probe, or an attenuating probe. These various terms are more or less interchangeable. A 10× probe has a built-in parallel resistor/capacitor combination, as illustrated in Fig. 4-12. The oscilloscope's input circuitry also looks to the signal like a resistor/capacitor parallel combination. For purposes of comparison, the effective circuit for a 1× probe is shown in Fig. 4-13.

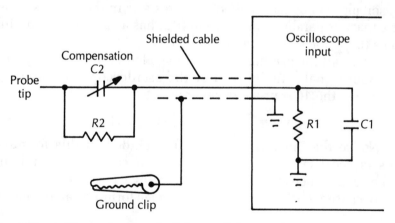

Fig. 4-12 *A 10× probe has a built-in parallel resistor/capacitor combination.*

If the two resistor/capacitor parallel combinations are made equal, the two capacitances will effectively cancel each other out. That is, if

$$R1C1 = R2C2$$

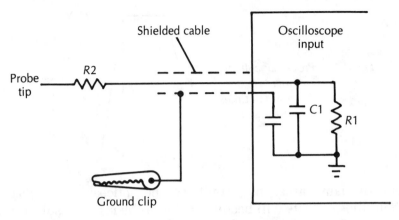

Fig. 4-13   *The effective circuit of the standard 1×probe.*

Then

$$C1 = C2 = 0 \text{ (effective)}$$

In practical 10× probes, the capacitance cancellation is not quite complete, but it is close. The probe capacitor (C2) is usually adjustable, allowing the probe to be precisely tuned to match the oscilloscope's input capacitance. The probe capacitor can be calibrated (usually via a screwdriver adjustment) to maximize the capacitance cancellation effect. The resistor in the probe's resistor/capacitor parallel combination (R2) has a value equal to nine times the scope's input impedance (R1).

If we call the original signal voltage fed to the probe V_s, and the input signal actually seen by the oscilloscope is called V_{in}, then when the 10× probe is calibrated,

$$V_{in} = (V_s \times R1)/(R1 + R2)$$

Notice that no capacitances are included in this formula. This is because the oscilloscope's input capacitance and the probe capacitance are effectively canceling each other out.

Because R2 = 9(R1), the input voltage formula can be rewritten as

$$V_{in} = V_s/10$$

The signal voltage is dropped by a factor of 10. This is why it is called a 10× probe.

Because of the capacitance cancellation effect, the 10× probe can be used over a much wider bandwidth without the problems of the pseudofilter effects that show up when the 1×

probe is used. In addition, circuit loading is reduced even further than normal with the 10 × probe. The circuit sees an input impedance of 10 megohms (instead of 1 megohm) for the probe/oscilloscope combination.

On the other hand, because of the inherent 10 times attenuation of the 10 × probe, the 1 × probe can be used to detect lower-amplitude input signals. The 1 × probe has a lower bandwidth and lower effective input impedance, but greater sensitivity. A serious electronics hobbyist or technician should have both a 1 × and a 10 × probe on hand, and select the one that is best suited for the particular job currently being performed with the oscilloscope.

To gain the maximum bandwidth advantage of the 10 × probe, the probe must be compensated. This means calibrating the probe capacitor to cancel out the oscilloscope's internal input capacitance. To compensate the 10 × probe, it should be connected to a calibrator, a square-wave source. Often this square-wave generator is built into the oscilloscope. The probe is then adjusted to make the sides and tops of the displayed square wave as flat and boxlike as possible, as shown in Fig. 4-14A.

If the probe is undercompensated, the square-wave pulses will tend to overshoot, as shown in Fig. 4-14B. Turn the capacitor adjustment a little further. Not surprisingly, if the probe is overcompensated, you'll get just the opposite effect. The square-wave pulses will tend to undershoot, as shown in Fig. 4-14C. Turn the capacitor adjustment back a little.

When properly compensated, a 10 × probe can be used with input signals with frequencies as high as 50 MHz (50,000,000 Hz). The effective capacitance load of the 10 × probe is only 10 pF, as compared to 30 pF for the 1 × probe. Attenuating probes with higher factors are available. For example, 50 × probes and 100 × probes are not at all uncommon.

Increasing the attenuation factor increases the bandwidth, but at a cost in sensitivity. For example, a 50 × probe can handle a bandwidth up to 250 MHz (250,000,000 Hz), but the signal amplitude is attenuated by a factor of 50. Similarly, a 100 × probe can handle signal frequencies up to 500 MHz (500,000,000 Hz), but the oscilloscope sees an input signal that is just 0.01 of the original signal amplitude fed into the probe. Obviously, these high-attenuation probes should only be used with oscilloscopes that have excellent sensitivity specifications. To offset the sensitivity problem somewhat, these high-attenuation probes are often

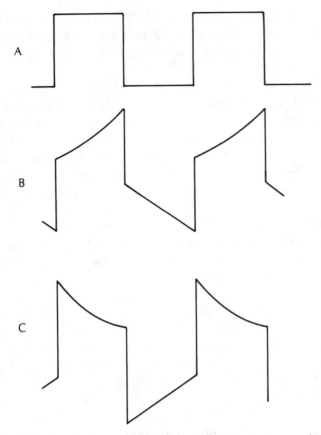

Fig. 4-14 *The 10× probe must be calibrated or "compensated" to display signals correctly: A) Correctly compensated; B) Undercompensated; and C) Overcompensated.*

used with the oscilloscope's 50-ohm input, rather than the normal 1-megohm (1,000,000 ohms) input.

So far, all of the oscilloscope probes discussed here have been simple passive devices. This is why there has been the trade-off between bandwidth and sensitivity. Passive probes are inexpensive, but inherently limited, as we have seen.

Active oscilloscope probes are also available. These probes feature a small active amplifier circuit within the probe itself. This amplifier circuit is specifically designed to have a very small input capacitance. The output is designed to be used with the oscilloscope's 50-ohm input, rather than the usual 1-megohm input. A length of standard 50-ohm cable can be used to connect the active probe to the oscilloscope without adding any extra capacitive loading effects.

Table 4-1 is a comparison of the various types of oscilloscope probes discussed here. Other, special-purpose oscilloscope probes are also available. The demodulator probe is often used in radio work. This type of probe is also sometimes known as an rf (radio frequency) probe.

**Table 4-1 Comparison of
various popular oscilloscope probes**

Probe type	Bandwidth	Resistive load	Capacitive load	Attenuation factor
1×	0–5 MHz	1 megohm	30 pF	1
10×	0–50 MHz	10 megohms	10 pF	1/10
50×	0–250 MHz	50 megohms	7 pF	1/50
100×	0–500 MHz	100 megohms	3.5 pF	1/100
Active	0–500 MHz	10 megohms	2 pF	1 (or more)

The name really tells the story here. The demodulator probe demodulates a measured rf signal into a proportional dc voltage that can be displayed by the oscilloscope. The basic circuitry of a typical demodulator probe is shown in Fig. 4-15. A small signal diode converts the peak rf signal into a proportional dc voltage. The RC network is similar to the standard attenuator probes discussed earlier in this section. This network reduces the input capacitance seen by the circuit under test and minimizes loading effects.

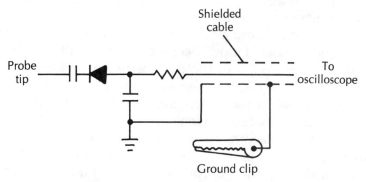

Fig. 4-15 *The basic circuitry of a typical demodulator probe.*

The oscilloscope is usually employed to measure voltages, but a current probe can be used for current measurements. Essentially, the current probe takes advantage of Ohm's law to convert the monitored current into a proportional voltage which can be displayed by the oscilloscope.

While there are a few exceptions, most current probes use a split-core arrangement. The core slides back to allow the current-carrying lead in the circuit being tested to be inserted into the center of the probe. With this system, the oscilloscope's test leads don't have to be inserted into the circuit under test, as with most current measurements. There is no need to physically open the circuit to be tested when this type of current probe is used.

Occasionally you may encounter an isolation probe. This type of probe is very similar to the direct 1 × probe, except the isolation probe contains a resistor in series with the probe tip. This resistor usually has a value between 4,000 and 10,000 ohms. The higher the resistance value, the more likely it is that the input waveform will be distorted. As the name suggests, the purpose of the isolation probe is to isolate the circuit under test from the input impedance of the oscilloscope.

Triggered and gated sweep

The horizontal (x-axis) and vertical (y-axis) signals must be synchronized in some way or the display will be a hopelessly indecipherable muddle. Most early oscilloscopes, and some low-cost modern oscilloscopes, use a method called recurrent sweep. A free-running oscillator built into the oscilloscope's circuitry generates the sawtooth-wave sweep signal. The frequency is manually adjusted until a stable display is achieved, indicating that the sweep has been synchronized.

The recurrent sweep method of synchronization is functional, but extremely limited for practical use. It is difficult to change the beginning trigger point of the display. In some cases, this will prove to be impossible. It is also extremely difficult to determine the actual period of the sweep signal when recurrent sweep is used, because the sweep frequency is actually changed to achieve synchronization. Recurrent synchronization also won't work for displaying transient or aperiodic signals, such as an occasional activated switching voltage. For these reasons (among others), the simple approach of recurrent sweep synchronization is rarely used in modern oscilloscopes beyond a few of the simplest bottom-of-the-line models.

A better approach to oscilloscope synchronization is known as triggered sweep. Instead of a free-running sawtooth-wave oscillator, a triggered sweep scope uses a one-shot circuit with a ramp output. One ramp is generated each time the one-shot circuit is triggered.

The time period of the ramp can be set with a single control. On most oscilloscopes this control is labeled "VOLTS/DIV" (volts per division). The time period of the ramp is not affected by the trigger signal in any way. The trigger is just used to determine when the ramp's time period will begin.

The triggering can be synchronized to any point in the input wave cycle or to a discrete, one-shot event of some sort. Thus the display can begin at any desired instant. This type of synchronization is usually offered in two variations called automatic synchronization (auto sync) and normal synchronization.

In automatic synchronization, the sweep signal is triggered each time the input signal passes through a baseline reference point. This will usually be 0 V, but it can usually be adjusted to account for any voltage offsets. A trace is displayed at all times, whether an input signal is present or not. This feature makes this mode particularly useful for monitoring weak signals with an amplitude that is too low for reliable triggering.

In normal synchronization, the sweep ramp is triggered after the input signal passes through a specific preset voltage. There is no imaginary baseline reference, as in the automatic synchronization mode. Therefore, it is important that the vertical (input) waveform does not cross this preset level, or the sweep circuit will not trigger.

On most oscilloscopes, a level control can be used to shift the voltage of the triggering point above or below the 0-V level. This permits even negatively biased waveforms to properly trigger the sweep circuit.

In a dual-trace oscilloscope, the trigger can be taken from either channel A or channel B, or it can alternate between the two. Channel A provides the first trigger, channel B provides the second trigger, then channel A provides the next trigger, and so forth.

Somewhat curiously, considering the names used for these two modes, the automatic synchronization mode is more commonly employed than the normal synchronization mode.

Some oscilloscopes use line-sync triggering. The sweep waveform is triggered by the 60-Hz ac power line. This type of synchronization is obviously only suitable for fairly low-frequency signals that are time related to the standard ac power-line frequency.

Many modern oscilloscopes also permit external triggering. With this option, an external trigger signal is used to drive the scope's one-shot circuit to generate the sweep ramps at the appropriate times. The frequency of this trigger signal should be harmonically related to the signal to be displayed, or the oscilloscope will be out of sync and the screen will display a lot of meaningless garbage.

Measuring dc voltages with an oscilloscope

The oscilloscope is designed primarily for the measurement and analysis of ac voltages, but it can be used to measure dc voltages too. Generally speaking, it is almost always more convenient and accurate to use a multimeter to take dc readings; but occasionally, when you are working with an oscilloscope you'll find you'll need to check a dc voltage or two. In this case, it may be less trouble to go ahead and use the oscilloscope for some quick dc measurements, rather than switch to a different instrument in midstream.

Throughout the remainder of this chapter, we will assume that all tests are performed on a single-trace oscilloscope, unless specifically noted. All dual-trace oscilloscopes can be used as single-trace scopes. Many of these single-trace tests can be performed just as well in the dual-trace mode. The only real difference is the position of the zero baseline on the screen. For a single-trace scope, there is one baseline, usually positioned halfway down the CRT screen. On a dual-trace oscilloscope, there are two zero baselines. One is offset above the midpoint of the screen, while the other is offset to a position below the center of the screen. The exact amount of these offsets depends on how much space is needed to display the two waveforms and the volts-per-division setting of the oscilloscope.

To measure a dc voltage with an oscilloscope, you must use the automatic mode for the sweep trigger. You'll get no display at all in the normal mode. An oscilloscope with a recurring sweep will also work for dc voltage measurements.

First, calibrate the offset control with no signal applied to the scope's test probe. For the clearest, most noise-free adjustment, it is helpful to ground the test probe to calibrate the offset. Then, turn the offset control until the displayed baseline is right on the center-most grid line of the CRT screen. The ground clip of the test probe should be connected to the circuit ground (0-V point) of the circuit under test. The probe tip is then touched to the circuit point to be tested. If a voltage is present, the displayed line will jump up or down from the center line.

To determine the magnitude of the test voltage, count the number of division lines between the displayed signal line and the center line. If the displayed line is not exactly on a grid line (and it rarely will be), estimate how much of a division is included—one-half, one-third, or whatever. Then look at the setting of the volts-per-division control of the oscilloscope. On most instruments, this control will be marked VOLTS/DIV or something similar. Multiply the number of divisions you counted by the volts-per-division factor.

For example, let's say the displayed line is 2.5 divisions above the center line, and the VOLTS/DIV control is set for 0.5 V/division. In this case, the measured voltage is approximately equal to

$$V_{in} = 2.5 \times 0.5$$
$$= 1.25 \text{ V}$$

If the displayed line is above the center line, the test voltage is positive. If the displayed line drops below the center line, the test voltage is negative.

Here's another example. Let's say the displayed line is 3.75 divisions below the center line, and the VOLTS/DIV control is set for 10. In this case, the measured voltage is equal to

$$V_{in} = -3.75 \times 10$$
$$= -37.50 \text{ V}$$

The accuracy of such measurements is limited by how well you can determine the fractions of divisions included in the measurement. For maximum accuracy, use the smallest volts-per-division setting that will leave the signal on the readable portion of the CRT screen. If the signal voltage is too large, the displayed line will be drawn above or below the edges of the screen and you won't be able to see it. No harm will be done to the oscilloscope under such conditions, unless the voltage is very large. Check the manufacturer's specification sheet to determine your instrument's safe limits.

Measuring ac voltages with an oscilloscope

Measuring an ac voltage with an oscilloscope is similar to measuring a dc voltage. With ac voltages, however, the oscilloscope's display offers a lot of additional information. For the time being, we will just consider the signal amplitude (voltage).

The same basic procedure is used for measuring ac voltages as for dc voltages. When calibrating the offset control, make sure the oscilloscope is set for the automatic mode of sweep triggering. Once the offset control has been adjusted so that the no-signal display line is on the center-most grid line of the scope's screen, you can switch the oscilloscope's mode control to the normal mode, if that is suitable for the particular tests you intend to run.

The ground clip of the test probe should be connected to the circuit ground (0-V point) of the circuit under test. The probe tip is then touched to the circuit point to be tested. If an ac voltage is present, a waveform will be displayed on the CRT screen. Usually, this waveform will be centered around the center line, although, the baseline may be shifted up or down if the ac signal being measured includes any dc offset voltage.

To determine the magnitude of the test voltage, count the number of division lines covered by the displayed waveform. If the displayed waveform does not cover a whole division (which is usually the case), estimate how much of a division is included—one-half, one-third, or whatever. Then, look at the setting of the volts-per-division control of the oscilloscope. On most instruments, this control is labeled VOLTS/DIV or something similar. Multiply the number of divisions you counted by the volts-per-division factor.

Of course, with an ac waveform, the instantaneous voltage, by definition, is continuously changing over time. At what point in the cycle do we measure the distance to the baseline? Measuring dc voltages is far more straightforward.

One obvious approach is to measure the peak value of the ac waveform. This is when the signal is at its maximum distance from the baseline. While a peak measurement is quite useful for certain purposes, such as determining the absolute maximum ratings of a component or circuit, it is somewhat misleading. As an example, let's say we have a sine wave that reaches a maximum (peak value) of 10 V. This waveform is illustrated in Fig. 4-16. Notice that the signal line is never further than 10 V from

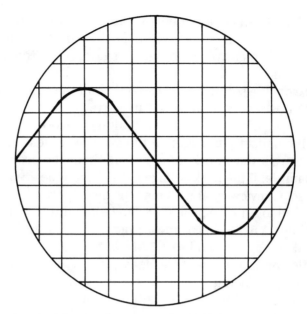

Fig. 4-16 *This sample waveform is used in the discussion of measuring ac voltages. It has a peak value of 10 V.*

the baseline. Because the sine wave is a symmetrical waveform, it also has a negative peak of – 10 V. This is the maximum deflection below the baseline.

You should be able to see from looking at this waveshape that to say we have 10 Vac is rather misleading, because the signal voltage actually reaches the full 10 V for only a brief instant during each cycle. The rest of the time, the actual signal voltage is less than 10 V. This signal will be considerably weaker and won't be able to do nearly as much work as a 10-Vdc signal.

Because the signal voltage varies between a + 10-V positive peak and – 10-V negative peak, there is a 20-V difference between the two peaks. That is, the signal voltage varies 20 V peak-to-peak. Again, peak-to-peak measurements are sometimes useful for certain purposes, but it would be very misleading to say that we have 20 Vac. Obviously, this signal wouldn't come close to being comparable to a 20-Vdc signal.

It might seem logical that we could take an average of the various instantaneous values passed through the complete cycle and come up with a meaningful average voltage. Unfortunately, with a symmetrical waveform like the sine wave, we won't get a useful result at all. The positive portion of the cycle is a mirror image of the negative portion. For every instantaneous positive voltage, there will be an equal instantaneous negative voltage. All of the individual values will cancel each other out, leaving use with an average voltage of zero, regardless of the amplitude of the ac signal.

A reasonable solution is to use only half the complete cycle—either the positive portion or the negative portion—and take the average of that. This can be rather tedious to work out, but it has been mathematically proven that the average value of half a cycle of a sine wave always works out to 0.636 times the peak value. So, in our example, if the peak voltage is 10 V, then the average voltage is 6.36 Vac. Conversely, if we know the average value of an ac signal and need to find the peak voltage, we can multiply the average voltage times 1.572327. For most practical electronics work, this can usually be rounded off to 1.57 (or even 1.6).

While the average voltage does give us a fair idea of how much voltage is being passed through a circuit, a major disadvantage of using this type of value is that the relationships of Ohm's law ($E = IR$) no longer hold true. This makes many circuit design calculations difficult or even impossible to perform. What we need is a way to express ac voltage in terms that can be directly compared to an equivalent dc voltage. In other words, we want 10 Vac to cause the same amount of heat dissipation in a resistor as 10 Vdc.

Such an equivalent value can be found by taking the root mean square (RMS) of the sine wave. The mathematics involved here are fairly complex; but for a sine wave, the RMS value works out to 0.707 times the peak value.

In our example, we have an ac voltage of

$$10 \text{ Vac (peak)} \times 0.707 = 7.07 \text{ Vac (RMS)}$$

The RMS value is the one most commonly used in the majority of practical ac measurements. By using RMS values, Ohm's law calculations can be used in exactly the same way as in dc circuits. Table 4-2 summarizes and compares the various ways used to express ac voltage. These same relationships hold for ac currents as well as ac voltages.

It is important to realize that these equations hold true only if the ac waveform is a sine wave. You won't get the correct results with other waveshapes. For comparison purposes, however, most nonsine-wave ac signals can be measured as if they were sine waves. This doesn't give strictly accurate results, but it will usually be close enough for most practical electronics work.

**Table 4-2 Ways to measure
the amplitude of an AC sine wave.**

RMS	0.707 × Peak
RMS	1.11 × Average
Average	0.9 × RMS
Average	0.636 × Peak
Peak	1.41 × RMS
Peak	1.57 × Average
Peak	0.5 × Peak-to-peak
Peak-to-peak	2 × Peak
Peak-to-peak	2.82 × RMS
Peak-to-peak	3.14 × Average

For example, a schematic may indicate that a square-wave signal at a certain point in the circuit should measure 12 V RMS. The measurement was probably made with an ac voltmeter calibrated for sine waves. If you measure the signal with a similar meter, or use an oscilloscope and take 0.707 of the peak voltage, you should get about 12 V too. This sidesteps the need to recalibrate all ac test equipment every time the waveshape changes, or to perform complicated mathematical calculations with every measurement made.

Measuring frequency with an oscilloscope

Besides voltage, an oscilloscope can also be used to measure the frequency of any periodic ac waveform. The first step is to adjust the sweep frequency and the scope's trigger controls to get a clear, stable display of the waveshape. The sweep control on most modern oscilloscopes is calibrated with time-per-division markings. For instance, a time base of 2 ms (0.002 second) per division may be selected.

Now count the number of vertical divisions on the screen of the oscilloscope from the beginning of one cycle to the start of the next. It is helpful if you can adjust the sweep frequency so the displayed signal covers a whole number of divisions, but this isn't always possible. It may be necessary to estimate the partial division left over at one end or the other—one-half, one-third, etc.

As an example, let's say the displayed waveform covers about 4.3 divisions. This number is multiplied by the time base time-per-division value to get the time period of the measured signal.

In this example, it works out to approximately

$$T = 4.3 \times 0.002$$
$$= 0.0086 \text{ second}$$
$$= 8.6 \text{ ms}$$

Now, to find the signal frequency, all we have to do is take the reciprocal of the time period; that is, divide 1 by the time period. For our example, the signal frequency is equal to

$$F = 1/T$$
$$= 1/0.0086$$
$$= 116.3 \text{ Hz}$$

The same frequency equations can be used for any periodic (repeating cycle) ac waveform. You can select any point as the "beginning" of a cycle, as long as you are consistent from cycle to cycle. Usually it is most convenient to assume the beginning point of the cycle as the point where the signal crosses the baseline (zero), moving in the positive direction. Be careful, though. Some complex waveforms can cross through the baseline more than one per cycle. An example of this is shown in Fig. 4-17. The same basic procedure can be used to determine the timing of an aperiodic (one-shot) electrical event, such as a change in a switching voltage.

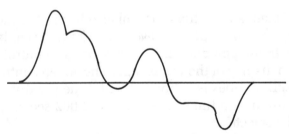

Fig. 4-17 *Some complex waveforms cross through the baseline (zero point) more than once per cycle.*

Analyzing distortion with an oscilloscope

Because an oscilloscope permits the electronics hobbyist or technician to directly view the waveshape of the signal being monitored, any distortion of the waveform can easily be spotted. Distortion, by definition, involves any undesirable change in a waveshape. If the waveform displayed on an oscilloscope doesn't look right, the monitored signal is presumably being distorted somewhere along the line. You must be aware that improper test procedures can make the displayed waveform look distorted, even though the signal passing through the circuit under test is fine.

To get a better understanding of distortion and its effects, you will need to understand the concept of harmonics. Most waveshapes include multiple frequency components. This is true of all possible waveforms, except a pure sine wave.

The nominal frequency of a waveform is called the fundamental frequency. This is the basic cycle repetition rate of the waveshape. Except for the sine wave, all ac waveforms include higher-frequency components above the fundamental frequency. These higher-frequency components are usually, but not always, lower in amplitude than the fundamental frequency. The amplitude normally continues to drop as the signal components increase in frequency. These higher-frequency components are sometimes called overtones. This term comes from acoustic theory, but it is often applied to electrical signals well outside the audible spectrum.

Usually these higher-frequency components are exact multiples of the fundamental frequency. That is, two times the fundamental frequency, three times the fundamental frequency, four times the fundamental frequency, and so forth. This type of overtone is called a harmonic.

Some waveshapes include overtones that are not exact multiples of the fundamental frequency. These overtones are called enharmonics. Any signal that contains enharmonics will inevitably change its waveshape at least a little from cycle to cycle. Enharmonics are fairly rare in most practical electronic circuits, so we will concentrate on harmonics.

The fundamental frequency of a complex waveform can be thought of as a simple sine wave. Each successive harmonic is like an additional sine wave at a higher frequency that is an exact multiple of the fundamental frequency. As an example, Table 4-3 outlines the harmonics for a 350-Hz signal.

Not all waveforms contain all possible harmonics, of course. As we've already mentioned, a sine wave (shown in Fig. 4-18) consists of just the fundamental frequency. It has no harmonic content at all. A sawtooth wave, like the one illustrated in Fig.

Table 4-3 Summary of available harmonics.

Fundamental	350 Hz	—
Second	700 Hz	2 × Fundamental
Third	1,050 Hz	3 × Fundamental
Fourth	1,400 Hz	4 × Fundamental
Fifth	1,750 Hz	5 × Fundamental
Sixth	2,100 Hz	6 × Fundamental
Seventh	2,450 Hz	7 × Fundamental
Eighth	2,800 Hz	8 × Fundamental
Ninth	3,150 Hz	9 × Fundamental
Tenth	3,500 Hz	10 × Fundamental
Eleventh	3,850 Hz	11 × Fundamental
Twelfth	4,150 Hz	12 × Fundamental

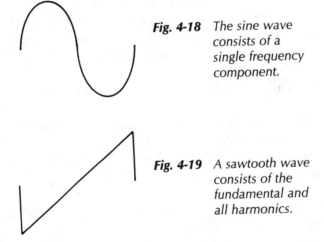

Fig. 4-18 *The sine wave consists of a single frequency component.*

Fig. 4-19 *A sawtooth wave consists of the fundamental and all harmonics.*

4-19, contains all possible harmonics, along with the fundamental frequency.

A square wave, like the one shown in Fig. 4-20 consists of the fundamental frequency and only the odd harmonics. All of the even harmonics (second, fourth, sixth, etc.) are omitted from this waveform. The structural makeup of a typical square wave is outlined in Table 4-4.

The harmonic content of a waveform is one of the primary factors involved in distinguishing one waveform from another. This, however is not the only difference between various waveforms. Another important factor is the relative strength of the harmonic frequency components as compared to the fundamental frequency signal.

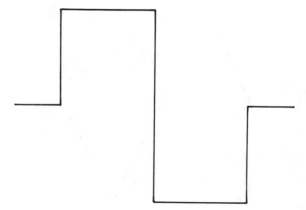

Fig. 4-20 *A square wave consists of the fundamental and all odd harmonics.*

**Table 4-4 Harmonics
of a square wave.**

Harmonic	Frequency	Amplitude
Fundamental	350 Hz	1
Third	1,050 Hz	1/3
Fifth	1,750 Hz	1/5
Seventh	2,450 Hz	1/7
Ninth	3,150 Hz	1/9
Eleventh	3,850 Hz	1/11

In a square wave, the harmonics are fairly strong. The amplitude of each harmonic is related to the amplitude of the fundamental frequency by the reciprocal of the harmonic's number. For example, the third harmonic has an amplitude that is one-third the amplitude of the fundamental frequency. The fifth harmonic is only one-fifth as strong as the fundamental frequency, and so forth.

The triangular wave, shown in Fig. 4-21, has the same basic harmonic structure as a square wave. That is, the fundamental frequency and all odd harmonics are included in this signal (all of the even harmonics are omitted). But the harmonics in a triangular wave are much weaker than the harmonics in a square wave. For this waveform, the amplitude of each harmonic is related to the amplitude of the fundamental frequency by the reciprocal of the square of the harmonic's number. For instance, the third harmonic has an amplitude that is equal to

$$\text{Fundamental} \times 1/(3 \times 3) = \text{Fundamental} \times 1/9$$

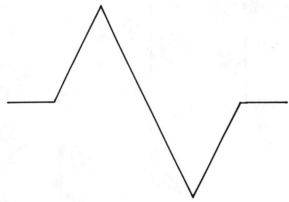

Fig. 4-21 *A triangular wave has the same basic harmonic structure as a square wave (see Fig. 4-20), but the amplitude of the harmonics is weaker.*

For the fifth harmonic in a triangular wave, the amplitude works out to

Fundamental × 1/(5 × 5) = Fundamental × 1/25

And so forth, for each of the higher harmonics. The structural makeup of a typical triangular wave is outlined in Table 4-5.

**Table 4-5   Harmonics
of a triangular wave.**

Harmonic	Frequency	Amplitude
Fundamental	350 Hz	1
Third	1,050 Hz	1/9
Fifth	1,750 Hz	1/25
Seventh	2,450 Hz	1/49
Ninth	3,150 Hz	1/81
Eleventh	3,850 Hz	1/121

There are several possible reasons why a waveform may be distorted. They include

- One or more harmonics may be attenuated more (or boosted less) than the fundamental frequency.
- One or more harmonics may be boosted or amplified more (or attenuated less) than the fundamental frequency.
- New harmonics or enharmonics are being added to the

signal from some undesired source. This may be due to rf pickup, signal leakage, or clipping.

Figure 4-22 shows a sine wave with severe clipping. Notice that the top of the waveform is flattened. This is usually an indication that the signal is too strong for the circuit under test. The circuit in question doesn't have sufficient power to reproduce the peaks of the signal. Clipping may show up on the positive peaks, as shown here, or on the negative peaks, or on both. When a signal is clipped, it more closely resembles a square wave. This implies that strong odd-order harmonics are being added to the signal.

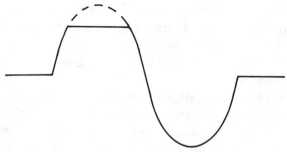

Fig. 4-22   *A sine wave with severe clipping on its positive peaks.*

Figure 4-23 shows a sine wave that is being distorted by severe overshoot. This might be an indication of miscalibration somewhere in the circuit under test (or more rarely, in the oscilloscope itself). Alternatively, this type of pattern might indicate that the sine wave is picking up a spike or pulse signal of the same frequency fro elsewhere in the circuit.

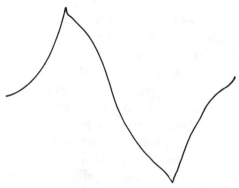

Fig. 4-23   *A sine wave signal distorted by severe overshoot.*

If the spikes, or other distortion, show up at regular intervals, but not at the same point in each displayed cycle, it means the interfering signal does not have the same frequency as the desired signal. In some circuits, this kind of display may not indicate a problem at all. Sometimes one signal rides on (or modulates) a second signal. It is always important to know what the monitored signal is supposed to look like before drawing any conclusions.

In waveshapes with straight edges, such as sawtooth waves, triangular waves, and square waves, make sure that the straight edges are, in fact, straight. Any curvature is an indication of distortion in the signal. (This may or may not indicate a problem, depending on the purpose of the circuit being tested.)

Undesired curvature of the straight edges of a waveform may be the fault of the circuit being monitored, or it may be the fault of the oscilloscope or its probe. An uncalibrated probe can cause this problem. The probe calibration process was discussed earlier in this chapter.

Typical types of straight-edge distortion include overshooting, undershooting, ringing, and poor slew rate. None of these symptoms are likely to be intentional results of the desired functioning of the circuit under test, although mild problems of these types may occasionally be normal and not problematic in the ordinary operation of the circuitry, especially in noncritical applications.

Overshooting occurs when the signal voltage exceeds its nominal peak level for an instant after a transistion. Overshooting may occur on either a low-to-high transistion or on a high-to-low transistion, or both. This type of problem is most noticeable on square waves and pulse waves. Overshooting is illustrated in Fig. 4-24.

Undershooting, as the name suggests, is just the opposite of overshooting. Here, the signal voltage does not quite reach its nominal peak level for an instant after a transistion. Undershooting, like overshooting, may occur on either a low-to-high transistion or on a high-to-low transistion, or both. Again, this type of problem is most noticeable on square waves and pulse waves. Undershooting is illustrated in Fig. 4-25.

Ringing is another problem common to square waves and pulse waves. After a transistion (either low-to-high or high-to-low, or both), the signal voltage briefly oscillates above and below the nominal peak voltage before settling down to its correct

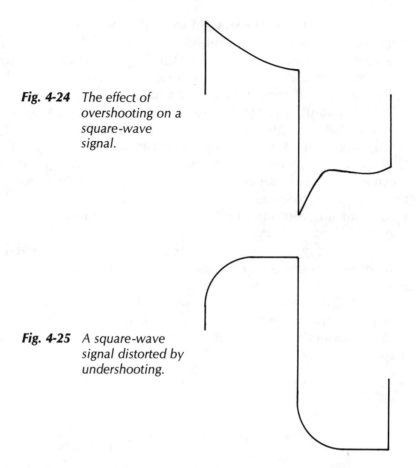

Fig. 4-24 *The effect of overshooting on a square-wave signal.*

Fig. 4-25 *A square-wave signal distorted by undershooting.*

value. This type of distortion can cause a lot of strange problems in many high-speed switching circuits. An example of ringing is shown in Fig. 4-26.

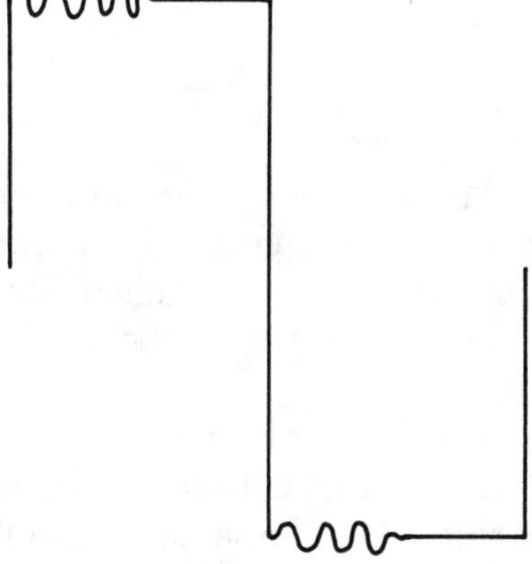

Fig. 4-26 *Ringing is often a problem with square and pulse waves.*

Slew rate refers to the straight up and down sides of a wave-form. This includes the low-to-high and high-to-low transistions in a square or pulse wave, as well as the flyback portion of a saw-tooth wave. Theoretically, the switching between states should be instantaneous. Of course, this is not possible in any practical electronic circuit. It always takes a finite amount of time to switch from one voltage to another. This transistion time is measured by the slew rate. On an oscilloscope, you can actually measure the slew rate in exactly the same way you measure the time period of a cycle (discussed earlier in this chapter). Slew rate measure-ments are usually stated as so many volts per millisecond (0.001 second) or microsecond (0.000001 second). The faster the slew rate, the better.

With a very good slew rate, the transistion lines will be straight up and down on the screen of the oscilloscope. In some cases, they may not leave a visible trace at all, as illustrated in Fig. 4-27. When the slew rate is poor, the transistion lines will be slanted. A square wave with a poor slew rate is shown in Fig. 4-28. A sawtooth wave with the same problem is shown in Fig. 4-29.

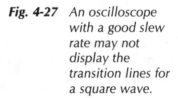

Fig. 4-27 *An oscilloscope with a good slew rate may not display the transition lines for a square wave.*

When isolating the source of any type of distortion, a dual-trace oscilloscope is very helpful. With this kind of test instru-ment, you can simultaneously monitor the input and output signals for any given subcircuit, making any differences very easy to see.

It's usually best to set the oscilloscope's volts-per-division controls so that both the input and output signals are displayed at the same size (the same apparent amplitude). This way you won't

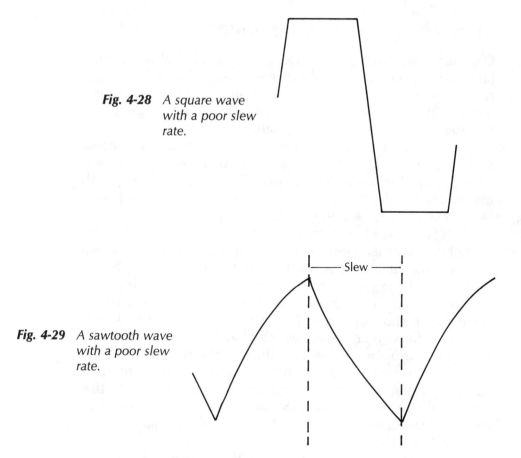

Fig. 4-28 *A square wave with a poor slew rate.*

Fig. 4-29 *A sawtooth wave with a poor slew rate.*

be misled by any differences in the overall signal amplitudes. Often, it is useful to bring the two (equal amplitude) signals together on the oscilloscope's display screen by moving their baselines until they are overlapping. Any difference between the two signals will now be plainly visible.

Remember, some circuits are designed to purposely change the waveshape between the input and the output. You must know what the circuit under test is supposed to do before you can draw any meaningful conclusions. Switching circuits often deliberately clip nonsquare input signals. Filters, by definition, change the amplitude of some frequency components, but not others. Any modulation system combines two or more signals into a new, more complex signal. There are many other possible examples of such deliberate "distortion." The electronics hobbyist or technician must know what he is looking for when he is working with electronic circuits.

Time and phase measurements

One way to describe the oscilloscope is to say that it measures (and displays) changes in voltage over time. A dual-trace oscilloscope can be particularly useful in monitoring time and phase relationships between pairs of signals. Does the voltage change the way it should, and when it should?

To compare the timing of two (or more) signals, you should avoid the "normal" triggering mode. In this mode, you should recall, trace A is completely drawn, then trace B is completely drawn. The two displayed signals are time shifted from each other by one complete cycle of the sweep frequency.

It is fairly easy to determine if a one-shot event occurs at the correct time with a dual-trace oscilloscope. For example, let's say a brief spike should be generated 3 ms (0.003 second) after a switching voltage goes from low to high. Assuming that the oscilloscope is set up for a time base of 1 ms/division, the displayed spike should show up three divisions after the low-to-high transition in the switching voltage. Obviously, there is no way to check this correlation in timing with a single-trace oscilloscope.

Often two signals must be in phase with each other, or phase shifted by a specific amount. When two signals are in phase, they begin and end their cycles at the same instant. Obviously they must be at the same frequency (or harmonically related) to stay in phase with each other.

A cycle is made up of 360 degrees. If two signals of the same, consistent frequency are exactly 360 degrees in phase with each other, then we might as well consider them in phase. A pair of inphase signals are illustrated in Fig. 4-30.

One-quarter cycle is 90 degrees. A 90-degree phase shift is illustrated in Fig. 4-31. Notice that with sine waves, the second signal begins its cycle as the first signal reaches its peak.

One-half cycle is 180 degrees. Assuming two signals have the same waveshape, frequency, and amplitude, but are 180 degrees out of phase with each other, mixing these two signals will cause them to cancel each other out. As one signal is going positive, the other signal is going negative by a like amount, resulting in an effective combined value of zero at each point throughout the entire cycle. Two signals that are 180 degrees out of phase with each other are shown in Fig. 4-32.

In many electronic systems, it is necessary to know how much phase shift a given circuit causes. This is easily deter-

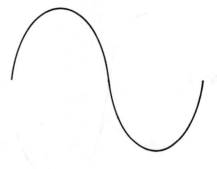

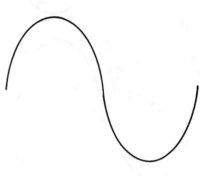

Fig. 4-30   These two signals are in phase with each other.

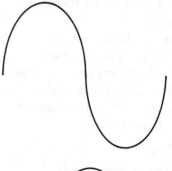

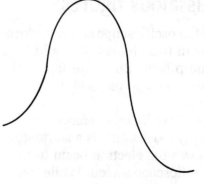

Fig. 4-31   These two signals are 90 degrees out of phase with each other.

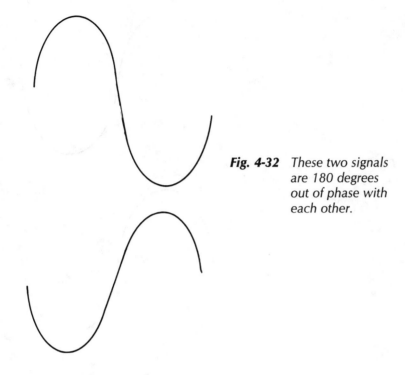

Fig. 4-32 *These two signals are 180 degrees out of phase with each other.*

mined by comparing the phase of the input and output signals of the circuit.

Phase relationships are particularly critical in many large-scale digital systems, such as computers and communications systems. If you only have a single-trace oscilloscope, phase relationships between two signals can be roughly determined by using Lissajous figures, which are discussed in the next section of this chapter.

Lissajous figures

If the oscilloscope could perform only the functions described so far in this chapter, it would be an extremely useful piece of test equipment. But there is an alternate mode of operation that is even more powerful and versatile. This is the use of Lissajous figures.

In ordinary operation, as we have already described, the vertical (y-axis) signal is a sawtooth wave, used as a sweep signal that moves the electron beam from left to right across the face of the oscilloscope screen. While frequency measurements can be made in this mode, as described in an earlier section of this chapter, such frequency measurements are inevitably rather crude and not terribly accurate. It is difficult to estimate partial divisions when the test (horizontal x-axis) signal is not an exact harmonic (whole-number multiple) of the sweep frequency. Also, phase comparisons require a more expensive dual-trace oscilloscope, and small phase shifts may be difficult to see. More accurate phase and frequency measurements can be made with Lissajous figures.

To create a Lissajous figure on an oscilloscope, two signal sources are required. The internal sweep-signal generator is not used. Signal A is connected to the x-axis (horizontal) input, just as in any standard oscilloscope measurement. At the same time, signal B is connected to the oscilloscope's y-axis (vertical) input. With these connections, a closed-loop pattern of some sort will be drawn on the oscilloscope's CRT screen. This pattern is called a Lissajous figure.

The exact shape of the Lissajous figure is determined by several factors, including the waveshapes of the two input signals, the relative amplitudes of the two input signals, the relative frequencies of the two input signals, and the phase relationship between the two input signals.

To keep things simple, for the time being we will assume that all input signals are sine waves. We will also assume that the applied signals do not contain any dc offset voltages.

First, let's assume that the same sine wave signal is simultaneously applied to both the x-axis input and the y-axis input. The resulting Lissajous figure will be a slanted line, as shown in Fig. 4-33. The length of the line reflects the amplitude of the signal and the setting of the oscilloscope's volts-per-division control.

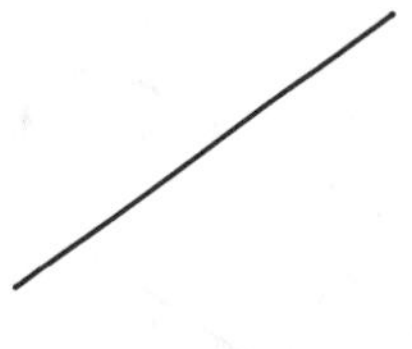

Fig. 4-33 *The Lissajous figure displayed when the same sine wave signal is applied to both the x-axis and the y-axis.*

When the instantaneous amplitude of the signal voltage is 0 V, the electron beam will strike the exact center of the CRT screen. At this point, there is no signal to deflect the electron beam.

During the first 90 degrees of the cycle, the signal voltage increases smoothly up to its peak value. This causes the electron beam to be deflected upward and to the right. (Remember, the same signal is controlling both the x-axis and the y-axis here.) In other words, the top half of the slanted line is drawn.

From the 90-degrees point to the 180-degrees point of the cycle, the signal voltage drops back from its peak value to zero. This is just the reverse of what happened in the first quarter cycle; the same line is redrawn, making no visible change in the displayed pattern. At the 180-degrees point, the instantaneous signal voltage is again 0 V and the electron beam is aimed at the center of the screen once more.

Now, during the next quarter cycle (from 180 degrees to 270 degrees), the voltage goes increasingly negative until it reaches a negative peak. This draws the second half of the Lissajous pattern, moving from the center of the CRT screen downwards and to the left. (Once again, keep in mind that identical signals are being fed to the oscilloscope's horizontal and vertical inputs.)

Finally, from the 270-degrees point to the 360-degrees point of the cycle, the signal voltage retraces the third quarter cycle, increasing from the negative peak voltage up to 0 V and retracing the bottom half of the line. Notice that the slant of the displayed line is 45 degrees. This is because the horizontal and vertical movements of the electron beam are always identical.

Now, what happens if the x-axis and y-axis input signals are sine waves that are equal in amplitude and frequency, but are not in phase with each other? As the phase relationship between the two input signals moves up from 0 degrees (in phase), the Lissajous figure will start to open up into a slanted oval, as shown in Fig. 4-34. When the phase shift reaches a difference of 90 degrees, a perfect circle will be displayed, as shown in Fig. 4-35.

Fig. 4-34 *If the x-axis and y-axis are slightly out of phase, the Lissajous figure will open up into a slanted oval.*

As the phase shift is further increased, the sides of the circle come together again, returning to an oval shape, until at 180 degrees, we again have a closed line (except it is slanted in the

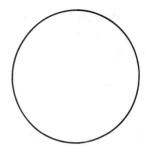

Fig. 4-35 *The Lissajous figure will be a perfect circle when the x-axis and y-axis signals are 90 degrees out of phase with each other.*

opposite direction). With phase differences between 180 degrees and 270 degrees, the slanted oval opens up again, reaching a peak circle at 270 degrees. From 270 degrees to 360 degrees, the oval closes up again, returning to the original closed, slanted-line pattern we started with. Remember, when two equal-frequency waveforms are 360 degrees out of phase with one another, there is no difference from the inphase condition. In effect, 360 degrees equals 0 degrees.

For our next example, we will again assume that the two sine wave input signals have equal amplitudes; but this time, let's say the vertical signal frequency is double the horizontal signal frequency. For each vertical cycle, only one-half horizontal cycle is displayed on the oscilloscope's screen. This is displayed as a closed loop on the CRT screen. The second half of the horizontal signal's cycle combines with a second complete vertical signal cycle, producing a second closed loop in the Lissajous figure displayed by the oscilloscope. In other words, we get a figure-eight pattern, as shown in Fig. 4-36.

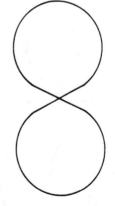

Fig. 4-36 *If the vertical signal frequency is exactly double the horizontal signal frequency, the displayed Lissajous figure will be a figure eight.*

What if the vertical signal frequency is only half the horizontal signal frequency. We get pretty much the same effect. It takes two horizontal cycles to draw a complete vertical cycle, so the Lissajous figure in this case is a sideways figure eight, as illustrated in Fig. 4-37.

Fig. 4-37 *If the horizontal signal frequency is exactly double the vertical signal frequency, the displayed Lissajous figure will be a sideways figure eight.*

Assuming the two input signals are harmonically related (one frequency is a whole-number multiple of the other frequency), the number of closed loops indicates the frequency relationship between the two signals. Fig. 4-38 shows the Lissajous pattern for a horizontal signal with a frequency three times that of the vertical signal. If the horizontal signal frequency is four times the vertical signal frequency, the Lissajous pattern shown in Fig. 4-39 will be displayed. If the vertical frequency is higher than the horizontal frequency, these patterns will be turned on their sides, as shown in Fig. 4-40 and Fig. 4-41. If you know the frequency of one of the signals, you can easily calculate the second signal frequency by counting the number of loops in the Lissajous figure displayed by the oscilloscope.

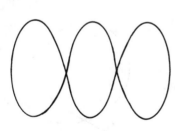

Fig. 4-38 *If the horizontal signal frequency is exactly three times the vertical signal frequency, this Lissajous figure will be displayed.*

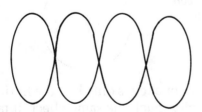

Fig. 4-39 *If the horizontal signal frequency is four times the vertical signal frequency, this Lissajous figure will be displayed.*

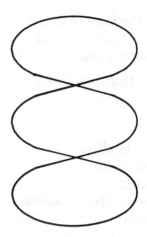

Fig. 4-40   If the vertical signal frequency is three times the horizontal signal frequency, this Lissajous figure will be displayed.

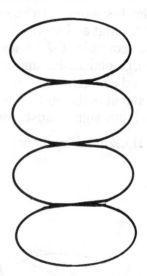

Fig. 4-41   If the vertical signal frequency is four times the horizontal signal frequency, this Lissajous figure will be displayed.

The 60-Hz line frequency is often used as the reference for relatively low-frequency Lissajous figure tests, because this frequency is very exact. If the 60-Hz line signal is used as the vertical signal, and three loops are stacked horizontally, then you know the horizontal signal frequency must be equal to

$$\text{Horizontal frequency} = 3 \times \text{Vertical frequency}$$
$$= 3 \times 60$$
$$= 180 \text{ Hz}$$

On the other hand, if there are three loops and they are arranged vertically instead of horizontally, then the horizontal signal frequency must be equal to

$$\text{Horizontal frequency} = \text{Vertical frequency}/3$$
$$= 60/3$$
$$= 20 \text{ Hz}$$

This is all very simple and straightforward. However, real-world electronic signals are rarely cooperative enough to be exact whole-number multiples of a convenient reference frequency. Fortunately, Lissajous figures can also be used to determine non-harmonic frequency relationships.

As the frequency relationship between the horizontal and vertical signals grows more complex, the displayed Lissajous figure grows nodes. With the simple cases we have been describing so far, the number of nodes along one axis has always been one. A complex Lissajous figure can have two or more nodes along both the horizontal and vertical axis.

For example, the Lissajous pattern shown in Fig. 4-42 has five horizontal nodes and three vertical nodes. This is usually expressed as a ratio—3:5 in this case. Assuming that the vertical input signal is the 60-Hz line frequency, then the unknown horizontal input signal must have a frequency equal to

$$\text{Horizontal frequency} = 3 \times (\text{Vertical frequency}/5)$$
$$= 3 \times (60/5)$$
$$= 3 \times 12$$
$$= 36 \text{ Hz}$$

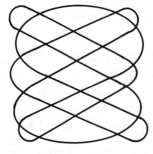

Fig. 4-42 *This Lissajous figure has five horizontal nodes and three vertical nodes.*

A 3:2 Lissajous figure is shown in Fig. 4-43, and Fig. 4-44 shows a Lissajous figure with a 5:2 ratio.

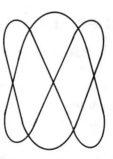

Fig. 4-43 *This Lissajous figure indicates a 3:2 frequency ratio.*

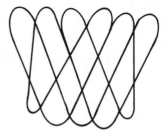

Fig. 4-44 *This Lissajous figure indicates a 5:2 frequency ratio.*

It is all too easy to miscount the nodes with very complex Lissajous patterns. The electronics technician using Lissajous figures should also be aware that sometimes certain phase relationships between the horizontal and vertical signals can obscure certain lines which are overlapping and, therefore, invisible in the displayed pattern. As a rule, a Lissajous figure is easiest to read when the two input signals have a phase difference of 90 degrees. Many oscilloscopes have a phase adjustment control to help make displayed Lissajous figures easier to read. If the displayed Lissajous figure is extremely complex, try changing the reference frequency. Often this will result in a simpler easier-to-read pattern. Minor frequency differences can also cause the displayed Lissajous figure to slowly rotate.

It's not a particularly useful test, but it can be fascinating to watch the Lissajous figures created by connecting a stereo music signal to the oscilloscope's inputs. Connect the right channel to the x-axis input and the left channel to the y-axis input. A constantly changing Lissajous pattern will be displayed, pulsating in response to the music. This works best with recordings of solo instruments or small ensembles. It also works quite well with electronic (synthesizer) music.

Reactance and impedance measurements

Ordinary dc resistance is easy to measure with an ohmmeter, but in ac circuits resistance becomes more complex. When ac signals are used, resistance is not a constant-value parameter. Instead, ac resistance (impedance) changes with frequency and phase.

Impedance is made up of dc resistance and two types of ac (frequency-dependent) resistance called reactances. A pure capacitor exhibits capacitive reactance, and a pure inductor exhibits inductive reactance. The capacitive reactance in any circuit is always 180 degrees out of phase with the inductive reactance.

The impedance of a capacitor is the sum of the dc resistance and the capacitive reactance. The dc resistance is a constant value for a given capacitor, regardless of the applied frequency. The capacitive reactance, however, is determined by both the capacitance and the applied frequency. The formula for capacitive reactance is

$$X_c = 1/(2\pi FC)$$

Where

F = frequency, Hz:

C = capacitance, farads (not microfarads or picofarads);

X_c = capacitive reactance, ohms; and

π = mathematical constant, approximate value of 3.14.

The formula may be rewritten as

$$X_c = 1/(6.28FC)$$

Assuming that the capacitance holds a constant value (which is usually the case), as the applied frequency increases, the capacitive reactance decreases.

A coil includes both a dc resistance and an inductive reactance. Once again, the dc resistance is a constant value, regardless of the applied frequency, and the inductive reactance is determined by the inductance of the coil and the applied frequency, according to the formula

$$X1 = 2\pi FL$$

Where

F = applied frequency, Hz;

L = inductance, henry (not millihenrys or microhenrys);

$X1$ = inductive reactance, ohms; and

π = mathematical constant, approximate value of 3.14.

We can rewrite the equation as

$$X1 = 6.28FL$$

Unlike capacitive reactance, inductive reactance increases as the applied frequency is increased.

The total ac resistance of the circuit (impedance) is equal to

$$Z = \sqrt{R^2 + (X1 - X_c)^2}$$

Where

Z = total impedance,

R = dc resistance,

$X1$ = inductive reactance, and

X_c = capacitive reactance.

Both capacitive reactance and inductive reactance are frequency dependent. Capacitive reactance decreases as the applied frequency increases, while inductive reactance increases with any increase in the applied frequency.

To monitor an ac resistance (impedance and reactance), connect the voltage waveform to the oscilloscope's vertical input and the current waveform to the horizontal input. A typical test setup is shown in Fig. 4-45. The relative values of the resistance (R),

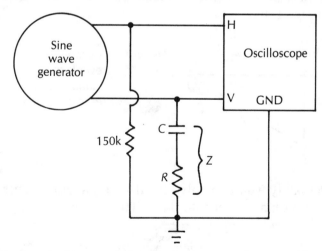

Fig. 4-45 *A typical test setup for monitoring ac resistance with an oscilloscope.*

reactance (X), and impedance (Z) will appear in the displayed Lissajous figure's proportions. The Lissajous figure displayed should be a single closed loop, usually at an angle.

The oscilloscope should be adjusted so that the displayed pattern is centered on the screen. That is, when no signal is applied to either input, all you should see is a single dot in the center of the CRT screen.

Count the number of divisions covered by the Lissajous figure along the zero line. This value represents the measured reactance (X). If the loop is slanted to the right, the reactance is primarily capacitive. If the loop is slanted to the left, the reactance is primarily inductive.

Next, count the number of divisions between the opposite peaks of the loop. This value represents the total impedance (Z). Obviously, Z (impedance) should always be greater than X (reactance). If the X value is larger, some mistake has been made in the test setup. If the reactance was really greater than the impedance, the dc resistance (R) would have to have a negative value.

You can find the R value by graphing the X and Z values. Draw a downward line on graph paper corresponding to the X value. Then, with a compass, draw an arc that has a radius equal to the Z value, starting from the bottom-most point of the X line. Now, draw a straight line perpendicular to the top of the X line until it intersects the Z arc. The length of this line will correspond to the value of R (the dc resistance). This process is illustrated in Fig. 4-46.

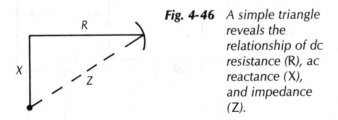

Fig. 4-46 A simple triangle reveals the relationship of dc resistance (R), ac reactance (X), and impedance (Z).

Alternately, you can solve for R using algebra. This is very easy to do with a pocket calculator. The formula is

$$R = \sqrt{Z^2 - X^2}$$
$$= \sqrt{(Z \times Z) - (X \times X)}$$

The test signal for such reactance and impedance measurements should be a sine wave, or a signal with very low harmonic content. Strong harmonics will distort the displayed ellipse and you won't get correct results.

There are many other potential applications for the oscilloscope, but we simply don't have the space to discuss them all here. To cover the capabilities of the oscilloscope with any degree of thoroughness would require a complete book in itself.

Storage oscilloscopes

Occasionally, while doing practical electronics work, a typical hobbyist or technician is probably going to want to study certain displayed waveforms for awhile. With a continuous periodic (ac) waveform, this is no problem. The pattern is repeatedly redrawn on each cycle of the sweep signal. But one-shot signals, such as those used in many switching circuits, come and go quickly. Often the entire signal of interest only lasts for a few milliseconds, and then it's over, leaving a flat trace on the oscilloscope's screen.

The persistence of the phosphors coating the inner surface of the CRT screen permit them to glow long enough for them to be seen, but the displayed trace fades away within seconds. This may not be long enough for the technician to read enough information from the displayed waveform.

The solution to this problem is to use a special type of oscilloscope known as the storage oscilloscope. A storage oscilloscope can be used as a regular oscilloscope, but it also has a special storage mode to permit relatively long-term display of nonperiodic signals. To accomplish this long-term display, the storage oscilloscope uses a special type of CRT. The basic structure of this device is shown in Fig. 4-47.

There are two main differences between this type of CRT and the simpler CRT used in most basic oscilloscopes. In the storage oscilloscope, the CRT has two electron guns (instead of just one) and a storage grid of tiny electrodes mounted just inside the phosphor-coated display screen. The two electron guns in the storage oscilloscope's CRT are called the main gun and the flooding gun. Some technical sources refer to the main gun as the writing gun.

The main gun functions just like the electron gun in an ordinary CRT. It produces the electron beam that draws the signal trace on the screen. In the basic (nonstorage) mode, the flooding gun is not used. The storage grid is also left unused in this operating mode.

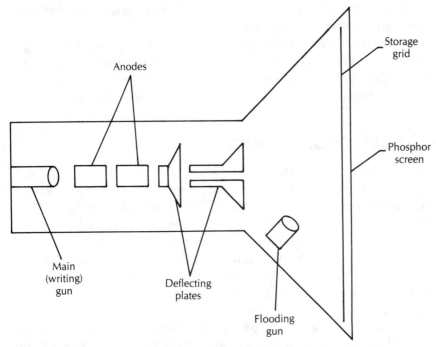

Fig. 4-47 *A storage oscilloscope holds the display of a brief signal so that it can be adequately examined.*

When the oscilloscope's storage mode is activated, the electrodes in the storage grid are saturated with a negative electrical charge just before the signal trace is drawn on the screen by the main gun. When the desired waveform appears on the face of the CRT, the saturating negative charge is removed from the storage grid. The electrodes that are struck by the directed electron beam from the main gun take on a localized positive charge. The other electrodes in the storage grid, which are not touched by the electron beam, do not pick up a positive charge.

The storage grid is specifically designed so that the positive charge on individual electrodes decays at a very slow rate, unless it is deliberately removed by resaturating the grid with an external negative charge.

The main gun has done its job now, and it's time for the flooding gun to take over. The flooding gun irradiates the entire storage grid, which prevents the electrons of the flooding gun from reaching the phosphor-coated screen except in those areas holding a localized positive charge. As a result, the original waveform continues to be displayed on the oscilloscope's screen.

The stored signal can be held as long as the user likes, usually up to several minutes. Infinite storage times are not possible, of course, because the storage grid electrodes cannot hold their charge indefinitely. The stored charge leaks off within a few minutes. Even so, the stored waveform is held long enough for the technician to examine it quite thoroughly. Not surprisingly, storage oscilloscopes are considerably more expensive than standard oscilloscopes.

Digital oscilloscopes

The big trend in electronics over the last decade has been the move from analog to digital circuitry. It should not be surprising that a number of digital oscilloscopes are now available.

Unlike the digital multimeters described in the last chapter, the final output of a digital oscilloscope is still in analog form—the waveshape is visually drawn. A digital oscilloscope is one that uses digital circuitry to prepare the signal for display. In a digital oscilloscope, the analog input signal is converted into digital form for processing and multiplexing, then it is converted back into analog form for the actual display.

Some digital oscilloscopes do not even have a CRT. A multiplexed arrangement of LEDs are used to display the waveform. More recently, LCDs have been used for this purpose, permitting simpler multiplexing circuitry and less expensive construction (each individual LED has to be soldered into the circuit).

An LED display tends to offer a little less detail than a CRT, but it is less bulky and less fragile. An LCD display can be even smaller still. A handheld dual-trace oscilloscope with an LCD screen is shown in Fig. 4-48. If a standard CRT were used, a handheld oscilloscope would not be a viable option.

Another type of digital oscilloscope uses either a CRT or an LED/LCD display, but digital circuitry is employed for signal processing purposes. The digital storage oscilloscope (DSO) is becoming increasingly popular among serious electronics technicians. This instrument is less popular among electronics hobbyists because of its considerable expense and complexity.

The DSO takes the idea of the analog storage oscilloscope (discussed in the preceding section of this chapter) one step further. In an analog storage oscilloscope, the stored signal will eventually fade away. A DSO, on the other hand, can hold the displayed signal indefinitely, as long as power is supplied to the

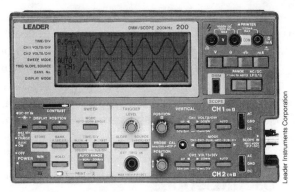

Fig. 4-48   *This handheld digital oscilloscope uses an LCD screen.*

instrument. The data about the displayed signal is stored in a digital memory, not just on the CRT screen. If a DSO is combined with a computer (see chapter 11), the signal can be recorded for permanent storage and eventual reuse.

Because the stored signal is in digital form, it can be manipulated in a number of ways. For example, certain features can be highlighted for emphasis, or the technician can enlarge the display to "zoom in" on areas of particular interest. Another advantage of the DSO is that, as a rule, digital timing can be more accurate than analog timing.

There are a couple of important new specifications to take into account when shopping for a DSO. All other factors being equal, choose the DSO with the longest record length specification. The record length determines how long the stored waveform can be.

In addition to the analog bandwidth specification (which is essentially the same for both digital and analog oscilloscopes), you also need to consider the sampling rate. The analog input signals are converted into digital form by sampling their instantaneous voltage many times per second. The speed at which this is done is called the sampling rate. According to the Nyquist theorem, the sampling rate must be at least twice the frequency of the signal to be digitized or aliassing will occur. Aliassing is a form of digital distortion that renders the display utterly meaningless.

If the sampling rate is just twice the signal frequency, the signal's frequency will be accurately measured, but all details of the waveshape will be completely lost. For this reason, some manufacturers of DSOs specify the sampling rate for four or more points per cycle or period. Other manufacturers list the Nyquist

Hewlett-Packard Company

Fig. 4-49 *The HP 5450A digital oscilloscope has two channels and a 400 MHz repetitive bandwidth.*

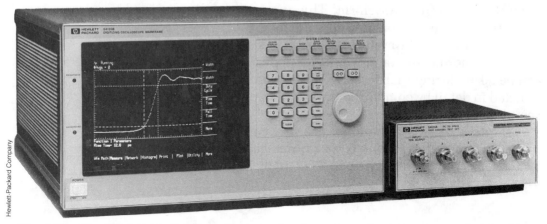

Hewlett-Packard Company

Fig. 4-50 *The HP 54123 digital oscilloscope has four channels and a 34 GHz bandwidth.*

rate. Before comparing sampling rate specifications, make sure you know how the figure was derived. The four-points system will give less impressive numbers than the Nyquist method; but in practical terms, the four-points system will offer more accurate results. Of course, the higher the sampling rate, the better the oscilloscope in question is.

Several different sampling methods are used in DSOs. Most DSOs offer the options of real-time sampling and repetitive sam-

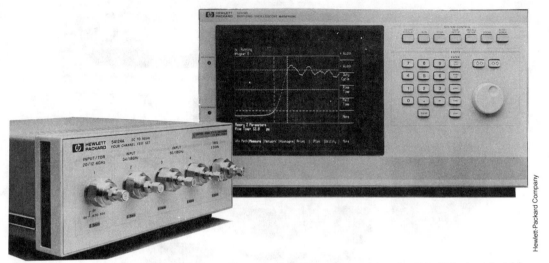

Fig. 4-51 *The HP 54124T digital oscilloscope has four channels and a 50 GHz bandwidth.*

pling. Real-time sampling uses a very high sampling rate to provide enough sample points in a single sweep for an accurate reconstruction of the waveform. This type of sampling is used primarily for one-shot or aperiodic events.

For periodic (ac) waveforms, repetitive sampling is used. Because the monitored waveform keeps repeating, fewer samples can be taken during each sweep, and the waveform can be reconstructed in detail by combining the sample points for several consecutive sweeps.

Digital storage oscilloscopes are very complex devices with many unique features, which we do not have space to discuss here. Some DSOs are shown in Fig. 4-49, Fig. 4-50, and Fig. 4-51.

❖ 5
LCR bridges and capacitance meters

MOST PRACTICAL ELECTRONIC MEASUREMENTS INVOLVE ONE OF the three basic electrical parameters—voltage, current, and resistance. As we've seen in chapter 3 and chapter 4, the multimeter and the oscilloscope can perform a wide variety of tests on these three electrical parameters. But it is not uncommon to need measurements of other electronic parameters, such as capacitance or (somewhat less frequently in modern electronics) inductance. Standard multimeters and oscilloscopes cannot measure capacitance or inductance, at least not directly. (A simple test for capacitor leakage or shorts using an ohmmeter was described back in chapter 3.) An oscilloscope can be used to determine signal frequency and impedance, and the capacitance or inductance can be algebraically calculated from that information. This chapter will look at test equipment specifically designed to measure capacitance and, in some cases, inductance.

The Wheatstone bridge

Most analog capacitance and inductance testers use some form of the Wheatstone bridge. The basic Wheatstone bridge circuit, shown in Fig. 5-1, is used to determine the value of an unknown resistance. This is done by comparing the unknown resistance to three known resistance values.

Usually, the input signal will be an audio waveform. A sine wave is usually the best bet for testing purposes because of its

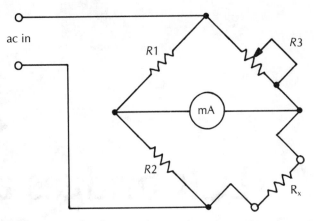

Fig. 5-1 *A Wheatstone bridge can be used to determine the value of an unknown resistance.*

lack of harmonics. Any audio signal generator may be used. Signal generators will be discussed in chapter 7.

The current meter in the center of the bridge should be the type with zero in the center of its scale. This type of ammeter is often called a galvanometer. To use the Wheatstone bridge, we need some way to detect both negative and positive currents.

As the input signal is fed through the Wheatstone bridge, variable resistor (potentiometer) R3 is adjusted until a null (zero current) reading is obtained on the meter. This indicates that the bridge is balanced. An alternate approach is to use a pair of reverse-parallel LEDs, as shown in Fig. 5-2. When the bridge is balanced, both LEDs will be dark, or both will be very dimly lit to

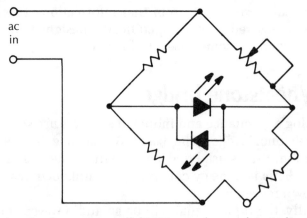

Fig. 5-2 *A pair of reverse-parallel LEDs can be used to indicate the null condition in a Wheatstone bridge.*

an equal degree. If just one of the LEDs is lit, the bridge is not balanced and R3 requires further adjustment.

Still another method of detecting the null balance condition is to use headphones in place of the current meter. Adjust R3 for the lowest sound level. Ideally, the signal should be blocked out completely. However, in most practical cases it will only be very strongly attenuated when the circuit is balanced.

When the Wheatstone bridge has been brought into balance, the unknown resistance can be calculated directly from the three known resistance values according to the simple formula

$$R_x = R3R1/R2$$

Usually, a calibrated dial is mounted directly on the shaft of potentiometer R3. (Resistances R1 and R2 are fixed and constant.) In this way, the unknown resistance value (R_x) can be read directly from the dial position without the user having to bother with any mathematical equations at all.

The same basic Wheatstone bridge can be used for capacitances and inductances, as well as for resistances. Of course, capacitors or coils should be used in the legs of the Wheatstone bridge instead of resistors, as appropriate for the desired type of test.

A modern, practical LCR bridge from a commercial manufacturer is shown in Fig. 5-3. This device can measure unknown resistances (R), capacitances (C), and inductances (L) over a variety of ranges. It usually takes some skill and practice to read the dial setting correctly on this type of device, but it is not a particularly difficult skill to learn.

A variation on the basic Wheatstone bridge is the Maxwell bridge, shown in Fig. 5-4. This circuit is designed to match

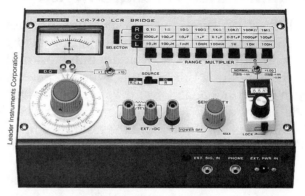

Fig. 5-3 *A commercially available LCR bridge.*

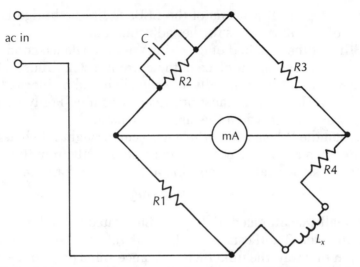

Fig. 5-4 *A Maxwell bridge is a variation on the basic Wheatstone bridge.*

capacitive and inductive reactances. The circuit is tuned until it goes into resonance. At this point the impedance of the known parallel resistor-capacitor combination is equal to (but phase shifted from) the impedance of the unknown series resistor-inductor combination. Of course, you could use a known-value coil to find the value of an unknown capacitance.

A nice thing about the Wheatstone bridge and the Maxwell bridge is that they don't require their own power source. They essentially "steal" their operating power from the ac signal source.

Simple capacitance measurement

Figure 5-5 illustrates a simple way to measure the approximate value of an unknown capacitance by comparing it to a known capacitance using an ac voltmeter (included in most multimeters (see chapter 3). To perform this test, place the unknown capacitor in series with a known capacitor and apply an ac signal across the two. The actual signal frequency isn't too critical here, as long as it is held constant throughout the test procedure. A 1000-Hz (1-kHz) audio signal generator (see chapter 7) is a good, convenient choice in most cases.

Use the ac voltmeter to measure the total ac signal voltage from the output of the signal generator. Next, measure the voltage

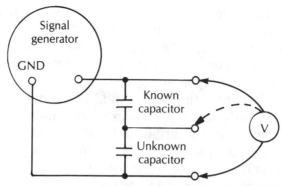

Fig. 5-5 *An ac voltmeter can be used to find an unknown capacitance by comparing it with a known capacitance.*

across the known capacitor and then across the unknown capacitor. Comparing the two measured voltages will give the approximate ratio of the capacitance values. What we're really doing here is putting two capacitive reactances in series across an ac voltage source. The capacitors act like an ac voltage divider, much like a pair of series resistors in a dc circuit.

As an example, let's say the signal generator is putting out an 11-V signal. We then measure 1 V across the known capacitor, which happens to have a value of 0.005 μF, and 10 V across the unknown capacitor. The voltage ratio is 1:10, so the capacitance ratio is 10:1. Remember, reactance is higher for smaller capacitances. In our example, the unknown capacitor has a value of about 0.0005 μF.

This test will generally work best if the difference between the known and unknown capacitances isn't too great. If the measured voltage ratio is awkwardly large, try the test again with a differently valued known capacitor as the reference. This certainly isn't a very sophisticated method of measuring capacitances, but it is fine for many practical quick and dirty test situations.

Digital capacitance meters

Once again, digital electronics has invaded the analog domain, but in this case, measuring the analog value (capacitance) is actually easier when digital techniques are employed. Analog capacitance testers tend to be awkward to use and are of limited accuracy. They usually require delicate calibration procedures.

A modern digital capacitance meter can be used as easily as a multimeter. Just connect the test leads across the capacitor (or other capacitive device) to be measured, push a button, and read the capacitance value directly from a numerical readout. Early instruments of this type used LED readouts, but LCDs are increasingly becoming the norm. An LCD readout typically consumes significantly less power than a comparable LED display, and it is easier to read in bright lighting. Test equipment using LCDs also tends to be less expensive than instruments equipped with LED displays because fewer solder connections have to be made during the manufacturing process.

A digital capacitance meter is basically similar to a digital voltmeter. A generalized block diagram for this type of test equipment is shown in Fig. 5-6.

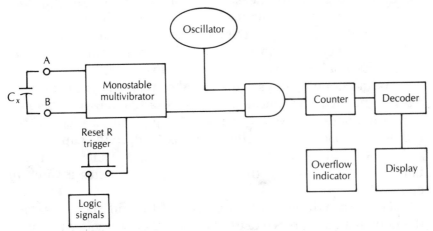

Fig. 5-6 *A block diagram of a digital capacitance meter.*

The first stage in this circuit is a monostable multivibrator. Any multivibrator, by definition, has two possible output states—logic 1 and logic 0. With a monostable multivibrator, only one of these states is stable (can be held indefinitely). In this discussion, we will assume that logic 0 is the stable state. The output of the monostable multivibrator remains at logic 0 until the circuit is triggered. At that time, the output switches to a logic 1 state for a specific period of time, which is defined by a resistor-capacitor combination. After this period of time, the output of the multivibrator returns to its normal, stable state (logic 0).

In a digital capacitance meter, the timing resistor has a fixed value. (In some instruments, different resistors may be switch selectable for different measurement ranges. But for any given test, the timing resistance has a constant, known value.) The monostable multivibrator's timing capacitor is the unknown capacitance being measured. Therefore, the output of this stage goes to logic 1 when triggered for a period of time that is directly proportional to the input capacitance at the instrument's test leads. The rest of the circuitry measures the length of this timing period.

The output of the monostable multivibrator controls an AND gate which blocks or passes a reference signal (generated by the reference oscillator stage) through to the actual counter stage. This reference oscillator generates square waves, or pulses, that are recognizable to the digital circuitry. When the monostable multivibrator is putting out a logic 0, the gate is closed and no pulses from the reference oscillator reach the counter. When the monostable multivibrator is putting out a logic 1, the reference pulses pass through the gate and advance the counter circuit one count per reference cycle.

The count is checked for a possible overrange condition and displayed. Obviously, the final count depends on how many pulses get through the gate. Because the reference oscillator operates at a consistent frequency, the number of pulses counted is directly proportional to how long the gate is held open; that is, how long the monostable multivibrator's output is at logic 1. This time period, in turn, is directly proportional to the unknown capacitance being measured, so the final count value displayed is directly proportional to the measured capacitance.

A digital capacitance meter can accurately and conveniently measure capacitances over a wide range of values. Most commercial capacitance meters are designed for handheld use and look very much like a handheld DMM, although some bench-top devices are marketed.

Do you need a capacitance meter?

For most electronics hobbyists and technicians a capacitance meter is a luxury item. Certainly, it is not an indispensable item on most electronics workbenches, but it can often be a very handy instrument to have available for those relatively rare occasions when a capacitance must be directly measured.

Capacitance meters range from the very simple to the highly

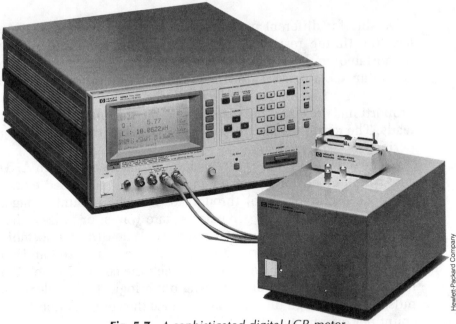

Fig. 5-7 *A sophisticated digital LCR meter.*

complex. For example, a very sophisticated digital LCR (inductance-capacitance-resistance) meter is shown in Fig. 5-7.

Is a capacitance meter a worthwhile investment? That depends on how often you have to deal with unmarked capacitors (or other unknown capacitances) in your electronics work.

A capacitance meter can be useful in tracking down stray capacitances which can cause problems in many electronic circuits, especially those that operate at high signal frequencies. Printed circuit boards with closely placed traces are often subject to stray capacitance problems, particularly in rf circuits.

Remember, a capacitor is nothing more than two conductors separated by an insulator. Air, wire insulation, or a section of copperless circuit board can all act as the dielectric (insulator between two conductors) in a phantom capacitor or stray capacitance.

A capacitance meter is primarily used to check specific capacitance values. An ohmmeter will do a perfectly adequate job for simple yes/no tests of a capacitor's quality (no excessive leakage or shorting). The procedure was described back in chapter 3. Certainly, there's no point in considering the purchase of a capacitance meter until you've taken care of your more basic test equipment—especially a good multimeter (see chapter 3) and oscilloscope (see chapter 4).

6

Frequency meters

FOR AC SIGNALS, FREQUENCY IS USUALLY A VERY IMPORTANT parameter. Frequency is a measure of how many complete cycles the waveform goes through in 1 second. The standard unit of measurement for frequency is the hertz (Hz). In some older technical texts, frequency is given in cycles per second (cps). These two terms (hertz and cycles per second) are fully interchangeable. In modern usage, hertz is the preferred term.

An ac signal with a frequency of 1 Hz goes through one complete cycle in 1 second. A 2-Hz signal goes through two complete cycles in the same time period (1 second). The frequency of a signal is not always a nice, neat whole number. For instance, if a waveform goes through 3 cycles in 1 second, it has a frequency of 3 Hz. The differences between these three hypothetical signals are illustrated in Fig. 6-1.

For many ac signals used in practical electronics circuits, the hertz is too small a unit to be practical. For higher frequencies, prefixes are applied. The two most common are the kilohertz (kHz) and the megahertz (MHz). The metric prefix *kilo* means thousand, so 1 kilohertz is the equivalent to 1,000 hertz. Similarly, the metric prefix *mega* means million, so 1 megahertz is equal to 1,000,000 hertz (or 1,000 kilohertz). Some typical frequency values are compared in Table 6-1.

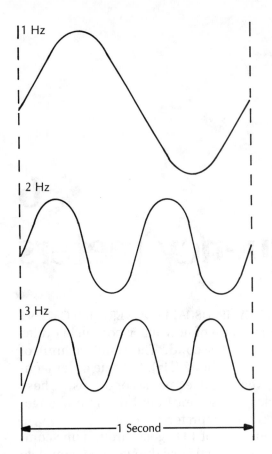

Fig. 6-1 *Frequency is a measurement of how many complete cycles occur in 1 second.*

**Table 6-1   Comparison of
some typical frequency values.**

1 Hz	0.001 kHz	0.000001 MHz
10 Hz	0.01 kHz	0.00001 MHz
100 Hz	0.1 kHz	0.0001 MHz
1,000 Hz	1 kHz	0.001 MHz
2,500 Hz	2.5 kHz	0.0025 MHz
10,000 Hz	10 kHz	0.01 MHz
100,000 Hz	100 kHz	0.1 MHz
350,000 Hz	350 kHz	0.35 MHz
690,800 Hz	690.8 kHz	0.6908 MHz
1,000,000 Hz	1,000 kHz	1 MHz
2,500,000 Hz	2,500 kHz	2.5 MHz
3,591,750 Hz	3,591.75 kHz	3.59175 MHz
25,000,000 Hz	25,000 kHz	25 MHz

Analog frequency measurement

Frequency is, more or less, an analog quantity. At least, it is a parameter of all analog ac signals. (It is also a parameter of all digital pulse (ac) signals.) But dedicated analog frequency measurement devices never proved to be very practical. A few analog frequency meters have been designed, mostly as hobbyist projects, and a few commercial models have been marketed over the years. They had limited reliability, accuracy, and usefulness, so they never caught on.

Until recently, virtually all electronic circuits were analog in nature. Most frequency measurements were made with oscilloscopes. If the sweep frequency is known, you can take the reciprocal to get the time period of a complete sweep:

$$T = 1/F$$

You then divide this time period by the number of divisions across the CRT's face from left to right. This gives you the time per division. Most oscilloscopes have a calibrated dial on the sweep frequency control. This allows you to read the time-per-division value directly.

Once you know the time-per-division value, just count how many divisions a complete cycle of the displayed waveform covers. This gives you the time period of the monitored cycle. Once again, take the reciprocal to find the signal frequency:

$$F = 1/T$$

The signal frequency can also be determined with an oscilloscope by creating a Lissajous figure with the unknown signal to be measured and a reference signal of a known frequency. Counting the loops in the Lissajous figure gives you the ratio between the two signal frequencies. These oscilloscope frequency measuring techniques were discussed in more detail in chapter 4.

Using an oscilloscope to accurately determine the frequency of a signal requires quite a bit of experience. It isn't too hard to get an approximate frequency using these methods, but precision measurements are difficult at best. Still, the oscilloscope is probably the best analog tool for measuring frequency.

Digital frequency measurement

The development of inexpensive digital circuitry has made frequency measurement devices relatively simple to design and manufacture. For quite some time, a digital frequency counter was the "sexiest" piece of test equipment around. Almost every electronics hobbyist and technician wanted a shiny new frequency counter on his workbench. Many of those shiny new frequency counters ended up as expensive dust collectors, because there simply aren't that many applications for this type of test equipment in most practical electronics work. In many cases, measuring frequency with an oscilloscope is still the most convenient approach.

In certain specialized testing applications, the high accuracy and direct numerical readout of a digital frequency counter can be a true blessing. This is especially true in complex digital systems (such as computers) that require precise timing and exact coordination between various signals. A digital frequency counter is also useful in some radio work, especially when extremely high frequencies are involved. Modern microwave circuits may utilize frequencies of millions of megahertz. Most electronic hobbyists and technicians can't afford an oscilloscope with a bandwidth that high, but a relatively inexpensive digital frequency counter can usually measure such extremely high frequencies.

Digital frequency counter circuitry

The basic circuitry of a typical digital frequency counter is quite similar to that of a digital voltmeter or a digital capacitance meter (see chapter 5). A simplified block diagram of a typical digital frequency counter is shown in Fig. 6-2.

Because the electronics technician is likely to measure a number of weak (low-amplitude) signals, most practical frequency counters include a preamplification stage of some kind. This amplifier boosts the signal amplitude to a usable level.

This type of instrument is built around digital circuitry and only recognizes the two discrete voltage levels of digital signals (high and low). This means reliable measurement of the signal frequency can only be made if the input signal is some form of rectangular wave. Of course, this would severely limit the general usefulness of the frequency counter.

Fortunately, it is not too difficult to "square off" almost any analog waveform. This is done with a circuit known as a Schmitt trigger. If the input voltage is above a specific level, the output of

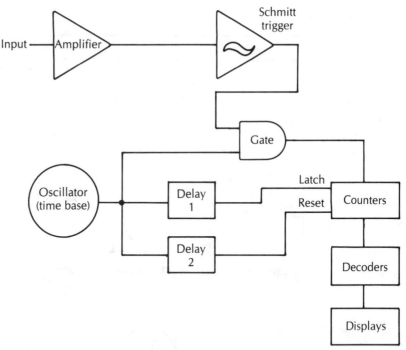

Fig. 6-2   *A block diagram of a digital frequency counter.*

the Schmitt trigger will be a logic high. If the input voltage drops below a specific level, the Schmitt trigger's output will be a logic low. Usually, two different switching points are used. The low-to-high transition point is higher than the high-to-low transition point. This gives an effect known as hysteresis, which permits more reliable and cleaner operation. The basic functioning of a Schmitt trigger circuit is illustrated in Fig. 6-3. If no hysteresis is used, the switching circuitry will be oversensitive to minor noise bursts that might show up in the signal. This problem is illustrated in Fig. 6-4.

Once the analog input signal has been pretreated into a form recognizable by the digital circuitry, the actual counting process can begin. Most of today's commercially available frequency counters use the "window" counting method. A sample of the input signal is allowed through a gate. This sample lasts a specific and fixed period of time. By counting the pulses during this sample period, the input frequency can be determined. If a window of 1 second is used, the output of the counter will be a direct indication of the signal frequency, because frequency is measured as the number of complete cycles in 1 second.

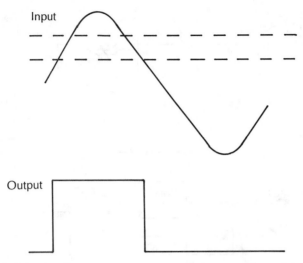

Fig. 6-3 *A Schmitt trigger can convert an analog waveform into digitallike pulses.*

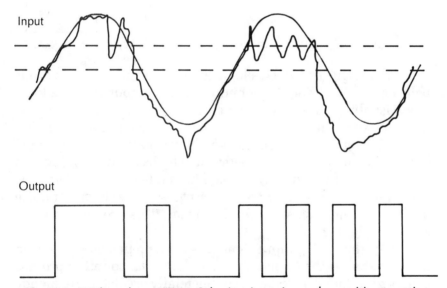

Fig. 6-4 *With no hysteresis, a Schmitt trigger is overly sensitive to noise.*

The squared-off signal from the output of the Schmitt trigger is fed into an AND gate, along with the output from an internal time-base oscillator. The input signal can pass through the gate only when the time-base oscillator is putting out a logic high (or 1). When the reference (time-base) signal is at logic low (or 0), the gate is closed and no signal can pass through it.

The time-base oscillator must produce three phase-shifted signals, as shown in Fig. 6-5. These three signals are referred to by their functions in the circuit—gate, latch, and reset. The gate signal controls the gate. The latch signal tells the counter to hold its final value, so it can be displayed. The reset signal sets the counter back to zero for the beginning of a new counting cycle.

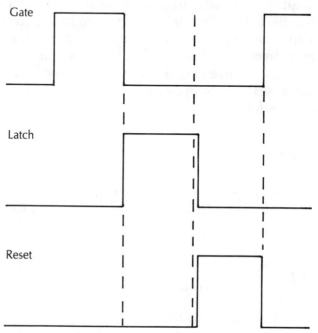

Fig. 6-5 *A digital frequency counter requires three precisely synchronized time-base signals.*

These three control signals may be independently generated by a special three-stage oscillator circuit, or a simple oscillator may be used to generate a single time-base signal (the gate signal). Delay or phase-shifting circuits are used to hold back the latch and reset signals until the appropriate times. This is the approach shown in the block diagram of Fig. 6-2. These three time-base signals must be precisely synchronized or the frequency counter will not function properly. The timing relationships between these control signals is very critical.

The digital counter is advanced one count for each input pulse it detects at the output of the gate. The decoder section adapts the counter's output signals into the electrical form required by the display device. Usually an LCD is used as the readout in modern commercial frequency counters, but some units still use seven-segment LED displays.

Accuracy and operating range

The accuracy of most commercial frequency counters is given as X% ±1 digit. It is virtually impossible to eliminate that ±1-digit inaccuracy. Because of the basic design used in digital frequency counters, the least significant digit may bob up and down on successive measurement cycles. This happens because the input signal is not synchronized to the time-base signal in any way. Sometimes a partial pulse may get through the window, as illustrated in Fig. 6-6.

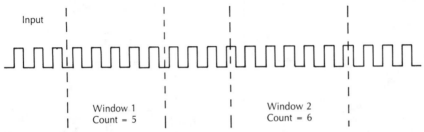

Fig. 6-6 *Digital frequency counters are always rated as ±1 digit, because sometimes a partial pulse may get through the "window," causing the count value to bobble.*

The time-base oscillator must be as precise as possible in its output frequency. If the time-base frequency drifts (changes value) at all, an accurate frequency measurement of the input signal cannot be made. The accuracy of the frequency measurement depends on comparing the unknown frequency to a precisely known reference frequency (the time base). If the time-base frequency varies, it will not be useful or meaningful as a reference. Most digital frequency counter circuits use crystal oscillators to generate the time-base signals for the best possible accuracy and stability.

The input frequency to be measured must be significantly higher than the time-base frequency. If the input frequency being measured is lower than the reference frequency, only zero or one pulse will ever get through the gate on any given count cycle. Most commercial frequency counters are not designed to read very low frequencies. Often, 1 kHz (1,000 Hz) is about the minimum frequency that can be measured. The exact lower limit will vary from model to model.

Some frequency counters allow the user to measure input frequencies lower than the time-base frequency. This is done by inserting a frequency multiplier stage between the Schmitt trigger and the gate. For example, if a 250-Hz signal is passed through a 10× frequency multiplier, it will look like a 2.5-kHz (2,500-Hz) signal to the counter circuitry. To get a correct readout, the decimal point in the display has to be moved.

The maximum measurable signal frequency depends on the design of the counter stage. There are two factors to consider here. The most important is the maximum count value of the counter. If a decimal counter has three digits, there is no way to count anything higher than 999. After a count of 999, the counter is forced to reset itself back to 000. (Most commercial instruments will light a warning overrange indicator if this happens.) If you tried to make a three-digit counter count 1,017 pulses, you'd get a reading of 017. Also, the majority of the counted pulses will be lost when the counter resets itself.

Another factor of importance is the switching speed of the counter circuitry. It is obviously impossible for the circuit to count pulses that are too fast for it to detect or respond to. If the input frequency is too high for the counter's range, a frequency divider stage can solve the problem quite easily. This works exactly the same way as the frequency multiplier discussed earlier, except in this case, the input frequency is divided by a factor of 10.

As an example, passing the 1,017-Hz signal described above through a divide-by-ten frequency divider circuit causes the counter to see the signal frequency as 101.7. This will be displayed as 101 or 102. (There's that ±1 digit again.) A switching circuit of some sort can move the decimal point appropriately in the display.

External frequency dividers, called prescalers, are often used to extend the range of digital frequency counters, especially older models. A modern prescaler can raise the range of a good frequency counter well up into the gigahertz (GHz) region.

Most commercial frequency counters have three to six counter stages for maximum counts of 999 to 999,999. As a rule, the more digits there are, the more expensive the instrument will be, but the greater the overall accuracy it will offer. Switchable frequency multipliers or dividers are also generally included to allow manually selectable ranges. Most modern digital frequency counters can handle signal frequencies ranging from a few kilohertz (thousands of hertz) up to several hundred (or even several thousand) megahertz (millions of hertz). This is the most useful range for most electronics work. If you need to measure a frequency that is too low for your frequency counter to cope with, you can always resort to using your oscilloscope for frequency measurement. Oscilloscopes offer the greatest accuracy and ease of reading with relatively low frequencies anyway. A couple of typical digital frequency counters are shown in Fig. 6-7 and Fig. 6-8.

Fig. 6-7 *A typical commercially available digital frequency counter.*
Leader Instruments Corporation

Fig. 6-8 *Another commercially available digital frequency counter.*
Leader Instruments Corporation

Advanced frequency measurement devices

For very advanced technicians working with highly critical circuits, specialized devices are available. Figure 6-9 shows a frequency and time-interval analyzer. This is basically a specialized digital oscilloscope with a built-in computer and special display features.

Fig. 6-9   *A frequency and time-interval analyzer is much like a highly specialized digital oscillo-scope.*

7

Signal generators

MANY TYPES OF TEST EQUIPMENT, INCLUDING MULTIMETERS, oscilloscopes, and frequency counters measure electrical signals passing through an electronic circuit. Many, and perhaps most, circuits do not generate an original signal from scratch. Instead, they accept an external input signal of some sort, processing and modifying it in some way before it reaches the output.

For example, an amplifier circuit accepts an ac waveform at its input and reproduces the same waveform (ideally with no distortion) at the output but at a higher amplitude. A filter circuit accepts an input signal and removes (or attenuates) some of the harmonic content before the signal reaches the circuit's output. There are countless other possibilities, of course, covering almost every type of electronic circuit there is.

A radio's input signal is the modulated rf signals in the air, which were generated at the transmitter. The radio's circuit modifies this input signal, mostly by amplification and demodulation. That is, the rf carrier wave is stripped off and the original modulating program signal is reproduced as audio from the radio's speaker.

It should be obvious that to test a circuit that modifies an input signal, some sort of input signal will be required for the monitored circuit to work on. Often, the normal input signal is too complex, irregular, or unpredictable to make meaningful comparisons. In such cases, we need to substitute a special test signal for the usual input. The test signal should be simple, easily recognizable, and consistent. The desired output signal should be very predictable. This allows the electronic technician to compare his measured results with the predicted results. Any deviation from the predicted results indicates some problem in the circuitry (or perhaps, in the test procedure).

Such cases come up often enough that any well-stocked electronics workbench should definitely include one or more signal generators. A signal generator is basically a highly accurate oscillator that is used to produce reliable and predictable test signals. There are many different types of signal generators available, for different purposes. In selecting a signal generator for a specific test procedure, you will first need to consider the frequency and waveshape of the generated signal.

Practical signal generators for general electronics work can be divided into two broad categories—af (audio frequency) signal generators and rf (radio frequency) signal generators. An af signal generator produces one or more simple waveforms within the audible spectrum (approximately 20 Hz to 20 kHz). An rf signal generator, on the other hand, operates at much higher frequencies for radio circuits. Most rf signal generators make some sort of provision for modulating the rf signal with an audio signal of some sort.

Sine wave oscillators

The simplest and most basic ac waveform is the sine wave, shown in Fig. 7-1. This waveform, unlike all others, consists of a single frequency component, the fundamental. A pure (undistorted) sine wave has no harmonic content at all. (Various waveshapes and their frequency components—the fundamental and harmonics—were introduced in chapter 4.)

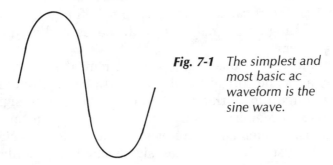

Fig. 7-1 *The simplest and most basic ac waveform is the sine wave.*

In most technical literature, a circuit that generates a sine wave is usually called an oscillator, while a circuit that produces some other waveform is called a signal generator. Other sources treat these two terms as more or less interchangeable. The distinction is usually made for test equipment, however. A signal generator that produces clean sine waves in the audio range is almost always referred to as a sine wave oscillator, or an audio oscillator.

A sine wave is a good input signal for many testing purposes because the absence of harmonics prevents any possible distraction from complex multiple-frequency components and sidebands. A sideband is a frequency component created by the interaction of two signals or frequency components, usually at the sum and difference (or multiples) of the original component frequencies.

In electronic circuits, distortion usually shows up as the addition of unwanted harmonics in the signal. Such harmonic distortion is easiest to spot if the test signal is a sine wave because there is no way for the distortion to be masked by any normal harmonic content in the test signal. Distortion in a sine wave is usually very visible when monitored on an oscilloscope, especially if a dual-trace oscilloscope is used. One trace (usually the upper trace) is the original test signal, straight from the signal generator, and the other trace (usually the lower trace) is the output signal of the circuit being tested. Any difference in the appearance of the two displayed signals is due to the effects of the circuit under test. Remember that the circuit's purpose is to make some change in the input signal. Clearly, it is quite impossible to draw any meaningful conclusions unless you know what the intended function of the circuit is.

For some test procedures, almost any input signal can be used. Sometimes, all that's necessary is to ensure that the signal is getting to where it is supposed to be. This is usually the case for the signal injection and signal tracing techniques described in the next chapter. In other test procedures, the exact waveshape is critical.

Still other test procedures require the technician to know the exact signal frequency. Most commercial audio oscillators have a calibrated frequency control dial. If you are working with some uncalibrated home-brew equipment, or if you suspect your instrument may be out of calibration, you can always check the actual signal frequency being generated with a frequency counter (see chapter 6) or an oscilloscope (see chapter 4).

If you have a frequency counter handy, you can often get away with a less sophisticated (and less expensive) audio oscillator on your workbench. The audio oscillator does not have to be accurately calibrated if you can measure the actual signal frequency externally. However, you should use caution if you opt for a less expensive sine wave oscillator. Some ''cheapie'' circuits are highly prone to frequency drift. That is, once you set the output to a specific frequency, it may start to shift over time. If you can continually monitor a frequency counter while performing the tests with the signal generator, this may not be a problem, but it could be rather awkward in many cases.

Many, if not most, commercial audio oscillators can also generate signals at frequencies well beyond the limits of audibility. These signals are in the form of audio signals, as opposed to rf signals. We will discuss rf generators later in this chapter.

When a precise, specific frequency is needed, a crystal oscillator is generally employed. A crystal oscillator usually exhibits very little frequency drift. On the other hand, it is often difficult to adjust the output frequency of a crystal oscillator over more than a very limited range (plus or minus a few hertz).

An audio oscillator with a truly variable range of output frequencies is often called a sweep oscillator. The instrument can ''sweep'' through a continuous range of frequencies. Some sweep oscillators can automatically sweep through their range. This is useful for testing the overall frequency response of a circuit. If the monitored circuit does not have a flat frequency response, the amplitude will fluctuate as the test signal is swept through its range.

The automatic sweep function is accomplished by frequency modulating the main oscillator signal with a low-frequency sawtooth wave or triangular wave. Ascending or descending sawtooth waves may be used. An ascending sawtooth starts the sweep at the low end of the frequency range and smoothly sweeps the signal upwards in frequency to a maximum value. It then snaps back down to the starting point and starts a new cycle. A descending sawtooth works in just the opposite way. The sweep moves in a downward direction (decreasing frequency), rather than upwards (increasing frequency). Ascending sawtooth waves seem to be more common than the descending variety.

When a triangular wave is used to sweep the frequency, the signal again starts at its minimum (lowest) frequency and smoothly sweeps upwards in frequency until the maximum point is reached. It then reverses direction and smoothly sweeps back down to the minimum frequency starting point, and the next cycle is begun.

There are certain inherent limitations to sine wave oscillators. It is virtually impossible to electronically generate an absolutely perfect, 100% distortion-free sine wave. Fortunately, it is not difficult to generate a sine wave that is close enough to pure for most practical purposes.

Sine wave oscillator circuits tend to be a bit bulky and inconvenient. Most classic designs require the use of bulky inductors and expensive variable capacitors. It is usually difficult to change the frequency of a sine wave oscillator except over a fairly limited range.

Some recent designs use specialized ICs that can generate good-quality sine waves without the use of any external coils. Many of these chips permit the frequency to be varied over a fairly wide range with a variable resistor (potentiometer) instead of the more inconvenient (and more costly) variable capacitor.

All in all, the basic audio oscillator is a fairly simple device, because it has a fairly simple job to do. It only has to generate a reliable and predictable ac waveform. Usually the front-panel controls are limited to frequency and amplitude adjustments.

A fairly typical commercially available audio oscillator is shown in Fig. 7-2. This instrument covers an extremely wide

Fig. 7-2 *A typical commercial audio oscillator.*

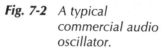

range, from 10 Hz to 1 MHz (1,000,000 Hz), divided into five decade ranges. This particular device can generate either sine waves or square waves, so it is more properly a function generator. This concept will be discussed in a later section of this chapter.

Pulse generators

Except for the sine wave, the most popular waveform used for testing electronic circuits is the rectangular wave, or pulse wave. Most analog ac waveforms have a linear range of values, sliding smoothly from one value to another value through an infinite number of intermediate steps. A rectangular wave, however, has just two discrete levels—high and low—as illustrated in Fig. 7-3. Theoretically, the transition time between the high and low states is infinitely short. That is, the reversal of states is assumed to take place instantaneously without passing through any intermediate values.

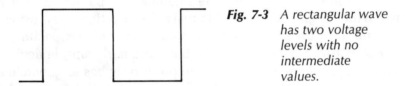

Fig. 7-3 *A rectangular wave has two voltage levels with no intermediate values.*

Any practical rectangular wave generator, however, won't be able to achieve truly instantaneous transitions between the signal states. It will inevitably take some finite amount of time (normally very, very brief) for the signal level to change from low to high (or vice versa). This transition time is known as the slew rate. Figure 7-4 shows a rectangular wave signal with a very poor slew rate.

Fig. 7-4 *A rectangular wave with a very poor slew rate.*

Most practical rectangular wave generators have much better slew rates than this. Usually the transition time between states is negligible for all practical purposes, and the electronics hobbyist or technician can usually ignore the transition time. But there are some exceptions to this. In some high-frequency circuits (especially high-speed digital switching circuits), the slew rate may become a critical factor.

Slew rate is usually measured in volts per second (V/s), or volts per millisecond (V/ms). This is an indication of how fast the signal can make large changes in its instantaneous voltage level. The concept of slew rate and its measurement with an oscilloscope were discussed in chapter 4.

There are many different rectangular waves possible. The difference is the relative amounts of time per cycle spent in the high and low states. Rectangular waves are usually defined by their duty cycle. The duty cycle is a ratio measurement of the high time compared to the total cycle time. For example, if the signal is in the high state for one-third of each complete cycle, the duty cycle is 1:3. Rectangular waves of various duty cycles are shown in Fig. 7-5.

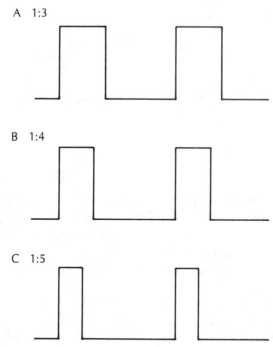

Fig. 7-5 *The duty cycle of a rectangular wave determines its harmonic content: A) 1:3; B) 1:4; and C) 1:5.*

The duty cycle ratio is usually written so that the first number (representing the high time) is a 1, even if this means that the second number is a fractional value; for example, 1:5.5. The duty cycle of a rectangular wave is important because it affects the harmonic content of the waveform. A rectangular wave consists of the fundamental frequency and all harmonics, except those which are exact multiples of the second number in the duty cycle ratio. For instance, a rectangular wave with a duty cycle of 1:3 would include all harmonics except those that are evenly divisible by three. A rectangular wave with a duty cycle of 1:4 would skip every fourth harmonic. Table 7-1 outlines the harmonic content of rectangular waves of differing duty cycles.

**Table 7-1 Harmonic content of
rectangular waves with different duty cycles.**

1:2	1:3	1:4	1:5
Fundamental	Fundamental	Fundamental	Fundamental
—	2nd	2nd	2nd
3rd	—	3rd	3rd
—	4th	—	4th
5th	5th	5th	—
—	—	6th	6th
7th	7th	7th	7th
—	8th	—	8th
9th	—	9th	9th
—	10th	10th	—
11th	11th	11th	11th
—	12th	—	12th
13th	13th	13th	13th
—	14th	14th	14th
15th	—	15th	—

For all rectangular waves, the amplitude of each harmonic is equal to the amplitude of the fundamental divided by the harmonic number. For example, the third harmonic has an amplitude that is one-third as strong as the fundamental. The fourth harmonic's amplitude is one-quarter of the fundamental's amplitude.

The square wave, shown in Fig. 7-6, is a special case of the rectangular wave. It has a duty cycle of 1:2. That is, the signal is in its high state for exactly one-half of each cycle and in the low state for the other half. (The transition times are generally ignored for these purposes.)

The square wave consists of the fundamental frequency and all odd harmonics, but no even harmonics. Because it is the only symmetrical rectangular wave, the square wave is particularly useful for many testing applications.

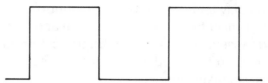

Fig. 7-6 *The square wave is a rectangular wave with a duty cycle of 1:2.*

In some technical literature the terms rectangular wave and pulse wave are often used more or less interchangeably. Strictly speaking, a pulse wave is actually a specific type of rectangular wave. A pulse wave has a very large duty cycle; that is, the signal is in the high state for only a small portion of each cycle. Naturally, this means that the pulse wave is very rich in harmonics, since all of the lower (higher amplitude) harmonics are included in the makeup of the signal. A typical pulse wave is illustrated in Fig. 7-7.

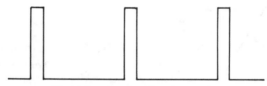

Fig. 7-7 *A typical pulse wave.*

As a piece of test equipment, a rectangular wave generator is usually called a pulse generator. Pulse generators range from simple, stable multivibrator circuits up to sophisticated, programmable units, like the one shown in Fig. 7-8. Most pulse generators designed for use on the electronics workbench offer manual control over the signal frequency and the duty cycle. More sophisticated pulse generators offer additional features,

Fig. 7-8 *A sophisticated, programmable pulse generator.*

such as signal delay and special triggering options. Some instruments permit the user to set the specific high and low voltages for the generated waveform. Not surprisingly, better-quality pulse generators usually offer a wider frequency range and faster slew rates than less expensive models.

Other waveforms

Most electronics testing using a signal generator will employ either a sine wave or a rectangular wave, but occasionally, other waveforms may be used. The triangular wave, illustrated in Fig. 7-9, is often used in electronics testing because it can be easily and inexpensively derived from a square wave. A triangular wave has the same harmonic structure as a square wave, except the harmonics in the triangular wave are weaker.

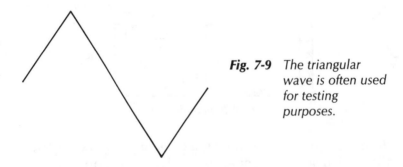

Fig. 7-9 *The triangular wave is often used for testing purposes.*

A square wave, as you should recall, is nothing more than a rectangular wave with a duty cycle of 1:2. This means that all even harmonics (multiples of two) are omitted from the signal; all odd harmonics are included. A triangular wave includes the fundamental and all of the odd harmonics, but no even harmonics.

The difference between a triangular wave and a square wave is the relative amplitude of the harmonic components as compared to the fundamental. For a square wave, each harmonic has an amplitude equal to the fundamental's amplitude divided by the harmonic number. For a triangular wave, the amplitude of each harmonic is equal to the amplitude of the fundamental divided by the square of the harmonic number. For example, in a square wave, the amplitude of the third harmonic is equal to

$$A_h3 = A_f/3$$

Where

A_h3 = amplitude of the third harmonic and

A_f = amplitude of the fundamental.

In a triangle wave, by contrast, the amplitude of the third harmonic is equal to

$$A_h3 = A_f/3^2$$
$$= A_f/(3 \times 3)$$
$$= A_f/9$$

A triangular wave can be derived by passing a square wave through an integrator circuit. Essentially, an integrator is rather like a low-pass filter. As the frequency (the harmonic number) increases, the signal is increasingly attenuated. Therefore, the amplitude of the harmonics will be weaker at the output of the integrator than at the input. Actually, the integrator circuit is performing a calculus function known as integration but the low-pass filter analogy is easier to understand and is adequate for our purposes here.

While a triangular wave is usually (though certainly not always) derived from a square wave, the signal is most commonly employed as a substitute for a sine wave. A triangular wave generator of a given quality will usually be less expensive than a comparable sine wave oscillator, especially if square-wave signals are also needed. Because the harmonics in a triangular wave are so weak, it is the next best thing to the harmonic-less sine wave. When viewed on an oscilloscope, a triangular wave shows most types of distortion almost as well as a sine wave. Some types of distortion are even more visible with the straight edges and sharp peaks of a triangular wave than with the smooth curves of a sine wave. For instance, Fig. 7-10 shows a sine wave with slight clipping, while Fig. 7-11 shows a triangular wave with a similar

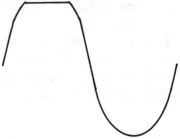

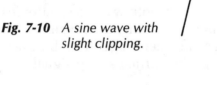

Fig. 7-10 *A sine wave with slight clipping.*

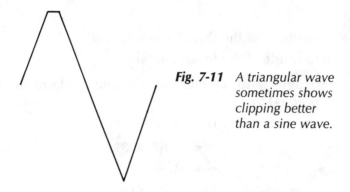

Fig. 7-11 *A triangular wave sometimes shows clipping better than a sine wave.*

amount of clipping. The flattening of the triangular wave's normally sharp peak is much more noticeable.

When feeding a test signal through a loudspeaker, a triangular wave also tends to be much less grating on the ear than a sine wave. A pure sine wave has a very piercing sound quality, while a triangular wave is much more mellow and almost musiclike. Triangular waves are sometimes referred to as delta waves.

Sawtooth waves, illustrated in Fig. 7-12, are sometimes used in electronics testing where a test signal with strong harmonic content is required. A sawtooth wave is comprised of the fundamental and all whole-number harmonics, both even and odd.

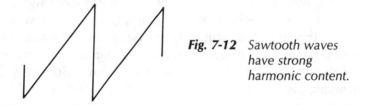

Fig. 7-12 *Sawtooth waves have strong harmonic content.*

Sawtooth waves come in two basic varieties: ascending and descending. The difference is the direction of the slope. Both types of sawtooth waves have the same basic harmonic structure, but the phase relationships between the various frequency components is different.

The most frequent use of a sawtooth wave in electronics testing is to sweep some other signal smoothly to a range. You should also recall from chapter 4 that an ascending sawtooth wave is also employed in a oscilloscope as the normal sweep signal.

Noise generators

For some types of broad-band testing, a noise generator is occasionally used. *Noise* in this sense is a randomized signal that covers a wide range of frequencies. When a noise signal is viewed through an oscilloscope, or otherwise measured, any deviations from a flat frequency response are usually quite apparent. In some cases, the differences in the sound quality produced through a loudspeaker will be readily apparent.

There are various types of noise, but the two most commonly used are white noise and pink noise. White noise is analogous to white light. It is made up of all audible frequencies. There is equal average energy for each individual frequency within the noise range. White noise has a flat frequency response; no frequency is stronger than any other frequency. When fed through a loudspeaker, white noise sounds like the no-signal static heard between stations on an FM receiver without muting.

Pink noise is basically filtered white noise. Instead of equal average energy for each individual frequency, there is equal average energy per octave throughout the noise range. An octave represents a doubling of frequency, so high octaves cover a wider range of discrete frequencies than do lower octaves. Therefore, low frequencies are emphasized in pink noise. When fed through a loudspeaker, pink noise sounds rather like a distant surf or falling rain.

Special white-noise generators and pink-noise generators are available. These are usually very simple and inexpensive circuits. Usually there are no controls on a noise generator except an on-off switch and perhaps a level (amplitude) control.

Function generators

A signal generator that can produce more than one waveshape is called a function generator. Usually, one base waveform is generated directly, and the other available waveforms are electronically derived from the base waveform. Most commercial function generators feature a rectangular wave (pulse wave), usually with an adjustable duty cycle; although some offer just a fixed square wave (duty cycle of 1:2). A triangular wave is also generated by just about every commercial function generator.

Most function generators also feature a sawtooth-wave output. This is sometimes called a ramp wave. In most cases, only an ascending sawtooth wave is produced, but some function generators can also produce descending sawtooth waves. Some deluxe function generators also produce sine waves. A few function generators may also offer one or more unusual waveforms.

A simple function generator has controls for the signal frequency and a switch to select the waveshape. There may also be a control to adjust the duty cycle of the rectangular wave output. The duty cycle control may or may not affect the other output waveforms, depending on the specific circuit design used in the instrument.

A level or amplitude control is often, though not always, included on commercial function generators. Obviously, this control adjusts the amplitude of the output signal.

More sophisticated function generators often offer some additional controls and special operating features. For example, a dc offset control is useful in many practical testing applications. By adjusting this control, the ac signal produced by the function generator can be made to ride on a dc voltage other than zero.

Many deluxe function generators have a sweep function. This sweeps the output frequency through a preset range. The sweep may be linear or logarithmic. Some equipment includes a switch that allows the user to manually adjust the type of sweep.

A function generator with a triggered mode can be externally controlled. One output cycle is generated each time the unit receives an external trigger signal. A similar feature is called gated tone burst. The function generator puts out a signal only as long as it is being fed a trigger pulse. When the trigger pulse stops, the output signal is cut off.

Another type of external control offered on many deluxe function generators is voltage control. An external analog voltage is used to control the frequency of the output signal. Increasing the control voltage increases the output frequency, and vice versa.

Besides the available frequency range, the number (and purity) of the available waveforms, and the controls and special features, the most important thing to look at when choosing a commercial function generator are the stability specs. To be useful on an electronics workbench, the generated signal must be consistent and not vary over time. The most variation is likely to appear as the instrument warms up.

Two types of stability specifications are usually given: amplitude stability and frequency stability. These terms should be pretty much self-explanatory. The amplitude stability rating indicates the consistency of the output signal level, and frequency stability indicates the amount of drift in the output signal's frequency.

Figure 7-13 shows a sophisticated commercial function generator. This unit features a digital LCD display panel to directly indicate the various parameters of the generated signal. Digital circuitry is used through much of this instrument, but the output waveforms are in analog form (except for the rectangular/pulse waves, of course).

rf signal generators

So far we have been looking at af signal generators. While af means audio frequency in this particular application, the term doesn't really refer to the frequency range. Instead, an af signal generator actually puts out analog signals as if they were audio signals, regardless of their true frequency. As we have seen, many (if not most) modern commercial af signal generators actually produce signals with frequencies well up into the rf region.

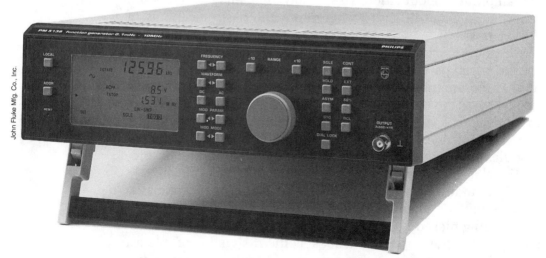

Fig. 7-13 *A function generator can produce multiple waveforms.*

Audio frequency signal generators with frequency ranges extending to tens, or even hundreds, of megahertz (millions of hertz) are not at all uncommon. The actual upper limit of audible frequencies is nominally just 20 kHz (20,000 Hz), so these af signal generators actually generate a lot more than just true af signals.

In the case of signal generators, the terms af and rf do not refer to the frequency range, per se. An rf signal generator is not just an af signal generator with a higher output frequency. It is a completely different instrument, for completely different testing purposes.

For most general electronics work, an af signal generator will probably be all that's needed. An rf signal generator is only needed when working on actual radio (transmitter and receiver) circuits. (This includes television sets and VCRs.)

In a radio transmitter/receiver system, an rf signal is comprised of two parts: a carrier signal and a program signal. The carrier signal has a very high frequency (in the rf range). The program signal is usually a true audio signal of some sort. (There are some exceptions to this, such as in digital communications and telemetry systems.) In any event, the frequency of the program signal is considerably lower than the frequency of the carrier signal.

The carrier signal is modulated by the program signal. That is, some parameter of the carrier signal is varied in step with the instantaneous level of the program signal. There are a number of different types of modulation, but the two most commonly used are amplitude modulation (AM) and frequency modulation (FM). It isn't too difficult to figure out the basic meanings of these terms.

In an AM system, the instantaneous level or amplitude of the carrier signal is controlled (modulated) by the instantaneous level of the program signal. In an FM system, the instantaneous frequency of the carrier signal is controlled (modulated) by the instantaneous level of the program signal. The frequency of the carrier signal at any given moment deviates from its nominal (no modulation) frequency value by an amount that is directly proportional to the instantaneous amplitude of the program signal.

The modulated rf signal is released into the atmosphere by the transmitter's antenna. This rf signal can travel great distances before being picked up by the receiver's antenna. The tuning circuitry in the receiver selects what specific rf signal is of interest on the basis of the carrier's frequency (its nominal center frequency in the case of an FM system).

The selected rf signal is then amplified and demodulated. Demodulation is a process of separating the modulating program signal from the modulated carrier signal. At this point, the rf carrier signal is discarded and the program signal is treated like any ordinary audio signal.

An rf signal generator, as you've probably anticipated, produces a modulated rf carrier signal. Usually the program signal is also generated internally by the rf signal generator. The program signal will usually be a simple waveform, like those produced by the af signal generators discussed earlier in this chapter.

An rf signal generator can be designed to use AM or FM, or both. In the last case, the choice of modulation will be switch selectable. Some rf signal generators also offer the option of less common types of modulation, in addition to the standard AM and FM.

A typical analog rf signal generator is shown in Fig. 7-14. Some sophisticated modern rf signal generators incorporating digital circuitry and displays are illustrated in Fig. 7-15, Fig. 7-16, and Fig. 7-17.

Most (though not all) rf signal generators feature sweep capabilities (as described earlier in this chapter) as in af signal generators. The concept of signal sweeping is pretty much the same for both af and rf signal generators. An rf signal generator with sweep will often inject marker pulses into its output signal to make certain key frequencies more readily identifiable when viewed on an oscilloscope. A typical sweep/marker generator is shown in Fig. 7-18.

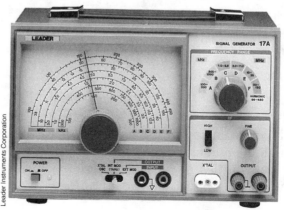

Fig. 7-14 *A typical analog rf signal generator.*

Fig. 7-15 *The HP 8657B digital rf signal generator.*

Fig. 7-16 *The HP 8673H digital rf signal generator.*

Recently, more and more use has been made of microwaves. The very high frequencies involved in microwave systems are beyond the capabilities of most standard rf signal generators. Some instruments, like the one shown in Fig. 7-19, are specifi-

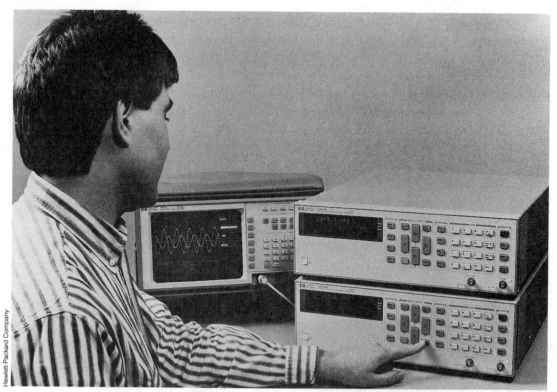

Fig. 7-17 Two HP 3324A synthesized function/sweep generators.

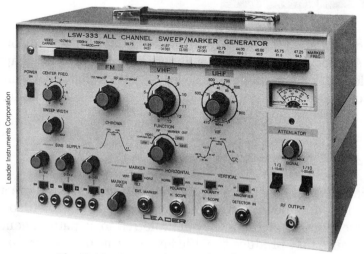

Fig. 7-18 A typical sweep/marker generator.

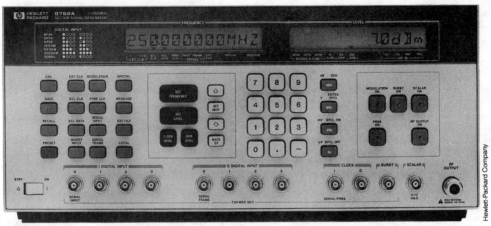

Fig. 7-19 *This rf signal generator is designed for use with microwave circuits.*

Fig. 7-20 *A typical video signal generator.*
Leader Instruments Corporation

cally designed for use with microwave circuitry. Like many of the sophisticated signal generators shown throughout this chapter, this device is an analog/digital hybrid. Notice that a convenient LCD display indicates the signal frequency and amplitude (or level) in direct numerical form.

Video signal generators

Special rf signal generators for television and VCR work are also available. These devices are called, naturally enough, video signal generators. Sometimes they are referred to as pattern generators because they produce specific test patterns on the screen of a television set. These test patterns are used to test the picture's alignment, resolution, and focus, as well as other parameters. A fairly typical video signal generator is illustrated in Fig. 7-20.

Signal injectors
and signal tracers

CLOSELY RELATED TO THE SIGNAL GENERATORS OF CHAPTER 7 ARE
signal injectors and, to a somewhat lesser extent, signal tracers.
These two types of test equipment are used to identify the defective stage in a multistage circuit. In our discussion of signal
injectors and signal tracers, we will assume we are testing the
audio amplifier circuit shown in the block diagram in Fig. 8-1.
Notice that this amplifier is made up of several amplification
stages and a few stages that perform other functions.

Both signal injectors and signal tracers are probelike tools.
They are always compact, handheld units. In appearance, signal
injectors and signal tracers look very much alike, except for the
actual controls and the fact that a signal tracer has a built-in
speaker, while a signal tracer does not. A typical signal injector
looks something like the drawing in Fig. 8-2.

Signal injectors

A signal injector is basically a small signal generator in probe
form. Compared to the signal generators described in chapter 7, a
signal injector has a very limited frequency range. Only frequencies in the true audible range are normally generated by this
instrument. Some signal injectors do not even have a frequency
adjustment control. The output signal frequency is fixed in such
devices. A typical frequency for a fixed-frequency signal injector
is about 1,000 Hz (1 kHz).

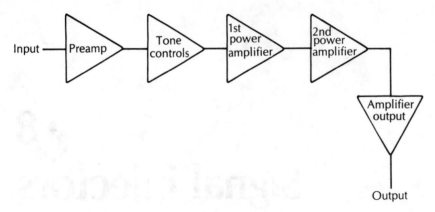

Fig. 8-1   *Signal injectors and signal tracers are useful in testing multistage audio circuits like this audio amplifier.*

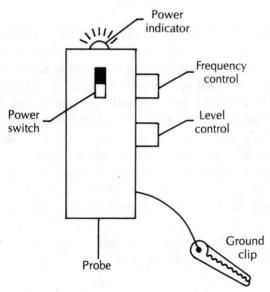

Fig. 8-2   *A typical signal injector.*

Most signal injectors include a volume or level control to adjust the amplitude of the generated signal. The waveshape generated by a signal injector usually isn't too critical. While there is no standardization, my observation is that the most commonly used waveshape for signal injection is the square wave. This is probably because it is very easy to generate a decent square wave with inexpensive circuitry. The relatively strong harmonic content of a square wave is also useful in some signal injection tests. Signal injectors are normally used only with multistage audio circuits.

To get an idea of how a signal injector works, let's assume we are troubleshooting the multistage audio amplifier circuit shown in Fig. 8-1. First, we will assume that the problem is the amplifier is dead—there is no output signal from the loudspeaker.

The first step is to test the amplifier's power supply with a multimeter. Is the circuit getting power? Is the supply voltage correct? Assuming that the power supply is OK, we now turn to the signal injector.

First, connect the signal injector's ground clip to a convenient ground point in the circuit being tested. Normally, once the ground clip is connected, it can be left alone throughout the rest of the test procedure; but there may be some exceptions. In certain types of equipment, separate and independent grounds may be used by different subcircuits. This prevents feedback, ground loop, and noise problems. Usually, separate grounds will be quite obvious to any experienced electronics technician or hobbyist, especially if a schematic of the circuitry is available.

Once the ground clip is securely attached, the signal injector is turned on. Its probe tip can be touched to the input of any subcircuit in the tested device, injecting a signal into the circuit at that point. The signal injection tests are made with no input connected to the amplifier. We are only interested in the injected test signals.

The probe is touched to the loudspeaker's terminal. Is a tone heard from the speaker? If so, the loudspeaker is OK and the problem is in an earlier stage. If no tone is heard, then you know the loudspeaker itself is defective. There may or may not be other problems at earlier stages in the circuit. There is no way to tell with a signal injector until the defective loudspeaker is replaced.

Assuming that the loudspeaker checks out OK, move the probe tip of the signal injector back to the final output amplifier stage. Is a tone heard from the loudspeaker again? If so, the problem stage is at some earlier point in the circuitry. If the output tone has disappeared, then the final amplifier stage is defective. The specific component or components causing the problem can now be tracked down with other test equipment. A multimeter will probably be most useful.

Notice that by using a signal injector to isolate the problem, you can save a lot of time and trouble. You don't have to perform component-level tests on any other subcircuits, just in the stage identified as bad by the signal injection tests.

If the final amplifier stage tests out fine, then move the probe of the signal injector to the next stage immediately preceding it. Continue to repeat these signal injection tests, moving backwards through the circuit until the problem stage is located.

Some readers might be wondering why we start at the output of the system and work our way backwards through the circuitry. What will happen if we start at the input and work through the individual stages from first to last, instead of from last to first? (Actually, this would work, but you'd probably end up making a lot more tests that way.) By starting at the back (output) of the system, each stage is cleared or implicated as it is tested. If you start at the system's input, the individual tests won't tell you as much. If you inject a signal into the second stage (for example) and get no output, what do you know? You know that the problem is somewhere between the input of the second stage and the system's output. The problem might be in the second stage, or it might be in the third stage, or it might be in the tenth stage.

You'll have to continue injecting the signal into successive stages until you get an output signal. When the output signal finally appears, the problem is somewhere in between the current test point and the previous test point. This approach will work, but it is hardly an efficient way to proceed.

Signal injection can be used to find problems other than completely dead subcircuits. For instance, if the problem is excessive distortion, you can use the signal injector to locate the stage in which the distortion first appears. Another problem that can usually be located with a signal injector is insufficient output signal level. Use the signal injection method to identify the stage where the signal amplitude drops inappropriately.

Signal tracers

A signal tracer is similar in concept to a signal injector, but it does not have a built-in signal generator. Usually the system's normal input signal is used for signal tracing purposes. If this is not possible, a standard signal generator (as described in chapter 7) can be used to provide a suitable input signal to the circuit under test. The test signal must be in the audible range. A signal tracer also has a small built-in speaker. It will almost always have a level or volume control to adjust the amplitude of the signal produced from the built-in speaker.

The first step is to connect the signal tracer's ground clip to a convenient ground point in the circuit being tested (just as we did with the signal injector described in the preceding section). Once again, after the ground clip has been connected, it usually can be left alone throughout the rest of the test procedure. But remember, in certain types of electronic equipment, separate and independent grounds may be used by different subcircuits. This prevents feedback, ground loop, and noise problems. Usually, separate grounds will be quite obvious to any experienced electronics technician or hobbyist, especially if a schematic of the circuitry is available.

Once the ground clip is securely attached, the signal tracer is turned on. Its probe tip can be touched to the input of any subcircuit in the tested device. If a signal is present, it will be heard through the signal tracer's built-in speaker.

With a signal injector, we started at the system's output and worked our way backwards through the various subcircuits. A signal tracer is normally used in just the opposite way. Start by checking the signal at the amplifier's (or other equipment's) input terminal. If there is no signal, there is no point in looking for a signal in later stages of the circuit.

Next, test the output of the first stage. If the signal is still heard from the signal tracer's speaker, that stage is fine. The problem must be in a later stage.

When the output of a stage is tested and no signal is heard from the signal tracer's speaker (or the signal is excessively distorted, the wrong amplitude, or whatever), you know you are at the output of the defective stage. Once again, the next step is to perform component-level tests on the identified problem stage using a multimeter or other test equipment.

Signal injectors and signal tracers are simple devices, and are therefore fairly inexpensive. It is easy enough for almost any electronics hobbyist or technician to whip up a simple homebrew signal injector or signal tracer. Basically, a signal injector is just an oscillator or simple signal generator mounted on a probe. A signal tracer is really nothing more than an amplifier and small speaker attached to a probe.

While these devices are very simple, and even a bit crude,

they can be very useful on the electronics workbench. They can quickly track down a troublesome stage in almost any multistage electronic circuit or system using audio signals. Other test methods can be used, but they tend to be more time-consuming.

9

Semiconductor testers

IN THE EARLY DAYS OF ELECTRONICS, ACTIVE CIRCUITS WERE BUILT around vacuum tubes. These were fairly hefty devices that worked with relatively large-voltage signals. Because of their bulkiness, cost, and high heat dissipation, few practical circuits contained large numbers of vacuum tubes. Tubes could be more or less tested in circuit by measuring the input and output voltages. It was also usually possible to visually check if the filament was glowing. One of the most common tube faults was a burned out filament. If the filament was burned out, current would not flow through it.

Tube testers were not uncommon. These fairly large devices had multiple tube sockets to accommodate various tube sizes. They had a complicated switching arrangement to apply the correct input voltages to the tube under test and indicate if its output voltages were in the appropriate range. Before actually testing a vacuum tube, the user had to first look up the tube's type number in a long chart to find out what switch positions to use and, sometimes, what the output readings should look like.

Besides being physically large, tube testers were very expensive. An independent electronics technician probably couldn't afford more than a very stripped down, semiportable model. Virtually all electronics hobbyists simply did without this piece of test equipment.

Fortunately, just about every store that sold vacuum tubes had a tube tester on the premises. Their customers brought in all the tubes out of a piece of equipment they were having problems with and tested them in the store. Hopefully, they'd made up an adequate diagram so they could put all the tubes back into the right sockets when they reassembled the equipment. Vacuum tubes were pretty simple on the technological level, but on the practical level, they were generally a pain in the neck.

Vacuum tubes are a relatively rare item in modern electronic circuits, except for CRTs which are used in television sets and oscilloscopes (see chapter 4). Today virtually all active circuits are solid state. This means that semiconductors are used as the active components.

Most substances are either conductors or insulators. A conductor passes electricity well; that is, it has a very low resistance. An insulator, on the other hand, passes electricity very poorly. Essentially, an insulator blocks the flow of electrical current; that is, it has a very high resistance.

A semiconductor, as the name suggests, is an in-between sort of substance. It conducts electricity much better than an insulator, but not nearly as well as a conductor. It has a moderate resistance. In its natural state, a semiconductor isn't really good for very much, except maybe making some overpriced resistors. Semiconductors are normally in crystalline form.

For use in electronic components, a semiconductor crystal is doped. This means an impurity is added to the semiconductor, in the form of a small amount of some other element. Only certain elements are used, ones which are automatically close to the semiconductor itself.

Some impurities give the crystal an excess of electrons, making it an N-type semiconductor. If a different impurity is used, the crystal will have a shortage of electrons (or a surplus of holes), making it a P-type semiconductor.

Again, N- and P-type semiconductors are no big thrill on their own. They don't really do anything special. But when they are put together, they can be highly useful. When a slab of N-type semiconductor is affixed to a slab of P-type semiconductor, the result is a PN junction, or a semiconductor diode. A bipolar transistor has two PN junctions. Other semiconductor devices have varying numbers of PN junctions and leads arranged in differing ways for different purposes.

A semiconductor, being in crystal form, is quite delicate. It can usually handle only fairly low voltages and currents. A semiconductor component can be easily damaged. Many modern semiconductor devices are much more durable than their earlier counterparts, but they are still relatively delicate. Obviously, this suggests that semiconductor components will be damaged or go bad from time to time. (But not nearly as often as vacuum tubes, which literally wore themselves out with normal use.)

Except for a few very simple circuits, most electronic devices use several transistors, diodes, and other semiconductor components. When something goes wrong, you need to know which device (if any) is bad, so you can replace it. Logical troubleshooting techniques can narrow down the list of possible culprits somewhat, but usually there will be several possibilities.

Electronics hobbyists often buy grab bags of surplus transistors or other components. Many of these devices will be good and usable, but almost any grab bag includes a certain number of "duds," which is why grab bags are such a bargain. If a dud is wired into an electronic circuit, it won't work. Often some of the items in a grab bag are not marked, so the hobbyist has no direct way of knowing the operating parameters of the device. Clearly, almost any electronics technician or hobbyist is going to need to test semiconductor components from time to time.

Testing semiconductors with a multimeter

Back in chapter 3 we discussed how a multimeter can be used to perform simple yes/no tests on semiconductor components, such as diodes and bipolar transistors. We will briefly review those principles here.

To test PN junctions with a multimeter, the ohmmeter section is used. It is possible to make these semiconductor resistance tests with the tested component wired into a circuit, but you will almost always get more reliable results if you remove the component from the circuit before testing it. Any parallel resistances in the circuitry could throw off the readings considerably, possibly making your results confusing or even totally meaningless.

As with all ohmmeter tests, no external power should be applied to the semiconductor component being tested. To prevent possible damage to some low-power devices, it is strongly advisable to use an ohmmeter with a very low-voltage battery—preferably 1.5 V, instead of a 9-V transistor battery. As a rule, make your semiconductor resistance tests with the multimeter set on its highest resistance range. The higher internal meter resistance on this range will cause more of the test voltage to be dropped internally, limiting the current flow through the component under test. Obviously, you don't want to risk damaging or destroying the component you are trying to test.

The idea behind these resistance tests is that any PN semiconductor junction will exhibit a fairly low resistance when forward biased, but a very high resistance when reverse biased. To test a semiconductor diode, attach the multimeter's red lead to the anode and the black lead to the cathode. This will forward bias the component. The multimeter should indicate a fairly low resistance—typically under 1,000 ohms. There will be considerable variation in the actual forward-biased resistance measured for different types of diodes.

Now, reverse the polarity of the diode. Connect the multimeter's red test lead to the cathode and the black test lead to the anode. Now the diode is reverse biased and the multimeter should give a very high resistance reading. The reverse-biased resistance reading should be considerably higher than the forward-biased resistance reading. With most diodes, the difference will be a factor of 10 or more.

For the most reliable tests, you should compare the resistance readings from your tests with those for a diode of the same type that is known to be good. As a general rule, however, if the measured resistance is significantly lower when the diode is forward biased than when it is reverse biased, the component is probably OK, although some of its other operating parameters may be off. This is more likely to be a problem with a transistor than with a simple diode.

This simple resistance test procedure can also be used to quickly determine the correct polarity for an unmarked diode. When you get the lower resistance reading, you know that the multimeter's red test lead is connected to the anode and the black test lead is connected to the cathode.

A bipolar transistor has two PN junctions, and is, in a sense, just a pair of back-to-back diodes. The same resistance test can be used for these devices too. There are now three leads and two individual PN junctions to test and keep track of. Of course, both PN junctions must test out OK or the component is worthless.

There are two types of bipolar transistors: NPN and PNP. An NPN transistor has two slabs of N-type semiconductor and one slab of P-type semiconductor. A PNP transistor is just the opposite, there are two slabs of P-type semiconductor and one slab of

N-type semiconductor. The diagram for an NPN transistor is shown in Fig. 9-1. For a PNP transistor, the polarities are simply reversed, as illustrated in Fig. 9-2.

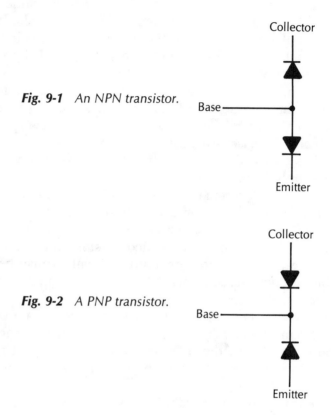

Fig. 9-1 *An NPN transistor.*

Fig. 9-2 *A PNP transistor.*

Each of the PN junctions in a bipolar transistor can be tested as if it was an independent diode. This way, the technician only needs to concern himself with two of the transistor's three leads at a time.

For an NPN transistor, you should get a low resistance reading when the black test lead is connected to the base of the transistor and the red test lead is touched to the transistor's emitter. Reversing the polarity of the leads (red to base and black to emitter) should reverse bias the PN junction, resulting in a very high resistance reading.

For a PNP transistor, these readings should be reversed. You should get a high resistance reading when the base is negative with respect to the emitter, and a low resistance reading when the base is positive with respect to the emitter.

The other PN junction in a bipolar transistor is between the base and the collector. Test this the same way you tested the base/collector junction. For an NPN transistor, you should again get a low resistance reading when the black test lead is connected to the base of the transistor and the red test lead is touched to the transistor's collector. Reversing the polarity of the leads (red to base and black to collector) should reverse bias the PN junction, resulting in a very high resistance reading.

Of course, these resistance reading will be reversed for a PNP transistor. There should be a high resistance reading when the base is negative with respect to the collector, and a low resistance reading when the base is positive with respect to the emitter. In each of these tests, the differences between the two resistance readings should be quite large.

It is important to remember that testing a diode or bipolar transistor with an ohmmeter using these procedures is just a crude yes/no check. This test procedure tells you nothing about the operating parameters of the semiconductor component being tested. It is either functional or nonfunctional. It may be functional, but its characteristics may be so far off spec that it may not operate properly in certain circuits.

Another serious limitation to testing semiconductor components with a multimeter is that not all semiconductor devices can be tested using this method. For example, you will not get any meaningful results if you test an FET using the ohmmeter method.

While this multimeter technique is often useful and convenient, serious electronics work very often requires more sophisticated testing of semiconductors. Several different types of specialized test equipment have been designed for just this purpose.

Transistor parameters

Obviously, before we can test any specific parameters of a transistor, we need to understand what those parameters are. To this end, we will briefly review the basic specifications for a transistor. Some parameters for a transistor are of importance to the circuit designer, but will rarely (if ever) need to be tested on the electronics workbench. These "fixed" specs include the transistor's internal impedances and the maximum amount of power it can safely dissipate.

Since a transistor is primarily a current amplification device, the most important parameter of a transistor is probably its current gain. The current gain of a transistor is defined by two inter-related specifications. These are alpha (α) or beta (β).

Alpha is defined as the current gain in the emitter and the collector. That is, for any change in the emitter current (with the supply voltage held constant), the collector current will change with a fixed relationship to the emitter. The basic equation for determining the alpha of a transistor is

$$\alpha = \Delta I_c / \Delta I_e$$

The triangular symbol in this equation is read as delta. It is used to identify a changing rather than a static value. In other words, ac signals are being assumed here. The dc form of this equation omits the delta symbols:

$$\alpha = I_c / I_e$$

In both of these formulas, I_c is the collector current and I_e is the emitter current.

For a typical bipolar transistor, a 2.6-mA (0.0026-A) change in the emitter current might result in a 2.4-mA (0.0024-A) change in the collector current. Notice that the collector current changes less than the emitter current. This is because there is always a negative gain from the collector to the emitter in a bipolar transistor. Only about 95% of the emitter current gets through to the collector.

For our example transistor, alpha works out to

$$\alpha = \Delta I_c / \Delta I_e$$
$$= 2.4/2.6$$
$$= 0.92 \text{ (approximately)}$$

Alpha will always be less than unity (one).

A small change in the base current, however, results in a large change in the collector current. Only 5% of the total current through a transistor flows through the base lead, while the remaining 95% flows through the collector.

For our sample transistor, the same 2.4-mA (0.0024-A) current change at the collector can be achieved with a mere 0.2-mA (0.0002-A) current change in the base circuit. The ratio between the base current and the collector current is the beta of the transistor. The formula for beta is

$$\beta = \Delta I_c / I_b$$

Notice that the beta formula is almost identical to the alpha formula, except the base current (I_b) is used instead of the emitter current (I_e).

The beta for our sample transistor is

$$\beta = \Delta I_c / \Delta I_b$$
$$= 2.4/0.2$$
$$= 12$$

The beta value is always greater than unity (one).

The alpha and beta values for any given transistor are closely interrelated. If you know one, you can calculate the other. For example, if you know the beta value and need to determine the alpha value, you can use the formula

$$\alpha = \beta/(1 + \beta)$$

Similarly, if you know the alpha value and need to find the beta value, you can use the equation

$$\beta = \alpha/(1 - \alpha)$$

Alpha and beta always increase together. If one is increased, the other is proportionately increased. By the same token, if one is decreased, the other is also proportionately decreased.

Inevitably, there will be some current leakage flowing backwards through the reverse-biased base-collector junction. In a transistor's spec sheet, this leakage current is usually labeled I_{cbo}, or sometimes just I_{co}. It's value is typically very small.

Another important specification for transistors is usually labeled H_{fe}. This is the transistor's forward current ratio when used in a common-emitter configuration. A large signal and a short circuit are assumed in forming this specification.

V_{be} is the transistor's base-emitter voltage. BV^r is the breakdown reverse voltage. This is the maximum amount of reverse biasing the transistor can withstand without breaking down.

There are numerous other specifications for transistors, of course, but the ones covered here tend to be the most important and most widely used. These specifications are for bipolar transistors. Other types of transistors (UJTs, FETs, etc.) may have somewhat different operating parameters.

Transistor checkers

A number of transistor checkers are available to extend the electronics technician's or hobbyist's transistor testing capabilities beyond the simple resistance tests of a multimeter. A simple home-brew yes/no transistor checker circuit is shown in Fig. 9-3.

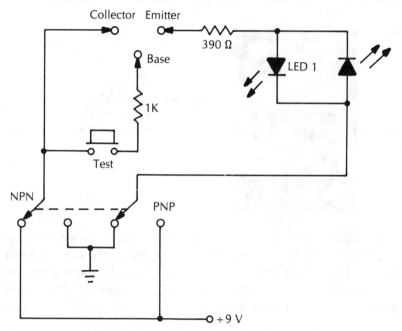

Fig. 9-3   *A simple transistor checker circuit.*

The three leads of the transistor to be tested are connected to the points indicated in the schematic diagram. This circuit is designed for out-of-circuit component testing. The DPDT (double pole, double throw) switch is used to set the voltage polarities in the circuit, so both NPN and PNP transistors can be tested with this device.

Essentially, this simple transistor checker circuit is just a more convenient variation on the multimeter/resistance test method discussed earlier. More advanced and sophisticated transistor checkers are also available, including a number of commercial models. A transistor checker of this type is lightweight and very portable. It is powered by a small internal battery. A fairly typical transistor checker from a commercial manufacturer is shown in Fig. 9-4. This unit can test diodes, bipolar transistors (low- and medium-power units), FETs, UJTs (unijunction transistors), and SCRs (silicon-controlled rectifiers). Some of the tests can be performed with the transistor in or out of the circuit. These include simple good/bad tests (much like those of a multimeter), lead identification, and identification of polarity (NPN or PNP types).

Fig. 9-4 *A typical commercial transistor checker.*

Several important dc parameters can also be tested with this unit, but these tests must be performed with the transistor removed from the circuit. This instruments dc parameter measurements include I_{ceo} (leakage current), V_{be}, and H_{fe}. These specifications were identified in the preceding section of this chapter.

Curve tracers

A more sophisticated type of transistor testing equipment is the curve tracer. A typical device of this type is shown in Fig. 9-5. A curve tracer is designed to be used with an oscilloscope. The displayed pattern gives detailed information about many transistor parameters, including beta gain, cutoff, leakage, and output admittance.

A number of sockets are provided to accommodate most types of semiconductor devices. Separate tests leads may be used with the occasional ''oddball'' component that won't fit into any of the available sockets.

This type of instrument is designed for use in a fixed location; that is, it is a workbench instrument not a portable, field-use device. An ac power source is required by the curve tracer. This is not unreasonable, since it must be used with an oscillo-

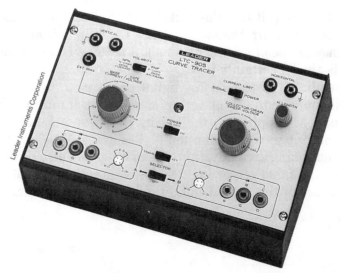

Fig. 9-5 *A curve tracer is a more elaborate tool for testing semiconductors.*

scope, and there are still very few truly portable, battery operated oscilloscopes available.

The curves are created by applying a sweep test signal to the transistor being tested. The concept of sweep test signals was explained in chapter 7. Most tests with a curve tracer can be performed either in circuit or out of circuit, although sometimes external circuitry may throw off some of the test results, giving false or misleading readings. It is usually best to make component-level tests out of circuit whenever practical.

Certainly, if an expensive transistor tests bad in circuit, its worthwhile to test it again once you've removed it from the circuit. If it tests bad in circuit, but looks OK out of circuit, there is probably something else in the circuitry that is confusing the test results. Believe the out-of-circuit measurements.

IC testing

More and more electronic circuits these days use ICs (integrated circuits). Unfortunately, these devices are difficult to design a generalized tester for. This is because there are so many different types of ICs. Specialized IC testers can be easily built. For example, I use a lot of op amps (operational amplifiers), so I've rigged up a simple yes/no op amp tester. It is nothing more than a simple oscillator circuit built around an op amp, with a small built-in speaker. Only a socket is wired into the circuit. To test an op amp IC, I just pop it into the socket and apply power to the circuit. If a tone is heard from the speaker, the chip is functional (it may or may not be operating on spec). If no tone is heard, the op amp IC is almost certainly bad.

Generalized IC testers for digital gates are now available. Each pin connection can be set up as either an input or output. Test signals are applied to the inputs in various combinations and the output pins are monitored. Besides testing whether a gate is functioning correctly, this type of tester can also be used to determine the function, or logic table, of an unknown gate. Just make a chart of the output condition for each combination of inputs.

10

Digital test equipment

UP UNTIL THE MID-1970s, VIRTUALLY ALL ELECTRONICS CIRCUITS were analog. Since that time, an increasing number of electronic devices have been designed around digital circuitry.

In some respects, analog and digital circuits aren't that dissimilar. After all, a voltage is a voltage. All ac signals in a digital circuit must be in the form of rectangular waves or pulses, while analog circuitry permits a wider variety of waveshapes.

There are many extremely important differences between analog circuits and digital circuits, particularly on the operational level. Standard analog test equipment, such as multimeters and oscilloscopes, are useful when working with digital circuits, but for detailed testing in the digital realm, specialized test equipment is needed.

Logic probes

The basic digital test device is the logic probe. This is an instrument that indicates the logic state at a given point in a digital circuit. Digital signals are often called logic signals. There are just two possible logic states (signal levels) for any single digital test point—logic 0 (a low voltage) and logic 1 (a high voltage). Intermediate values are not allowed.

An extremely simple, but functional, logic probe can be made from an LED and a current-dropping resistor, as illustrated in Fig. 10-1. The resistor prevents the LED from drawing too much current and self-destructing.

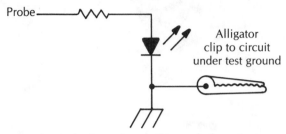

Fig. 10-1 *A very simple logic probe can be made from just two components.*

In use the ground clip is connected to a convenient ground point in the digital circuit to be tested. The tip of the test probe is then touched to various inputs and outputs in the circuit. If the monitored connection is carrying a logic 1, the LED will light up. If there is a logic 0 at the test point, the LED will remain dark. What could be simpler than that?

A simple logic probe like this can be built by an electronics hobbyist or technician in less than 10 minutes, at a cost of well under a dollar. Unfortunately, this super-simple logic probe may actually be a little too simple to be truly useful as a piece of test equipment. It has several serious limitations.

First the logic 0 condition is not unambiguously indicated by this device. If the LED remains dark when the probe is touched to a test point, there may be a logic 0 signal there. But it is possible that due to some circuit defect there is no signal at that point at all. Perhaps the IC being tested is not getting power. It is even possible that the probe is not making a good electrical contact with a test point that is actually carrying a logic 1 signal.

Another problem is that when the LED lights up, you still don't know for sure that you have a logic 1 signal. The signal at the test point may be a rapid train of pulses. The LED is actually blinking on and off at too fast a rate for the human eye to see the individual blinks. Depending on the actual frequency of the pulse signal, the LED may or may not appear to be glowing a little dimmer than normal.

Another problem with this simple logic probe is that it is easy to miss brief, one-shot pulses which can come and go in a millisecond (0.001 second) or less. If you blink, you could miss it. If the pulse duration is extremely brief, the LED flash may be too quick for the human eye to see even under the best of conditions.

A simple passive logic probe circuit, like the one shown in Fig. 10-1, can present an excessive load to some test circuits, resulting in erroneous operation and, therefore, incorrect readings. Practical logic probes include additional circuitry to take care of these problems. However, all digital logic probes are ultimately based on the simple concept illustrated in the circuit of Fig. 10-1.

An improved logic probe has active circuitry to avoid loading problems. In most cases, inverters are used. The output of an inverter is always at the opposite state from its input. That is, if the input is a logic 1, the output will be a logic 0, and if the input is a logic 0, the output will be a logic 1. A second inverter stage will reinvert the signal to its original input state, as illustrated in Fig. 10-2.

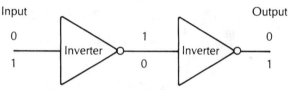

Fig. 10-2   *A pair of back-to-back inverters buffer the signal, but the final output state matches the input state.*

Practical logic probes are almost always equipped with at least two LED indicators. One LED lights up when a logic 1 signal is being monitored. The other LED is lit only when the probe tip is in contact with a logic 0 signal.

If both LEDs are lit, the monitored signal must be a pulse train with a frequency of at least 10 to 20 Hz (and probably considerably higher). The two LEDs are actually alternately blinking on and off with each individual pulse, but the human eye cannot see the individual flashes due to a phenomena known as the persistence of vision.

A two-LED logic probe eliminates much of the ambiguity that is inevitable with a single-LED unit. Four possible signal conditions are clearly and unambiguously indicated:

- Neither LED is lit means no signal;
- LED #1 is lit, LED #2 is dark means logic 1;
- LED #2 is lit, LED #1 is dark means logic 0; or
- Both LEDs are lit means pulses.

Adding the second LED to a logic probe does not require a

substantial increase in circuitry. The signal for the second LED indicator can be derived with a simple inverter stage.

A simple, but improved, two-LED logic probe circuit of the type described here is illustrated in Fig. 10-3. Notice that this circuit consists of just five components. The two inverter stages are both contained within a single IC chip. Inverter ICs typically contain six independent (except for the power supply connections) inverters. The inputs of the four unused inverter stages should be grounded to prevent possible stability problems in the IC.

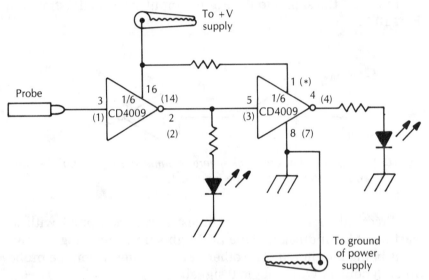

Fig. 10-3 *A two-LED logic probe gives less ambiguous results.*

CMOS inverter chips are used in most modern logic probe circuits, because they tend to be more versatile and durable than their TTL (transistor-transistor logic) counterparts. A TTL IC is very fussy about its supply voltage, and can easily be damaged by an incorrect voltage.

The actual high and low voltage levels are slightly different for CMOS and TTL circuits. It may be necessary to include a pull-up resistor to use this CMOS logic probe in a TTL circuit. This is illustrated in Fig. 10-4.

A two-LED logic probe neatly sidesteps most of the problems of the super-simple logic probe, but there is one problem still remaining. It is all too easy to miss brief, one-shot pulses which can come and go in a millisecond (thousandth of a second) or less. Such short isolated pulses are quite common in many prac-

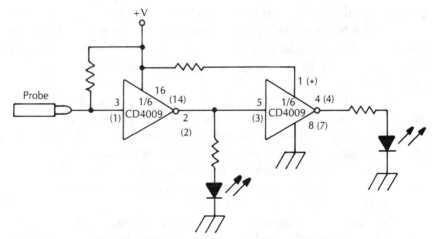

Fig. 10-4 *A CMOS logic probe can be easily modified with a pull-up resis-tor to test TTL gates.*

tical digital circuits. If you blink, you could miss the entire pulse. If the pulse duration is extremely brief, the LED flash may be too quick for the human eye to see even under the best conditions.

The solution to this problem is to add another circuit to the logic probe, as shown in Fig. 10-5. This added circuitry is called a pulse stretcher, and the name clearly describes its purpose.

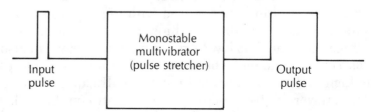

Fig. 10-5 *A pulse stretcher helps catch brief, one-shot pulses.*

Brief pulses are "stretched out," causing the LED to stay lit for awhile after the pulse is over. In a way, this is a little like the concept of a storage oscilloscope (as discussed in chapter 4).

A pulse stretcher circuit is actually pretty simple. It is nothing more than a monostable multivibrator. A monostable multivibrator, of course, has just one stable state. When it is triggered, its output goes to the opposite (unstable) state for a fixed period of time, which is determined by resistance and capacitance values in the monostable multivibrator circuit. The length of the trigger pulse is irrelevant. The output pulse will always have the same length. In a logic probe's pulse stretcher, the trigger pulse is the monitored pulse picked up at the probe's tip. The output (the stretched pulse) from the monostable multivibrator is used to light the LED.

The pulse stretcher circuit will always be switchable. In ordinary operation, the pulse stretcher will get in the way of clear readings, so it must be bypassed. A similar feature to the pulse stretcher that is included on many commercial logic probes is a latch. When the latch circuitry is activated, once the LED is lit, it will stay lit until the user pushes a reset button (or power is interrupted, of course.)

An extremely simple logic probe consisting of just an LED and a resistor can effectively "steal" its operating power from the test point in the circuit being monitored. More sophisticated logic probes, however, include one or more ICs in their circuitry, and they require a definite power source. Most logic probes use a built-in battery, but some steal power from the circuit being tested. In addition to the ground clip, there is a supply voltage clip, which is attached to the test circuit's $V+$ bus.

A logic probe is simple, but it is the most versatile and useful type of purely digital test equipment. The average electronics hobbyist and most technicians can get by with the logic probe as their only digital test device. In a sense, a logic probe is more or less the digital circuit's equivalent of the analog circuit's multimeter.

Of course, multimeters are used with digital circuits too, to test supply voltages and the actual logic levels—how much voltage is high, how much is low? An analog multimeter can also be used as a crude logic probe because it can indicate if the test signal is high or low. A pulse train signal will cause the meter's pointer to waver or give a reading midway between the high and low voltages. This will depend on the actual frequency of the pulses being monitored.

Logic clips

Logic clips are becoming increasingly popular among electronics technicians, and especially hobbyists working with digital circuits. Basically, a logic clip is a compact combination of multiple logic probes that can indicate the logic state at each of the pins on a digital IC.

An ordinary logic probe lets you monitor just one point in a digital circuit at a time. Often this is fine, but sometimes it can be a problem. For example, suppose you need to simultaneously monitor an input signal and the resulting output signal. The situation is analogous to what led to the development of the dual-trace oscilloscope (see chapter 4).

A logic clip is connected to the pins and body of an IC with a special clamp that resembles an oversized clothes pin. This clamp, called a Glomper clip, makes simultaneous electrical contact with all of the pins on a single DIP IC chip.

Usually a 16-pin Glomper clip is used for the greatest versatility. If an 8-pin or a 14-pin chip is to be monitored, the extra unused connections are simply allowed to hang unconnected over the end of the IC body. This works fine, except in very tightly packed digital circuits, where there simply isn't room to insert the logic clip.

Glomper clips can only be used with ICs housed in DIP packages. Round can ICs cannot be tested with a logic clip. Fortunately, digital gate ICs are almost always manufactured in DIP housings.

Because of space considerations, the signal state of each pin in a logic clip is indicated by a single LED, with the resulting ambiguity described in the preceding section. If you need more detail about one of the signals, use a more sophisticated logic probe or an oscilloscope.

A regular logic probe can fit into many places and get to some connections where a Glomper clip won't fit. But the logic clip offers the advantage of indicating (even with some ambiguity) the logic state at each pin of a complete IC. It's a trade-off, and the decision will ultimately depend on the specific requirements of the actual testing situation.

Each pin in a logic clip drives its own individual logic probe circuit. A typical circuit used in a logic clip is shown in Fig. 10-6. All of the components shown here are repeated for each pin connection; however, in some logic clips, resistor R1 may be used just once.

Logic pulser

In analog servicing, a signal generator (see chapter 7) or a signal injector (see chapter 8) is often used to help find a defective circuit stage. A signal tracer might also be used. A logic probe is

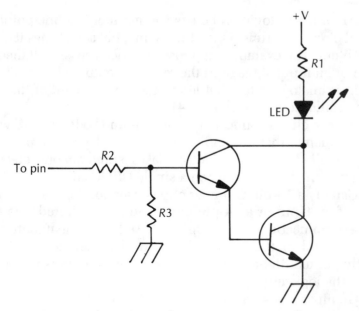

Fig. 10-6 *Each pin in a logic clip uses a circuit something like this.*

essentially the digital equivalent of a signal tracer. The digital equivalent of a signal injector is called a logic pulser.

A signal injector, as you should recall from chapter 8, is an instrument that can feed a known signal into any desired point in the circuit under test. Since the signal's characteristics are known, and under the control of the technician (or hobbyist), tracing the operations of the various circuit stages is made much easier than might otherwise be possible. This same basic technique can also be useful in servicing digital electronic circuits.

As its name suggests, a logic pulser is a circuit that emits logic pulses through a probe tip. A simple square-wave oscillator can generate a continuous string of pulses at a desired frequency. In some cases, it will be more useful to monitor the results of a single isolated pulse. To accomplish this, most logic pulsers also include a manual switch that can trigger a monostable multivibrator, producing a single pulse at the desired logic levels and with the desired duration. Usually, a control for manually adjusting the timing period of the monostable multivibrator is also included. Many commercially manufactured logic pulsers include built-in logic probes to monitor their own signals.

Logic analyzer

Digital test equipment is either very simple and inexpensive or very sophisticated and costly, with very little middle ground. Most electronics hobbyists and technicians with any experience can easily build and even design their own logic probes, logic clips, or logic pulsers. Commercially, manufactured models of these devices are becoming increasingly available, and they are usually quite inexpensive, by test equipment standards. But the serious technician, or the advanced digital electronics hobbyists, may need more sophistication and power.

One specialized tool that will tell you almost everything you might want to know about the inner workings of a digital circuit is the logic analyzer. This device is basically a specialized digital oscilloscope (see chapter 4). Logic analyzers always offer multiple simultaneous displays. Eight to sixteen simultaneous traces are not uncommon. Since all digital circuits take on just two voltage levels (high or low), the CRT does not need to directly display as much waveform detail. All that matters is the beginning and ending points of each pulse. Everything in between can be digitally re-created. Most logic analyzers also display certain alphanumeric data about the test signals. The multitrace display of a logic analyzer provides detailed and unambiguous information on such things as timing interrelationships between signals, input and output patterns, pulse lengths, and signal frequencies.

A logic analyzer is a very expensive piece of test equipment, and the price is not likely to come down substantially any time in the foreseeable future. It's not a must-have item for every electronics workbench, even if most of your work is done on digital circuitry. I'd say, if you can get by without this instrument, don't bother shopping for one. On the other hand, if someone offers you one as a gift or at a ridiculously low price, by all means take it. A logic analyzer is an incredibly powerful and versatile piece of test equipment, but it is scarcely indispensable to the average electronics hobbyist or technician.

Digital IC testers

While there are many different types of digital ICs, digital gates all function more or less the same, and generalized IC testers for this type of component are now available. The IC to be tested is plugged into a socket or connected (in circuit) with a Glomper clip. Each pin connection can be set up as either an input or output. Test signals are applied to the inputs in various combinations and the output pins are monitored.

Besides testing whether a gate is functioning correctly, this type of tester can also be used to determine the function, or logic table, of an unknown gate. Just make a chart of the output condition for each combination of inputs.

For example, let's say that a certain output responds to two inputs in the following pattern:

Inputs	Output
A B	
0 0	1
0 1	1
1 0	1
1 1	0

From this, we know the gate in question is a two-input NAND (not AND) gate.

A digital IC tester of this type can usually be set up to work with various popular logic families, such as TTL and CMOS. Different logic families have differing supply voltage and signal level requirements. Some advanced digital IC testers can also test timing functions and flip-flops. This makes the instrument suitable for testing digital chips that are more sophisticated than simple gates.

The computer
on the workbench

MODERN ELECTRONICS DEFINITELY HAS A HEAVY EMPHASIS ON digital circuitry. As we've seen throughout this book, even test equipment for the measurement of analog parameters often is built around digital circuits, and this trend shows every indication of continuing into the foreseeable future.

Wherever digital circuits are used, can the computer be far behind? All digital signals are essentially alike—just a string of ones and zeros (high and low voltages). There is no reason why the ones and zeros produced within digital multimeters, digital oscilloscopes, digital frequency counters, or whatever, can't be used as input data for a computer.

It is also entirely possible, and not particularly difficult, to use the computer's output data to control digitally based test equipment. The result is ATE (automated test equipment).

A/D converters

Before we can truly understand the place of the computer on the modern electronics workbench, we need a clear understanding of how analog signals are put into digital form. The process is called analog-to-digital conversion (or, more commonly, A/D conversion). Not surprisingly, a circuit that performs this function is called an A/D converter.

Digital electronics is based on the binary numbering system. That means each digit can take on either of two possible values:

zero or one. Most people are more familiar and much more comfortable with the decimal numbering system, which has ten available values: 0, 1, 2, 3, 4, 5, 6, 7, 8, and 9. The base of the binary
numbering system is two, and the base of the decimal numbering
system is ten.

Suppose we need to express a numerical value that is more
than the largest available digit (9 in the decimal system)? We start
another column to the left. Each new column has a value that is
raised by an additional power of the base. As an example, consider this multidigit decimal number: 41,754. We can break
down the value of this number as follows:

$$41{,}754 = (4 \times 10^4) + (1 \times 10^3) + (7 \times 10^2) + (5 \times 10^1)$$
$$+ (4 \times 10^0)$$
$$= (4 \times 10 \times 10 \times 10 \times 10) + (1 \times 10 \times 10 \times 10) +$$
$$(7 \times 10 \times 10) + (5 \times 10) + 4 \times 1)$$
$$= (4 \times 10{,}000) + (1 \times 1{,}000) + (7 \times 100) + (5 \times 10)$$
$$+ (4 \times 1)$$

Notice that any number raised to a power of zero (such as 10^0) has
a value of 1.

The binary numbering system works in exactly the same way,
except that the highest digit value for each column is one. This
means that when the value goes to two, or higher, a new column
must be added to the left. For example, consider this binary number: 1101 1011. (Binary numbers are usually broken up into
groups of four (or occasionally three) digits when they're written
down. This convention just makes the numbers a little easier to
read.)

$$1101\ 1011 = (1 \times 2^7) + (1 \times 2^6) + (0 \times 2^5) + (1 \times 2^2)$$
$$+ (1 \times 2^3) + (0 \times 2^2) + (1 \times 2^1) + (1 \times 2^0)$$
$$= (1 \times 2 \times 2 \times 2 \times 2 \times 2 \times 2 \times 2) + (1 \times 2 \times 2$$
$$\times 2 \times 2 \times 2 \times 2) + (0 \times 2 \times 2 \times 2 \times 2 \times 2) +$$
$$(1 \times 2 \times 2 \times 2 \times 2) + (1 \times 2 \times 2 \times 2) + (0 \times 2$$
$$\times 2) + (1 \times 2) + (1 \times 1)$$
$$= (1 \times 128) + (1 \times 64) + (0 \times 32) + (1 \times 16)$$
$$+ (1 \times 8) + (0 \times 4) + (1 \times 2) + (1 \times 1)$$
$$= 128 + 64 + 0 + 16 + 8 + 0 + 2 + 1$$
$$= 219\ \text{(decimal)}$$

If you are one of the many people who don't particularly like
doing math, don't worry about it. In practical work with digital

electronic circuits, you will rarely, if ever, actually have to convert between binary and decimal numbers. Modern digital devices do this work for you.

For instance, this is what happens in the common pocket calculator. The user punches in the numerical values in decimal form. The calculator's switching circuitry converts the input into binary form for processing (the calculations), then converts the results back into decimal form for the display.

The binary numbering system is not used in digital electronics simply out of any perversity of the technicians and circuit designers. The binary numbering system is actually easier for electrical circuits to cope with, because only two discrete and unambiguous voltage values are required—high and low (one and zero). No intermediate voltages are needed.

A digital circuit using the decimal system would require 10 separate and unmistakable voltage levels for each digit. Obviously, this would be awkward and inconvenient, and ultimately, extremely expensive.

A number is a number. It can represent anything we want it to represent. Let's say we are measuring an analog voltage. How much voltage is there at such-and-such a point in a circuit? Let's say it's 5 V. We've used a decimal digital value to express the analog voltage. In binary form, this same voltage would be represented as

$$0101 = (0 \times 2^3) + (1 \times 2^2) + (0 \times 2^1) + (1 \times 2^0)$$
$$= (0 \times 8) + (1 \times 4) + (0 \times 2) + (1 \times 1)$$
$$= 0 + 4 + 0 + 1$$
$$= 5 \text{ (decimal)}$$

As you can see, we really aren't doing anything fundamentally different when we move from the decimal numbering system to the binary numbering system. We're just writing down the numerical values in a different format.

When we are dealing with an ac analog signal, such as a sine wave, the situation becomes just slightly more complex. In this case, we repeatedly sample the instantaneous voltage at different points in the waveform, as illustrated in Fig. 11-1. This gives us a string of numbers which can be used to reconstruct the original analog waveform, as illustrated in Fig. 11-2. Clearly, the more samples per cycle there are, the better the digital representation and ultimate reconstruction of the analog waveform will be.

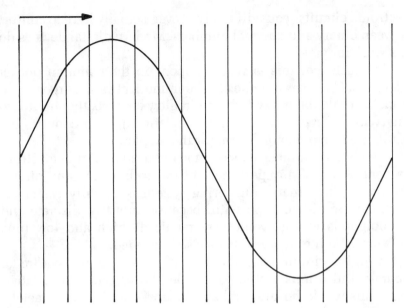

Fig. 11-1 *An A/D converter samples an analog waveform several times per cycle.*

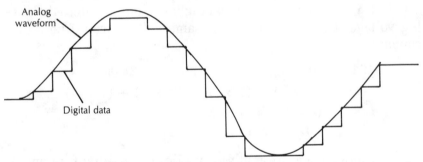

Fig. 11-2 *The original analog waveform can be reconstructed from the digital samples.*

While the data is in digital form, it can be stored or manipulated in almost any desired way. For example, if each sample value is multiplied by a fixed value, the reconstructed waveform will be effectively amplified. The gain in this case will be equal to the fixed multiplication value.

Digital measurements of analog parameters almost always involve a great many samples per second. The sampling frequency will be at least several tens or hundreds of kilohertz (1 kHz =

1,000 Hz). Whenever possible, the sampling frequency will be in the megahertz range (1 MHz = 1,000 kHz = 1,000,000 Hz).

There are several different types of circuits used to perform A/D conversion. Most are fairly complex because of the inherent difficulties of the task. One popular method of A/D conversion is based on the integrator. Essentially, an integrator is an op amp circuit that creates a ramp voltage from the input voltage. A simple integrator circuit is illustrated in Fig. 11-3.

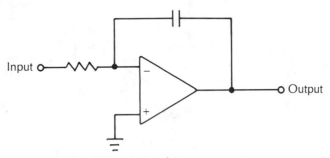

Fig. 11-3 *A simple integrator circuit.*

There are two common forms of A/D converter circuits using integrators. They are called single-slope converters and dual-slope converters. The dual-slope converter is sometimes called a double-slope converter. Figure 11-4 shows the block diagram for a typical single-slope A/D converter circuit. Note that it is made up of a number of simpler subcircuits, as summarized in Table 11-1.

A sample-and-hold circuit is one that samples the instantaneous value of an analog input signal whenever it is triggered. The sampled output is held at the subcircuit's output until it is retriggered. This stage gives the integrator a constant input volt-

Table 11-1   Subcircuits in a single-slope A/D converter.

Sample and hold
Integrator
Electronic switch
Voltage comparator
Reference voltage source
Gate
Clock
Gate generator (or timing coordinator)
Counter

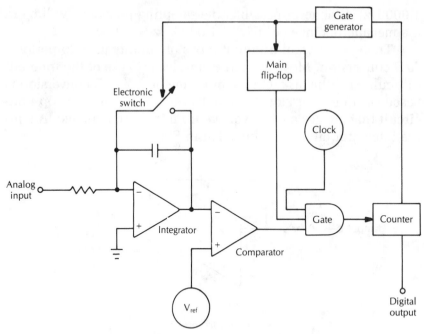

Fig. 11-4 *A block diagram for a typical single-slope A/D converter.*

age to work with for each conversion. In other words, the sample
voltage doesn't change until the last sampled value has been
processed.

The switch is used to clear the circuit to zero. When this
switch is closed, the capacitor is allowed to discharge. In a practical A/D converter, this is not a mechanical switch, but an automated electronic switching circuit controlled by the gate generator. The output of the integrator rises from zero in a linear
fashion at a rate determined by the sample input voltage.

The next stage after the integrator is the comparator. A comparator, logically enough, is a circuit that compares two analog
input voltages and issues an output to indicate which one is
higher. The output of the integrator is compared with a constant
reference voltage.

Meanwhile, the clock puts out a continuous stream of evenly
spaced pulses. As long as the output of the comparator is high
(i.e. the reference voltage is greater than the integrator's present
output voltage), the clock pulses can pass through the gate to the
counter. When the integrator's output voltage exceeds the reference voltage, the gate is closed, and no more clock pulses can get
through to the counter.

The counter simply counts how many clock periods (pulses) occur before the gate is closed. This produces a multidigit binary value that is proportional to the system's analog input voltage.

The single-slope A/D converter is relatively simple (as A/D converters go) and fairly inexpensive, but it doesn't always offer the best accuracy. The last digit will tend to bobble because partial clock pulses may be included in the timing period, thus confusing the counter circuitry. The same sort of problem can occur with frequency counters (this was discussed in chapter 6).

An improvement in accuracy and stability can be obtained by using a dual-slope A/D converter circuit. The block diagram for this type of circuit is shown in Fig. 11-5. As you can see, the dual-slope A/D converter is quite similar to the single-slope converter, incorporating many of the same subcircuits. The added "reference" stage is a precision voltage or current source, which is used as a comparison for the unknown analog input signal.

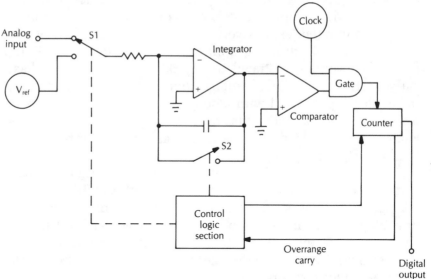

Fig. 11-5   *A block diagram for a dual-slope A/D converter.*

At the beginning of the conversion cycle, the input voltage is fed through the integrator and the number of clock pulses are counted, as in the single-slope A/D converter. But the clock pulses are not gated here. The counting continues until the counter exceeds its maximum count value and overflows. At this point, the output of integrator is proportional to the input signal.

Now, the control logic section will change the integrator's input to the reference, which has the opposite polarity as the original analog signal. Therefore, the new integration process will begin to discharge (rather than charge) the capacitor. This means the integrator's output ramp will slope downwards, rather than upwards. Because the reference has a precisely constant value, this discharge slope will have a constant rate. The steepness of the slope will be directly proportional to the analog input signal.

Because the counter has just overflowed before the discharge process began, the count is zero. The count will continue to increment during the downward integration slope until the integrator output voltage reaches zero (ground potential), cutting off the comparator/gate network. The count at this point will be directly proportional to the level of the analog input signal.

The dual-slope A/D converter is relatively immune to noise errors in the input signal and to clock frequency inaccuracies. However, this type of circuit is relatively slow (although it is still fast enough for most practical purposes). The chief disadvantages of the dual-slope A/D converter circuit are that it is fairly complex and rather expensive.

A completely different approach to A/D conversion is the parallel converter, illustrated in Fig. 11-6. This circuit is basically a series of paralleled voltage comparators, each comparing the analog input signal with a dc reference voltage. A precision resistor network is used to bias the individual comparator stages. Each comparator is biased one LSB (least significant bit) higher than its neighbor.

There are some serious limitations to the parallel A/D converter, especially in terms of the number of output bits. The number of comparator stages can rapidly result in an extremely unwieldy circuit. In addition, there is a practical limit to how small an LSB the comparators can reliably recognize. The smaller the LSB value, the greater the precision required of the voltage-divider resistors.

The chief advantage of the parallel A/D converter is speed. Conversion takes place almost instantly. Parallel A/D converters are often called flash converters for this very reason. Parallel converters tend to be popular among electronics hobbyists, because this type of circuit is easier to understand and build than single-slope or dual-slope converters.

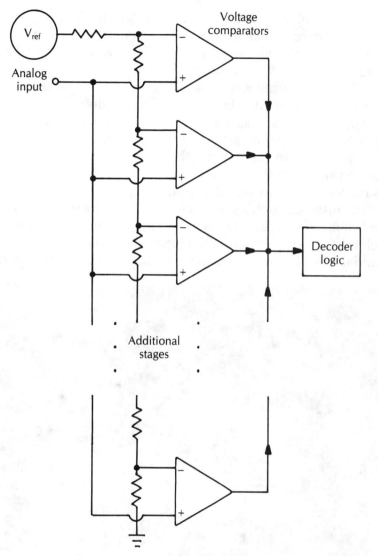

Fig. 11-6 *A parallel converter.*

ATE

With the astonishing growth of the computer industry in the last couple of decades, more and more technicians are turning to the advantages of ATE (automated test equipment). As the name suggests, what we are dealing with is test equipment that is programmable under computer control. In some cases, a dedicated built-in computer is included within the test equipment. In other cases, an external general purpose computer is used to control one or more pieces of test equipment. Some examples of ATE are illustrated in Figs. 11-7 through 11-12.

ATE offers several special advantages. All test measurements are in the form of digital data which can be indefinitely stored on a floppy disc, a hard disc, or any other digital storage media. The test results can then be called back for review at any later time. The computer can manipulate the data in any way desired. A common application of this feature would be to average a number of samples over an extended period of time.

For instance, in a system that is being continuously monitored, hourly and daily (24-hour) averages could be calculated. Such continuous monitoring is a big advantage of ATE systems. It would not be reasonable to expect a human operator to perform a

Fig. 11-7 A network protocol analyzer is used in circuit development.

ATE   233

Hewlett-Packard Company

Fig. 11-8 *A network analyzer combines precision network analysis with high-throughput device evaluation.*

series of tests every 5 minutes, 24 hours/day. A computer would not mind in the least. Sometimes it is necessary to continuously monitor a signal to see when or if it exceeds or drops below a specific level. This would be tedious beyond belief for a human operator, and mistakes would be likely. It would be all too easy for a human operator to miss a brief transient signal. A computer, on the other hand, never blinks, and can monitor any signal indefinitely without fatigue or any drop in accuracy over time. Also, the computer can be programmed to compare two or more test signals, either instantaneously or over an extended period of time. A graph of the signal data can be stored in memory or drawn out on a printer.

Under a computer's control, testing operations can be automated. In effect, the computer sets the controls on the test equip-

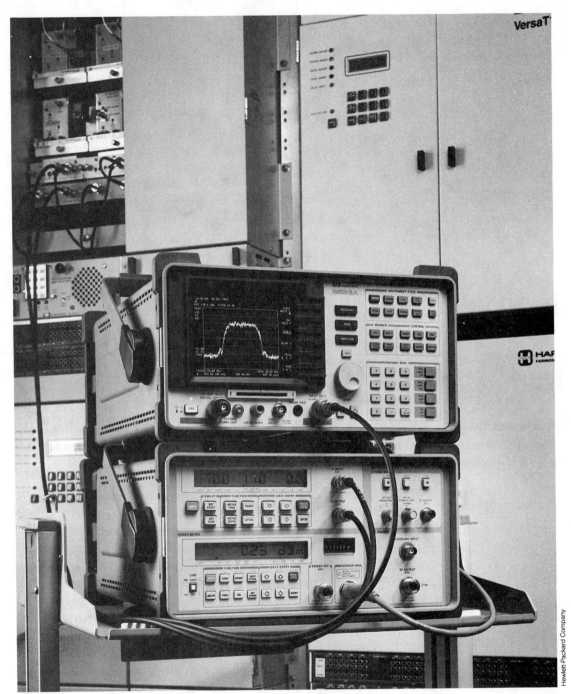

Fig. 11-9   *The HP 11758T digital-radio test system combines many test functions in two portable cases.*

Fig. 11-10 *The HP Industrial Touch terminal is designed to optimize application development.*

ment. This permits near-perfect repeatability of test settings, and can save quite a bit of time when a number of similar tests must be made in sequence.

As you can see, ATE offers some very powerful and exciting possibilities. Unfortunately, at the present time, true ATE tends to be extremely expensive, and is generally only feasible for technicians in large laboratories. Independent electronics technicians and hobbyists probably can't afford such equipment.

This situation is likely to change some in the near future. Electronics is one field where prices tend to come down rather quickly, while capabilities go up. There is certainly a demand for reasonably priced ATE. Several of the electronics hobbyist magazines have run construction articles on projects that utilize the

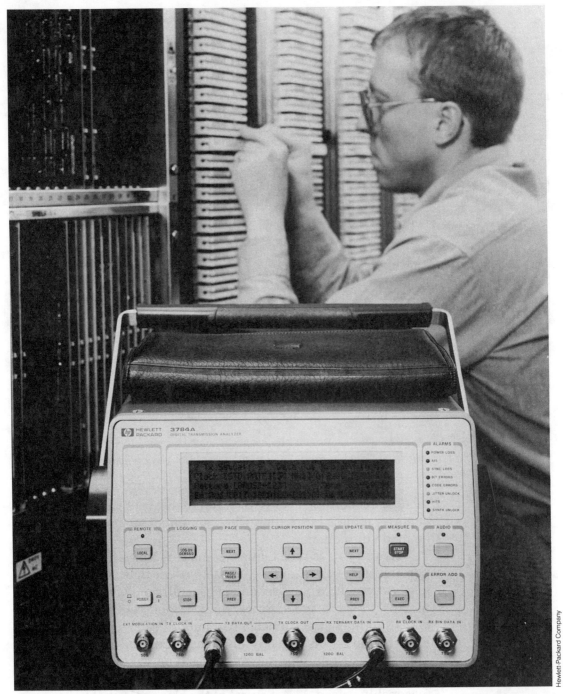

Fig. 11-11 *This digital transmission analyzer offers BER and jitter measurements for telecom and general purpose applications up to 50 Mbits/s.*

Fig. 11-12 *A high-speed computerized troubleshooting system.*

ATE concept. Almost all of these projects are more or less based on the A/D converter circuits discussed earlier in this chapter.

Because ATE is so new, there aren't any industry standards yet. But I think it's very likely that we'll soon see the day when ATE is the norm for all serious electronic work.

❖ 12

Electronics safety

WE WILL END THIS BOOK WITH A REVIEW OF SAFETY PRINCIPLES in electronics. This issue was addressed briefly in chapter 1, but it certainly bears repeating. We will go into a little more detail here.

Safety is a vital issue that is too often ignored, even by people who really should know better. Is it worth risking serious injury or even death to save a little money or a few seconds of your time? Once you get into the habit of good safety practices, you'll find they really don't take that much time at all, and they're the cheapest form of insurance there is. Stop accidents before they happen.

Fuses and circuit breakers

Make sure all of your equipment is properly protected by a fuse or circuit breaker. Never replace any fuse with one of a higher value. The fuse is blowing for some reason. Find out why and correct the problem; don't bypass the protection of the fuse. If you substitute a larger fuse, you may find that another component in the circuit (usually an expensive semiconductor) will blow to protect the fuse. Obviously this is a case of false economy, both in time (to replace the blown component) and money.

Occasionally a fuse will blow with no real circuit defect at all. This is usually due to a peak transient on the power line. The most efficient approach when a fuse blows is to unplug the equipment and replace the blown fuse with an identically rated unit. Plug the equipment into the line socket and turn it on. If everything works OK, don't worry about it. There is apparently no problem. The first fuse was probably the victim of a transient. It did its job—it prevented that transient from getting through to more expensive components in the circuit.

If the replacement fuse blows right away, or within a minute or so, there is definitely something wrong with your equipment. Disconnect the power and troubleshoot the circuit before attempting to use it again. If you can't find the problem, call a qualified technician. In most cases, when fuses keep blowing, the problem is some sort of short circuit within the equipment. Such problems are usually relatively easy to find with an ohmmeter.

The same basic principle applies to circuit breakers too. If the circuit breaker pops, try hitting the reset button. If the equipment then works OK, the problem is solved. If the circuit breaker repeatedly pops, there is something wrong. Repair the equipment. Never consider bypassing a circuit breaker.

Besides risking damage to components in the circuit itself, an overrated fuse or bypassed circuit breaker could cause damage to other equipment connected to the unprotected device. There is also a very real possibility of a shock hazard. At best, an electrical shock is painful. At worst, it can be fatal. To top off the risks of inadequate fusing is the possibility of an electrical fire.

Don't take foolish chances. Use fuses and circuit breakers in all your equipment, and use them properly. Add a fuse to any home-brew project you build that uses ac power. It won't add more than 50 cents or so to the cost of the project, so its incredibly cheap insurance.

For added protection, especially against fire, use a fused power strip for all the equipment on your workbench. Don't overload a wall socket with an array of cube taps. A power strip has several ac sockets, and usually a master power switch and a circuit breaker. The master switch is a good way to ensure that everything is off when you're through working.

If the circuit breaker in the power strip pops once, it may be due to a transient. If it pops repeatedly, something is wrong. You are probably overloading the strip's power-handling capabilities. Try unplugging some of the equipment. If the power strip's circuit breaker pops only when one specific piece of equipment is plugged in, there is almost certainly a short circuit in that particular piece of equipment.

Use the same rules with your main fuse box or circuit breaker panel in your home (or office). If something blows, try resetting the circuit breaker or replacing the blown fuse with one of the same value. If it blows again, something is wrong. Find the problem and correct it. If necessary, call a qualified electrician. A problem in your main wiring lines could result in a fire. Usually such an electrical fire will start in some inaccessible and invisible nook or cranny, and by the time you're aware of it, the fire could be out of control.

How many major fires have been started because some idiot put a penny in the fuse box? Yes, it will work. The penny fits in most standard home fuse sockets, and being copper it will conduct electricity. But it totally defeats the purpose of the fuse box. If too much current is drawn through your power lines, there will be excessive heat, and that can result in combustion. Changing fuses may sometimes seem like a lot of fuss and bother, but consider the alternative.

Power supplies and cords

We often see warning signs saying "Danger, High Voltage." Actually, high voltage in and of itself isn't all that dangerous. It's high current that is potentially harmful, and even deadly. Of course, in most cases high voltage and high current tend to go together, so it makes sense to heed such warning signs.

Adequate fusing, as described in the preceding section, will help reduce the danger of electrical shock on your workbench. For added protection, it is a good idea to use a power supply with current limiting to power any test circuit you might be working on. If the case is open, and electrical connections are exposed while power is applied, current limiting is more than a good idea. A good power supply, like the one shown in Fig. 12-1 also lets you precisely adjust the power conditions, making more accurate testing possible.

Always be on the lookout for frayed or worn power cords. When in doubt, replace the cord, just to be on the safe side. A replacement power cord usually costs less than a dollar, and anyone who knows which end of a soldering iron to hold can make

Fig. 12-1 *A good power supply is a must on any electronics workbench.*

the replacement in just a few minutes. The insulation on a power cord should not be cracked or brittle. If you can see the copper wire, replace the cord immediately. An exposed wire in a power cord is an open invitation to a fire or a deadly electrical shock.

Sometimes in an emergency, you can cover the bad insulation with electrician's tape, but remember, this is just a temporary fix. Do not leave the cord plugged in unattended, and replace the entire cord as soon as possible. Use only actual electrician's tape. This type of tape is designed to provide electrical insulation. Duct tape or ordinary friction tape are not good insulation materials.

I once saw somebody actually use masking tape for this purpose. This was a very stupid thing to try. Not only is masking tape a very poor insulator, but it is combustible and actually added to the fire hazard. Fortunately, there were no ill results on this occasion, but that was just dumb luck.

Fire hazards and liquids

There is always a risk of fire when electricity is used. On the electronics workbench, electrical connections carrying large voltages or currents may be exposed. In addition, a hot soldering iron can easily start a fire. It is particularly vital to be careful if you don't have a soldering iron stand. If you set the hot iron down in the wrong place, it could easily burn through its own cord, causing an extremely dangerous situation. A soldering iron holder is very strongly recommended for that very reason (see chapter 2).

It is a good idea to keep a small fire extinguisher on hand near your workbench. Hopefully, you'll never need it, but it's a good thing to have available, just in case. Never pour water on an electrical fire. Remember, water is a good conductor. It could help the fire grow, rather than putting it out.

A power strip with a master switch that can quickly shut down everything on your workbench could also be a life saver if a fire does get started. Hit the master power switch and prevent any further electricity from making the problem worse.

Because of the conductivity of liquids, it is a good idea to ban all drinks from the immediate area of your workbench. I keep a small table within arm's reach, and if I have a drink while I'm working, that's where I keep it. Never place the drink on the workbench itself. When you take a drink, move back a little ways from the work area. Don't try to simultaneously work (especially on a live circuit) while taking a sip. It would probably be best not to allow any drinks in the same room as your workbench, but some allowances have to be made for human nature.

Always remember, if you spill a drink into an electronic circuit, you're going to have problems. You may get a fire. You may get an electrical shock. You may get one or more damaged components in the circuit. You may well find yourself faced with an extensive repair job.

If you do spill any liquid into any electrical circuit, disconnect all power to the circuit immediately. This is vitally important. Make sure every drop of liquid is cleaned out of the circuit before reapplying power. This precaution could easily save your life. It is never a waste of time or effort.

Colas and coffee can be particularly troublesome. These liquids can be highly corrosive to many materials used in the manufacture of certain electronic components. The faster you can clean up a spill, the better. But even if you can't perform the full repair right away, for whatever reason, always disconnect the power without hesitation. Nothing is worth exposing yourself to the enormous fire and shock hazards of such a situation.

Proper grounding

Always make sure all of your electronic equipment is properly grounded. If the equipment has a polarized plug, make sure it is oriented correctly. Do not attempt to force it in the wrong way. Never shove a polarized plug into an unpolarized extension cord. Often this is physically possible, but it is never a good idea. The manufacturer used a polarized plug for a reason. If you use an unpolarized extension cord, the polarity may or may not be correct. A metal chassis could be hot, resulting in a very, very dangerous shock hazard.

It is best to avoid extension cords whenever possible, but if you must use one, make sure it is polarized if it is to be used with a polarized plug. Also, make sure that the extension cord is heavy enough to carry the required current. If the extension cord ever gets warm to the touch when the equipment is used, it is not heavy enough. Use a heavier duty cord.

A lot of people use a great deal of ingenuity to defeat three-prong plugs. Don't do it! Manufacturers never use a three-prong plug just to annoy you. They are used because the extra ground line is a necessary safety precaution.

If you use a three-prong to two-prong adapter, the ground connection must be made to the center screw of the wall socket. In some older buildings, the ground connection may not be made to this screw. If there is the slightest room for doubt, have a qualified electrician check it out.

Never leave the ground connection unattached. If I had a nickel for every misused three-prong adapter I've seen in use, I'd be a very rich man. Often, the connection wire will be hanging there right beside the screw, and nobody bothered to connect it. More often, the adapter is used to force the three-prong plug to fit into a two-prong extension cord. Sometimes, people will shove the plug into the socket directly with no adapter, with the unused ground connection jutting out awkwardly. Don't these people realize that third prong is there for a reason, and if it's just sticking out in the open air, it's not accomplishing any purpose?

Yes, most three-prong plug equipment will function without the ground connection, but it is dangerous. Why take unnecessary risks of fire or electrical shock? Not making the required ground connection is just asking for trouble.

Static electricity

Finally, we'll consider another type of risk; although this time, the only risk is to certain electronic components, not to your person. Still, that can be bad enough.

Many electronic circuits, especially those using CMOS ICs are sensitive to static electricity, especially in environments with low humidity. Handle all CMOS devices with care. Do not touch the individual pins.

Many electronics technicians and hobbyists use a grounding strap. This is a metallic bracelet, rather like a watchband, with a length of wire that is connected to a good ground point. This grounds your body and reduces the chance of a static discharge while you're working.

A grounded soldering iron is also a very good idea when working on circuits using CMOS ICs. This is not essential, but it reduces the possibility of occasional problems.

Conclusion

There's no denying that electricity is a potentially dangerous force, but with a few simple precautions and a little common sense, there's no reason why any electronics hobbyist or technician should ever be hurt by electricity. However, thousands are injured or killed every year, almost always due to their own carelessness. That's something worth keeping in mind.

Don't be afraid of electricity, but always treat it with the proper respect. If you take foolish chances, when the worst happens, you have no one to blame but yourself.

Index